Professions

Professions

Conversations on the Future of Literary and Cultural Studies

Edited by Donald E. Hall

University of Illinois Press
Urbana and Chicago

© 2001 by the Board of Trustees
of the University of Illinois
All rights reserved
Manufactured in the United States of America
1 2 3 4 5 C P 5 4 3 2 1

Library of Congress Cataloging-in-Publication Data
Professions : conversations on the future of literary
and cultural studies / edited by Donald E. Hall.
p.   cm.
Includes bibliographical references and index.
ISBN 0-252-02651-9 (cloth : alk. paper)
ISBN 0-252-06961-7 (paper : alk. paper)
1. English literature—Study and teaching
(Higher)—United States. 2. Literature—Study and
teaching (Higher)—United States. 3. Humanities—
Study and teaching (Higher)—United States.
4. Culture—Study and teaching (Higher)—United
States. 5. Education, Humanistic—United States.
6. Education, Higher—United States. I. Hall,
Donald E. (Donald Eugene), 1960–
PR51.U5P76   2001
820'.71'173—dc21   00-012209

Contents

Introduction:
The Functions and Dysfunctions of Criticism at the Present Time

Donald E. Hall

Conversations can take us places that we never imagined going. Unlike mono-logues (and their print counterparts, monographs) multivoiced discussions do not proceed according to any one individual's plan; they develop by way of negotiations and can turn in surprising ways through chance occurrence and spontaneous articulation. Certainly we can *learn* from participating in a dialogue in ways that we cannot when we simply state our own ideas and present evidence backing them up. At the very least, good conversations teach us patience: if we are polite and engaged we usually wait until the other(s) finish speaking before we proceed with our own argument and pursue our own agenda. And just through delay that agenda almost inevitably changes, often doing so dramatically through the exchange of information that conversations entail.

Professions: Conversations on the Future of Literary and Cultural Studies has been a learning experience for everyone involved. It actually started with a conversation, held in a graduate class a couple of years ago. As my students and I talked about the changing nature of literary and cultural studies and, more locally, the changing department of English in which we all work in some form or fashion, our conversation turned to the difficulty that critics have engaging in dialogue with each other, especially when their methodologies, readings, or professional practices differ significantly. Of course, the students' own opinions on the texts we were reading, on their methodological bases for interpretations, and even on what a graduate education should entail varied widely, and they were quite capable of speaking to each other calmly and at length about their divergences and convergences in viewpoint; why, they asked, were their professors unable to speak in similarly restrained but productive fashions, for both their own and their students' benefit? They suggested and I offered a few platitudes about ego, stress, and generational differences, but the question hung in the air, for the most part, unanswered. The next day, continuing to muse on the previous evening's discussion, I decided to try to put together a dialogue-based collection that would help address their question and meet some of the needs that generated it, thinking that I could draw productively on both my previous editorial experience and administratively honed facilitation skills (I went on to complete forty additional hours of para-professional training in facilitation as the project developed). Thus *Professions* was born as something of a challenge to myself to meet an articulated demand from students: to read and have as a point of reference a collection of essays that helps define some of the most important issues facing literary and cultural critics in their professional and scholarly lives, but that also demonstrates a genuine respect for divergent opinions and diverse practices. I imagined it as a comprehensive textbook of sorts, to which students could turn to find a range of opinions concerning major methodologies and professional controversies, something like Lentricchia and McLaughlin's *Critical Terms for Literary Study,* except one based in dialogue rather than single-authored entries, and that addressed numerous aspects of our work as professionals, as well as the concepts underlying our critical practices.

Well, that was the plan, anyway. What you have before you is both more and less than that. *Less* in that it is far from comprehensive (as if such a thing were ever possible)—you will notice that the dialogues it contains examine broad currents in our professional and critical work rather than attempt to cover major theoretical fields and critical concepts—and *more* in that it offers the reader a series of unique, "meta"-discussions on where we are and where we might go as a profession. Its plural title captures both the activity involved in being a "professor"—*professing*—and some of the varied working conditions and senses of vocation that characterize a dynamic and diverse *profession.* As a multivoiced work, *Professions* strives to capture the dynamism of literary and cultural studies at the start of a new millennium, both in some of its divergent applications and its changing professional practices. Thus in ways that far exceed its original plan, it bridges a discussion of critical methodologies with discussion of the methods whereby one *becomes* a critic. It reflects both the breadth of and some of the disagreements concerning the processes involved in "professionalization," including (necessarily, to my mind) some attention to critical methods but more importantly attention to the ways our applications of them are disseminated—in print, in the classroom, in graduate programs, and in our work beyond the institutions that house us as students and professors.

What *Professions* retains from its earliest drawing-board manifestation and initial prospectus is its optimism that talking about differences has certain advantages over sitting in resentful silence or speaking about them only in sustained monologue. Those advantages include, but certainly are not limited to, the ability to test and hone our ideas by explaining and defending them to each other, the opportunity to learn something new and potentially useful by hearing about the opinions and diverse career experiences of our colleagues (and perhaps to come to understand something about our own epistemological limitations in the process), and the chance thereby to alleviate our suspicion and resentment of others so that common cause in areas of mutual interest and need can be found. But beyond how we as participants in conversation can change in opinion and awareness, the auditor of the conversation also can benefit from it in ways that our standard practices often make impossible. Diversity of opinion and a recognition that thoughtful and good-willed scholars can disagree for *very good reasons* on some fundamental issues in their work are almost invariably lost in monographs, which, following the norms of scholarly writing and publication, have an interpretation or thesis to advance that is usually highly circumscribed and often oppositionally stated. And with very few exceptions (notably works of feminist critique such as Linda Kauffman's *Gender and Theory*) collections of essays to date also have tended to argue in defense of a critical premise or methodology in response to the mistaken notions of some implicitly or explicitly designated group of "other" critics. To be sure, I must now argue for my own methodological premise in contrast to what I perceive as a mistaken notion, but as you will see, my goals here are rather modest. I am not suggesting that we all become methodological eclectics, or that we attempt to come to grand forms of consensus on our professional practices, only that we can, as writers, teachers, and colleagues, do a better job at representing and finally respecting a range of thoughtful opinion.

Indeed, one could say that the present project puts into print form some of the basic principles underlying Gerald Graff's concept of "teaching the conflicts"—here, professional and methodological conflicts. Its formal dialogues, informal conversations, and wide-ranging interviews allow insight into the varying perspectives, diverse methodologies, and differing career paths of some of the most successful and intellectually supple academics working in the field of literary and cultural studies today. Yet it also demonstrates that while there may be significant, even irreconcilable, differences of opinion among practicing scholars, disagreement does not have to devolve into bitter argument or summary, sweeping refutation. In foregrounding some of the "conflicts" my contributors work to clarify the premises and priorities underlying divergent professional and critical practices, but they also point to areas of agreement on/in the work they do in literary and cultural studies and, more generally, to the need to return to a sense of collegiality in a profession that is, and has been for many years, strife-torn. Indeed, this collection suggests that any simple notion of "conflict" in either our critical writing or our teaching practices is inadequate, that a less binary model acknowledging both conflict and convergence captures more accurately the complexity of our opinions and existences. Models of professional dissensus, I suggest below, are quite useful, but they ignore the overlaps of belief and behavior that usually exist even among individuals whose disagreements over interpretations, methodologies, or points of professional practice are profound. In seeing only the divergences and ignoring the convergences we do as much injustice to the multidimensionality of our professional lives as a Pollyannaish denial of the sometimes profound differences that do occur.

The dissensus model (which J. Hillis Miller references in my interview with him near the end of this book) is that of the late Bill Readings. In the last chapter of *The University in Ruins*, "The Community of Dissensus," Readings suggests a model for the university that has important implications for the profession as a whole and for individual departments of literary and cultural studies within it. In Readings's dissensus model, proponents of profoundly different professional practices, critical methodologies, worldviews, et cetera should be able to coexist with each other within institutions while making no attempt at all to reach consensus; instead, they should value the strength of their thoughtful individuality (what Miller calls their "vital diversity"). Given the wholesale crumbling of traditional notions of cultural homogeneity and practically any agreement on fixed or standard notions of value, Readings suggests instead that we imagine a community that is "heteronomous" rather than "autonomous. It does not pretend to have the power to name and determine itself; it insists that *the position of authority cannot be authoritatively occupied. . . .* Thought can only do justice to heterogeneity if it does not aim at consensus" (187, emphasis in the original). Readings imagines a university in which the social bond is one that "exceeds subjective consciousness" (186), and in which that bond is preserved as simultaneously a question and an obligation.

Yet even Readings admits that "To abandon consensus says nothing about limited or provisional forms of agreement and action, rather it says that the opposition of inclusion to exclusion (even a total inclusion of all humanity over and against the space alien) should not structure our notion of community, of sharing" (187). His institutional model is a powerful and intriguing one, and certainly his destabilizing of the inclusion/exclusion binary is important. But to forego consensus as an express or implicit goal does not mean, to my mind, necessarily abandoning an explicit recognition and appreciation of overlap when it does exist. "Limited" and "provisional" simply do not capture adequately the manifold and multilayered ways that our individual practices as critics, teachers, department members, and professionals are at times quite homogeneous. We may be a very disparate group of individuals but we do, with surprising regularity, show up in a city and hotel on a given day and expect to find an academic conference there (with book exhibits and slide projectors in place). We may disagree vehemently on which poems to teach in class, but we do agree generally that poetry as a genre is important and worth teaching (unlike some who may think of higher education as only advanced vocational training). Indeed, we often seem eager or at least oddly determined to fracture an actually preexisting unity by wholly ignoring or quickly dismissing those commonalities; we too often demonize those closest at hand while ignoring broader institutional and extra-professional groups and forces that can be far more divergent and even destructive in their beliefs and agendas regarding the work we do in the classroom, in our writing, and as public intellectuals.

Of course to chart those professional norms and shared beliefs will be seen by some as inevitably to oversimplify them or perhaps to reify them without sufficient skepticism. Critical attachment to our common professional behaviors is clearly necessary, but one of the primary behaviors that will be critically engaged throughout this collection is our tendency to focus solely on disagreements and faultfinding. Indeed, to concentrate only on disagreements over methods and practices has consequences beyond jeopardizing, by ignoring, a preexisting, multifaceted social bond; it also does a grave disservice to professionals-in-training and other disenfranchised individuals. As a hiring committee member for my department, I can tell the difference rather quickly between job seekers who are knowledgeable about and prepared for the multiple responsibilities that await them as new assistant professors and those who are fairly clueless about the myriad of professional norms of the work that they must do. "What does 'refereed' publication mean?" asked one applicant, whose lack of that bit of information was symptomatic of her many, many problems as a would-be professional. Presumably her professors in graduate school knew what a "refereed" publication was, but they had never told her about that or the many other commonplaces in their own professional lives.

Perhaps they were too busy arguing and plotting against each other. Readings states with deadly accuracy that "Anyone who has spent any time at all in a University knows that it is not a model community, that few communities are more petty and vicious than University faculties" (180). Indeed, acrimony and pettiness have been, themselves, "normalized" in many sectors of our profession, but are hardly the most productive forms of scholarly and professional behavior to engage in (sniping and revenge-seeking wastes endless amounts of time) or to pass along to students (if such behavior doesn't actually keep most information from getting passed to them). And I am not alone in such thoughts, for I know that many of my colleagues, contributors, and students share my distress over the rancor we see (and hear) around us, over the internecine warfare that is threatening (and often halting the work of) some of our departments, graduate programs, professional organizations, and the publishing houses and journals that we both support and depend upon. Of course this divisiveness and rancorous behavior has its own long institutional history. Graff in *Professing Literature* points out that "As early as the turn of the [last] century, MLA addresses start to bewail the disappearance of the sense of solidarity and shared goals that had supposedly marked the first generation of modern language scholars of the [eighteen] eighties and nineties" (130–31). But to find that such behavior has been around for a century now is hardly to find good, or indeed any, reason for it to continue without serious and continuing challenge.

But, admittedly, such long-standing norms are difficult to disrupt. The question posed by Jane Tompkins and Gerald Graff in the first dialogue in this book—"Can We Talk?"—haunts the rest of the collection. In many ways, of course, the answer is quite obviously "yes," for we talk, as scholars and professionals, at/to each other and at/to audiences of students, readers, and colleagues, almost incessantly. Perhaps the more crucial question, therefore, is "Can we listen?" And to that question there is no obvious answer. Of course, many of us listen quite well and engage—if not easily then certainly earnestly—in a give and take and multilayered and dimensional process of common ground–finding, intellectual growth, and, inevitably, change. We demonstrate thereby that the supple, inquiring, and dynamic selfhoods that were ours early in our formative years remain vibrant and open. But for some—too many—a process of closing down seems to set in, an ever "touchier" defensiveness that ends most productive dialogue, recognition of commonalities, and openness to morphic possibilities. We may continue talking, but listen with answers to all real or imagined challenges already at hand and often on a hair trigger.

This is the academy's dirty little (not so) secret, though of course to say that it is peculiar to the academy or to English and humanities departments would also be to ignore broad social norms. Living in a city, Los Angeles, which is dominated by the entertainment industry, and having known intimately many individuals "in the industry," I realize that dysfunctional behaviors abound across the landscape of the professions. Acrimony and rigidity are common when senses of professional selves and even employment itself are precarious and dependent upon individual achievement and one's continuing success at arguing for the singular legitimacy of one's own ideas or interpretations. We are told that, and are often treated as if, we are only as successful as our last solo effort, film, book, article, or lecture. And if we add into the mix the many, muddled narratives of aging and gendered behavior that are often enacted without thought or reflection, it is hardly surprising that we find "bitter old men" (actually, bitter women and men of various ages) everywhere: in law, politics, retail, the police force, the entertainment industry, and certainly, the academy.

But there is something particularly surprising and disturbing about manifestations of insularity and rigidity in the particular field addressed by this book: those who would and do teach, write, and talk about language, literature, and culture. For one thing, our teaching and our research are devoted to "communication"—in our mentoring of students, in our interactions with texts, and in our love of words, images, and ideas. If we are unable to communicate effectively, then certainly we are open to charges of hypocrisy—"do as I say, not as I do" seems at times to be the message to students, who are told to consider audience in their writing, to listen carefully, and certainly to grow and expand intellectually, but who may encounter more than one instructor who is rigid and convinced that he (or she) has already found all of the answers, and needs only to profess and pronounce.

But to my mind, the more disturbing aspect of such behavior is broader than the disconnect between our practices and those that we expect in others (students, the writers whom we study, the authors of the books which we review), it is quite simply the unnecessary failure of our own enormous potential as organic thinkers. The Readings model makes sense largely as a synchronic one; while "consensus" may be expressly disavowed as a goal, we still should be eager to learn from each other and certainly we should be able to change our opinions over time. We enter a profession and lifework that is (supposedly) *intellectual,* that grapples with questions and does not accept easy answers, and we demonstrate through the long process of our own educational formation that we can incorporate new ideas and learn to deploy sophisticated critical methods, that we can, in the graduate seminars we attend as students and in our interactions with mentors and friends, listen, learn, and change as new information comes our way. We should be, by our training and proven abilities, the group most likely to continue to do the same, to struggle joyously, intensely, and unfailingly with the many complex questions and problems that we will continue to encounter. We ask our students to be "lifelong learners" (or something to that effect, even if we avoid that particular cliché). How often do we realize the same potential ourselves? Why, finally, do so many academics seem so isolated, angry, and either uncommunicative or trapped in modes of unproductive, because closed-ended, communication?

Others besides Readings have suggested useful answers to these questions. Readings makes no mention of Wayne C. Booth, who has long talked about pluralism and difference in our work as critics. That lack of citation itself tells of our unnecessary isolation from each other, for while certainly there are quite clear differences between Readings's dissensus and Booth's pluralism, why would their common desire to find a way of coexisting without rancor be wholly unacknowledged by Readings? Here as elsewhere our function and success as "critics" seems to be defined by our ability to distinguish our own voice, while dismissing or leaving unexamined consonance and similarity, thereby disabling alliance and even stoking the very acrimony that Readings diagnoses as endemic. Booth, in *Critical Understanding* (1979), points to much the same "chaotic warfare" (4) addressed by Readings almost two decades later, and discusses in exhaustive ways some of the models that underlie and account for vehement critical disagreements. In particularly incisive terms, he reveals the "monism" of many critics who demand a final, definitive solution to interpretive and methodological questions (one that, of course, they have already discovered). That concept of "monism" would allow Readings to account for some of the individual personality traits and methodological presuppositions that stand in the way of functional dissensus. Booth's *goal* of finding ways of "living with variety [rather than] subduing it" (3) is Readings's, though the particulars of his *program* for doing so are different (perhaps because it predates the English publication of Lyotard's *The Postmodern Condition* and the communication theory that informs Readings's work). There is little need to retread familiar ground by critically engaging Booth's "pluralism" here, since it has been examined carefully in the pages of *Critical Inquiry* (especially 12.3 from 1986) and by Ellen Rooney in *Seductive Reasoning*. Rooney usefully points out that "pluralism" as a construct often subsumes and silences disruptive voices instead of fomenting or allowing a limitless variety of readings and interpretations. But certainly what links Booth's project with that of Readings, and that makes both laudable in ways that Rooney fails to acknowledge in her response to Booth, is a sincere desire to find a working model for coexistence rather than combat, to normalize thoughtful discussion rather than sneering dismissal.

Yet even sneering dismissals can take up an inordinate amount of time. Booth points out that "some forms of critical exchange are needlessly wasteful of energy and spirit, destructive of life itself" (7). As I suggest above, internecine arguments often obscure and deflect attention away from much more serious problems. Even as the profession sparred over "pluralism" and sought to pin down fine points of distinction concerning the term during the 1980s, it did surprisingly little to challenge the new "business" ethos that was beginning to dominate our colleges and universities. Today this ethos further inflames tensions and heightens insecurities concerning our long-term employment prospects and academic freedom. In *Higher Education under Fire*, Cary Nelson and Michael Bérubé among others have discussed pervasive anxiety and other consequences of such trends in corporatization and growing exploitation of graduate and part-time labor, as well as the generational divides that continue to plague departments. Lauren Berlant too has touched on these and others issues as she has mused on the "atmosphere of distrust [that] characterizes many literature departments (and departments in other fields)" ("Collegiality, Crisis, and Cultural Studies," *Profession 1998*, 114). Berlant, Graff, Readings, Booth, Rooney, Nelson, and Bérubé offer divergent but important answers to the question "why" we are at such loggerheads today; a study different from the one before you would spend numerous pages picking apart their perspectives and attacking the perceived flaws in their answers to that question "why." And so the cycle would continue.

But I am going to try to disrupt that cycle here. Indeed, given the common critical practice of discovering and disclosing the (appalling) a prioris of others' work, I will simply attempt to work through and reveal as many as possible now to save readers (and reviewers) time. This collection assumes that a broadly defined "pluralism" (in the sense that undeniably there are numerous interpretive mechanisms in play at the present time) is simply a fact of our professional/departmental lives. Dissensus is here; we can either waste time denying or deploring it or we can learn to live with it and make it work. It also assumes that active forms of professionalization—seminars, workshops, roundtables, and so on—are very worthwhile components of graduate programs in literary and cultural studies today, that "anti-professionalism," as Stanley Fish has pointed out in *Doing What Comes Naturally*, is simply a professional stance in itself, and a fairly unproductive, dead-ended one at that. But what is not assumed here is exactly what form that professionalization should take—is it "descriptive" or is it "prescriptive," and if the latter, in what overtly revisionary ways? Indeed, what are the desired "ends" of graduate education? What skills, employment prospects, and behaviors are nurtured there? To what extent are graduate instructors interested in training supple thinkers and eager participants in scholarly and professional conversations? Indeed, is the outcome of "professionalization" a next generation of academics who are confident and authoritative or who are rigid and authoritarian?

Of course these questions would seem to indicate a blank-slate quality to the graduate student mind, one that programs inscribe either positive or negative qualities upon. That, to be sure, is a condescending and simplistic construct. What *draws* people to this profession is a question too rarely asked and one only touched on here. Indeed, I would urge graduate student readers of this book to engage critically their own desires and expectations and those of their peers in open and energetic conversation. What is leading you to seek a career as an English or French or comparative literature professor? Is it a love of reading? A love of writing and research? A desire to teach? Or is it, perhaps, a covert desire to find a way of constructing an irrefutable argument, a chance to learn how to *be* an authority and to deploy that authority, with the opportunity to provide answers and opinions to a captive audience of students—and then through testing to make sure that they heard and can repeat back to you those answers and opinions?

That is meant to be provocative, of course, and may sound cynical, but it is not. I do not impute dishonorable motives to the great majority of my colleagues or of those individuals who wish to work in the academy. But certainly I saw some nascent, rather grim and rigid personality types among my fellow graduate students ten years ago; as much as graduate instructors may like to think of students as uniformly "nice" (even if differently skilled), graduate students themselves are certainly able to speak with greater attention to their own population's complexities and differences. And I am equally sure that the process of "professionalization" can work to bring out the best or worst aspects of complex personalities, characters, and work habits of professors-in-training. Even if we enter graduate school with the most supple minds and earnest desires to learn and talk about books and other texts, what skills are exercised and what professional character traits are validated there? In learning to articulate successfully and defend strenuously a thesis, do we also come inevitably to lose the ability to self-reflect, to change our opinions, to listen carefully, and to see multiple possibilities rather than stark impossibilities? Why so often do we become skilled polemicists and difficult colleagues, even as we seem to become wholly unable to talk about texts, our work, and our profession without a comforting buttress of jargon and footnotes?

You will find few notes and little jargon here. Both have their places, I believe. I depend upon notes in the research I read in order to exploit fully the learning potential represented thereby, and provide them for the same reason to my own readers. Specialized language has as legitimate a function in literary and cultural studies as it does in any other field of inquiry. But certainly informal conversations and even more formal dialogues, at their liveliest and riskiest, are rarely burdened with daunting language nor do they often slow down long enough to perform the exhaustive research that one would demand in a scholarly monograph. Evidence is necessary in any conversational presentation of an opinion or a cherished practice, but it is often experientially based, with a few key references included in empowering but unobtrusive ways. Books on the successful presentation of research abound, as do those demonstrating such skill; this book is unabashedly different in that it is about, and attempts to demonstrate, successful collegial behavior.

I want to spend a bit of time now talking about its process of construction, its organization, and its specific contents, elaborating some on what it does and does not do. On that morning of decision when I decided to launch this project, my first thought was that I should begin the process by deciding what specific issues I wished the collection to address, and proceed with constructing it around those topics. But then I changed my mind, seeing that prescriptive move as far too monologic in itself. I decided instead to contact individuals whose profiles in the profession and whose distinct voices excited my own interest, to ask them what *they* thought were the most pressing issues that needed airing for the benefit of graduate students and the broader profession, and to ask them also to suggest individuals with different views with whom they wished to engage in dialogue. Of course those initial choices predetermined many of this book's broad characteristics and outcomes, but no project would be possible without choosing and committing to a process; I chose and committed to mine. I negotiated with some contributors when their topics seemed too narrow or their partners appeared to hold opinions too close to their own positions. Some asked me to pair them with another critic who expressed an interest in the collection but whom they had never met before. Others found that their topics changed dramatically as they engaged in their dialogue. Some agreed to participate but later withdrew with apologies; others simply disappeared without a trace or even a "goodbye" to their dialogue partners. More than a few individuals whom I contacted initially told me that the project was futile or worthless, especially if I couldn't involve in dialogue individuals representing every imaginable stance, including very conservative and very leftist ones. However, when I dutifully approached individuals representing those perspectives I was turned down cold (though one well-known Marxist did tell me that he would grant an interview, he refused to give me a firm time or date, expecting, it seems, that I would simply fly across the country and wait for an audience). That the individuals who accepted my invitation to join the collection and who completed their work could be said to represent the "mainstream" of the academy may or may not be regrettable. If this collection works partly to prepare students for successful careers in the academy, then these are the individuals whose behaviors are, to my mind, most worth emulating. That I did not find a hostile, accusatory voice or several to include from among the hostile and accusatory "far right," "far left," and "middle-of-the road" voices in our profession does not trouble me very much. They will have their say in reviews of this book, and so the dialogues will continue . . .

The list of contributors and topics that I did end up with is one that I hope you will find provocative. Indeed *Professions* is intended to spark and further conversation rather than end it, offering few definitive answers but posing many questions. My editorial hand has been light (except in the interviews, which I will discuss below). I have allowed people to "have their say" without telling them that I believe their arguments are flawed or their perspectives are problematic; you as a reader can take your own stand on the issues raised here. Write me, write the contributors, *talk among yourselves.* After musing for some time on the pros and cons of standardization across the contributions, I also decided not to mandate a single format or process for the contributors, preferring instead that individual dialogues retain their idiosyncratic, conversational tones; some tend therefore toward formality, others toward informality. Some are a little testy, most are very cordial, all are sincere. Here is our profession, living and breathing, with all of its intellectual energy but also a few of its scars and bumps fully displayed. One well-known scholar whom I contacted about participating was horrified that someone might hear him speak in anything other than finely polished form and discover thereby the imperfection of his thinking processes. He declined, fearing that the world would find out that, for all of his academic fame, he is indeed human. Frankly, my contributors are far braver and far more generous than he was.

The dialogues have arranged themselves (with a bit of prodding on my part) into three broad categories, covering certain bases that I believe are worthwhile for any classroom or extracurricular discussion of our "practices" and "profession." Part 1 addresses some of the broadest constructs that underlie and give defining shape to our work as intellectuals and scholars, talking over their legitimacy and morphic possibility. Indeed, the gerund form of "change" that begins each of the three part titles indicates not only a descriptive discussion but also more active forms of change that these discussions attempt to further. "Changing Paradigms" opens with Gerald Graff and Jane Tompkins posing the question mentioned above, "Can We Talk?" Their answers are tentative but not pessimistic, and indeed their hopefulness is born out in the productive "talking" that the next two dialogues evince. Regenia Gagnier and John McGowan speak across and about epistemological and other differences, as they investigate a variety of possible ways that we can define ourselves as public, professional intellectuals. James Kincaid and James Phelan then explore a range of possible critical stances vis-à-vis the texts which form the subject matter (really object matter) of much of our work. Their witty piece (written for this collection but published first in *Critical Inquiry*) demonstrates that just because we disagree does not mean we have to lose our senses of humor or senses of our own limitations.

Part 2 of this collection, "Changing Applications," explores both the ways discrete fields of inquiry are metamorphosing and how we can speak about those changes. Marjorie Perloff and Robert von Hallberg's "Dialogue on Evaluation in Poetry" covers an enormous amount of territory in contemporary studies in poetics as the two participants converge and diverge in their readings and responses to the field and its participants. In the "Changing Practices of African American Studies," Judith Jackson Fossett, a literary critic, and Kevin Gaines, a historian, find common ground across disciplines as they both discuss and participate in a process of negotiation. Finally, Dennis W. Allen and Judith Roof discuss but refuse to participate in their own version of a "star search," in an exchange in which their individual voices are at times distinct and at others indistinguishable, demonstrating that "who speaks?" (a question addressed by Roof and Robyn Wiegman in their collection *Who Can Speak?*) is often far less important than what is said.

Part 3 of this collection, "A Changing Profession," shifts the discussion from critical applications to professional practices and protocols. In "The New Challenges of Academic Publishing," Gordon Hutner, Niko Pfund, and Martha Banta investigate both why norms of academic publication have changed dramatically in recent years and how scholars and scholars-in-training may wish to respond to those changes. In "The End of Theory, the Rise of the Profession," Geoffrey Galt Harpham "rants" in hopes of eliciting responses from his audience concerning the changes he has witnessed in intellectual and academic work over the past twenty years; my editor's headnote provides just a few of my responses that come out of my own generational and theoretical positions. And, finally, those generational differences take center stage in my dialogue with Susan Lanser, who was a mentor from my graduate school years and who has remained a friend and confidante. Our discussion explores both the changing nature of graduate education and the wide variety of work that the two of us perform in the academy, for which graduate school did and did not train us well.

The last group of dialogues in this collection, ones that also concern a changing profession, are of a different sort. J. Hillis Miller, Herbert Lindenberger, Sandra Gilbert, Bonnie Zimmerman, Nellie McKay, and Elaine Marks all agreed to give candid interviews on the changes that they have witnessed around them over the course of their careers, and to discuss openly their hopes and fears for the profession. The perspectives and experiences they reveal are thought-provoking and often surprising. The wide range of their opinions on graduate training, administration, women's and ethnic studies, and possibilities for joy and personal fulfillment in a stressful profession will no doubt serve to spark many and perhaps heated conversations among readers. While my editorial hand in shaping the final drafts of these interviews was somewhat heavier than in other sections of this collection (I had many dozens of pages of wide-ranging conversational material from which to draw in each case), the interviewees themselves always had "final cut" (as we say here in Hollywood) and were, without exception, frank and earnest in their commitment to this project and to sharing information with colleagues and a new generation of professionals.

ᴄ₰

A final bit of "disclosure" and I will be done: as I was working on this introduction, I was informed of my early promotion to "full" professor, at the ripe old age of thirty-eight. Why do I mention this? Because as much as we might like to consider our work *timeless*, of course it is not; it is thoroughly enmeshed in time. Speaking out of actuarial probabilities, I have thirty or so more years in this profession. What kind of profession it will be is of intense and continuing interest to me. Susan Lanser speaks of her own position as full professor as one of increased responsibilities locally as well as increased interest in pursuing "her own work"; I agree but believe also that being past the hurdles of tenuring and promotion allows one to speak candidly, and that, indeed, candor and an open, even brave, engagement with controversial issues is one of the most important responsibilities of senior professors; it *is* our work.

So let me be very candid in the remaining paragraphs of this introduction. I equivocated quite awhile before deciding to try to become an academic. Unlike some of my contributors and interviewees, a position as a professor was not something that I dreamed of or even desired through most of the years of my undergraduate and graduate education. And, in fact, an English department in particular was the last place I wanted to be. From my freshman year in college on, I found many English professors to be strange, arrogant folk, with a tendency to sneer at and belittle each other. Through my years in a B.A. program in German and political science and an M.A. program in comparative literature, I pursued studies in literature and language for the joy of it, and with the thought that eventually I would enter a degree program in library science. Even when I decided that university teaching was something that I really would like to pursue as a career (after a stint as a visiting professor at the National University of Rwanda in the mid-eighties) and entered a Ph.D. program in English to maximize any very slim employment chances that I might have, I still thought that I would eventually end up working as a librarian or a civil servant. And that was not a wholly unpleasant prospect, because the atmosphere in English departments seemed tense, the work there joyless, and the vitriol of the sniping back and forth between professors over matters of methodology and their own senses of personal prestige and professional standing astounding. I loved the teaching, I loved my writing, and I loved many of my peers and teachers, but I was shocked by the norms of academic behavior.

I mention in my dialogue with Susan Lanser (who, along with Deirdre David, Martha Nell Smith, and Neil Fraistat were truly wonderful graduate school mentors) that it was a long time before I finally received a job offer in the late spring of 1991. I want to relate one last anecdote here that helps explain the perspective I bring to the matters discussed in this book. One day in mid-1989, I took a break from dissertation writing to go to a movie at a suburban shopping mall. I was a little early for the film so I stopped at a used bookstore on the way to the mall to look around and kill time. Digging around aimlessly in a section of old hardbacks I came upon a little red book called *Victorian Tales for Girls*. It cost $4. I only had about $10 with me, but finally decided to forego a soda at the theater and bought the book. A few weeks later, I happened upon a posted announcement for the Victorians Institute Conference of 1990 that asked for papers on Victorian imperialism. No primary text that I was well acquainted with seemed appropriate, so I dug out that little red book and found in it a story by the British children's writer Juliana Horatia Ewing that sparked a few ideas. The conference wanted longish papers; mine ended up running fifteen or so pages. The paper was accepted and well received. Again, somewhat later and while on a search for some other piece of information, I noticed (by chance) a call for articles for a special issue of the *Children's Literature Association Quarterly* on imperialism; they wanted essays of about fifteen to twenty pages. The deadline was just two weeks away; I hesitated momentarily but sent in the conference paper unrevised. It was accepted. In the fall of 1990, when I was applying for jobs, I constructed a version of my application letter that marketed myself as a "children's literature specialist" on the basis, primarily, of that one essay (as well as a chapter of my dissertation on *Tom Brown's Schooldays* and a sincere interest and solid base of knowledge in the field). I got lots of interviews that year, but only one in "children's literature," at Cal State Northridge. As time wore on, every job I was interviewed for went to another candidate; even CSUN offered their position first to someone else, who eventually turned it down. It was late spring before I heard that I had a firm offer from them. Though I have been on the market several times since then, I have never received another job offer for an academic position.

The reason I occasionally tell the story above to graduate students and repeat it here is simple. I am where I am today because I had an extra fifteen minutes to kill before a movie and decided to buy a little red book instead of a diet Coke. No *Victorian Tales for Girls,* no full professorship at CSUN. Now, of course (and I can hear Sue Lanser's voice, because she has heard and responded to this narrative before) I have worked very hard, and wouldn't be where I am if I hadn't written a publishable dissertation, et cetera, et cetera. I'm not saying that merit has nothing to do with professional advancement. But the "merit" aspects of our work are over-discussed and certainly over-relied-upon, while we almost never talk about how our careers, practices, positions, and successes are very, very chancy. I think it would help all employed and especially all high-profile academics to trace back a series of arbitrary occurrences that account for where they are and the successes that they have had. It might foster a humility that would allow us to speak to one another without the rigidity and implicit belief in our own semidivine "mastery" that seems to account for at least some our rancor. It would also allow us to speak to graduate students in ways that acknowledge their difficulties and also assure them that if they do not end up in the careers that they (sometimes desperately) want that it is *not necessarily their fault.* Not a single one of us, in or out of this profession, has finally and definitively mastered anything. We are all fallible and rather frail no matter how long our vitae, how thick and ivy-covered the stone walls that buttress our offices and classrooms, or how enviable and mighty our positions of privilege.

And with that final provocation, I will bring this introduction to its end. Let me thank sincerely my contributors, who have approached this work with a remarkable openness and goodwill, and to my many friends and colleagues in this profession who do their work joyously, largely because they retain their good humor and senses of their/our own inevitable limitations. And those limitations, mine and yours, mean that we need each other to help fill in each other's gaps.

Now, what do *you* have to say?

PART ONE

Changing Paradigms

1

Can We Talk?

Jane Tompkins and Gerald Graff

Dear Jerry,

No, not very well. Too many things get in the way.

Pride . . . and envy, for example. Academic people are afraid they might make a mistake, or not have all the evidence they need, or not look smart or have all the good arguments on their side; so they keep quiet. They're afraid to risk what they really think for fear they'll get shot down.

People don't get involved, really involved in conversations about issues in their fields because they have so much invested in their ideas, they're afraid to risk exposure. If the other person wins the argument, what's left? They're too proud to put their ideas out there, so they keep them to themselves, except for the journal articles they write. But everybody's too busy writing their own stuff to read those.

And that's another thing. People are too damn busy to talk. Nobody has time. It doesn't count toward tenure or promotion. You can't put a good conversation on your vita. You can't use it as a basis for applying for a fellowship or a study leave. And you can't put in for a sabbatical saying: I really need to have a lot of good conversations about my topic, so please give me some time off to talk with my colleagues.

The trouble is, nobody *values* conversation. All anyone cares about is productivity. "Is he productive?" they ask. And they don't mean, can he talk well? Does he like to engage people in lively debate? They mean, what has he published lately? There's no intellectual life left in universities, or precious little, because people are too busy getting ahead professionally—which is to say, doing their research—to stop and talk to each other. They're all bottled up inside themselves; there's no free flow of ideas, no excitement, no thrill of testing your mind against someone else's, no feeling of exploring unknown territory together with another person.

Dear Jane,

We agree that there's a lack of real intellectual community in the university. Despite the tremendous apparent potential on campus for exciting discussion and debate, these things rarely occur, and then only on intermittent occasions that leave us feeling frustrated. Why is this?

Here I think we differ: I gather that you see the lack of good discussion as a feature of our professional culture, whereas I see it as a local condition of campus life, and one that actually stems from the *failure* of campus life to reflect the intellectual liveliness and sociality of our professional culture. So when you complain that "there's no free flow of ideas, no excitement, no thrill of testing your mind against someone else's, no feeling of exploring unknown territory together with another person," my response is, yes, that's the case for many of us at home but it's not necessarily the case in our professional lives.

I don't think it describes the mood at academic conferences, for example, or in academic and other intellectual journals, where there's no lack of lively discussion and debate, if also no lack of back-stabbing and one-upping too, but I think that's another matter. I'd put the question differently, then: why is it that the lively conversation that flourishes at conferences and in print seems to end for most of us when we return to our home campuses?

To me the problem lies in our local institutional structures rather than in any special proneness of academics to the sin of pride, to the fear of being shot down, to being too damn busy, or to worshiping at the altar of Productivity—where, as you note, we can't put having had a good conversation on a vita. Not that academic life isn't marked by all these unpleasant traits, but aren't these traits that, in the right environment and circumstances, greatly stimulate good vigorous talk rather than shut it down? Professional ambition and the cult of productivity do have their ugly sides, but they also motivate and energize discussion. What curtails and blocks discussion, it seems to me, is a local institutional structure that keeps people isolated and contains few arenas in which discussion can take place—or rather contains that discussion within the cozy confines of in-groups that endlessly reinforce our pet prejudices while protecting ourselves from the criticism of outsiders.

I mean, if we don't have time or occasion to talk to our colleagues, it's no wonder when we spend so much of our time separated from those colleagues either teaching our courses or preparing to teach them. And by the end of the day or the week, when we might want to attend a faculty workshop or a visiting talk, we're naturally so burned out from teaching along with the other stuff we have to do that as often as not we don't have time. We then blame ourselves or our profession for being too busy or compulsive, but it's not these things that are cheating us out of a community but the way our working time is organized. And what enables our working time to be organized as it is is the assumption that teaching is just by nature a solo performance, something we do by ourselves with our students and in ignorance of what our colleagues and their students are doing.

It seems to me, then, that the place to begin creating intellectual community on campus is the place to which so much of our energy is necessarily devoted—the curriculum itself. Given the pressures of teaching, committee work, and the rest—pressures that don't figure to abate—it seems to me that if we don't begin to create intellectual community within our day-to-day teaching we're not going to be able to create it at all. Extracurricular symposia, workshops, readings, and other such events will never create an enduring community because sooner or later they will conflict with the demands of courses (as well as with other extracurricular events), and it's virtually an Iron Law of Academe that whatever conflicts with the demands of courses always loses. If we start thinking in a new way, however, we could begin integrating what is now extracurricular into the curriculum itself.

Dear Jerry,

Yes, I agree. You have to build community and conversation into the *structure* of the educational enterprise, or they'll never happen, given that everyone is already maxed out. Like you, in the last chapter of *Beyond the Culture Wars*, I've been impressed by the idea and track record of learning communities, groups of three or four courses clustered around a theme that are taken by a single cohort of students and taught by professors who meet regularly to talk with the students and each other. That way, the student's experience is integrated and coherent, instead of being atomized socially and intellectually as is normally the case. In the current smorgasbord system, a student chooses courses as if he or she were picking food on a cafeteria line, taking one of these and one of those. Everyone has different combinations of courses which don't necessarily fit together, and everyone is going through their courses alone— there's no carryover either in the human domain or in terms of course content. Faculty are completely isolated from one another; each professor can teach and go home; there's no necessity to exchange ideas with a colleague, and no sense of being engaged in a joint enterprise, either in pedagogical terms, or in the exploration of an idea.

What the learning community does is build in to the regular conduct of classes the kind of interaction you and I feel the lack of.

For instance, the learning community frequently replicates the conference model you're talking about, when three or four sections of a megacourse meet to discuss a film, say, with faculty and students taking part in discussions, which can be organized in a variety of ways. The social interaction characteristic of conferences can come about spontaneously in student-initiated events, and at regularly scheduled small group dinners that include both students and faculty.

But the larger point I want to make is not about learning communities as such. It's about the principle involved in making higher education work socially and intellectually. That principle—to make a stab at it—has to take into account the human side of being human. By which I mean, people's physical, social, emotional, and spiritual needs. Pretty much everyone realizes that you can't stick four hundred people in a room, give them numbered seats, hire someone to talk at them for fifty minutes three times a week, give them a couple of exams, and expect to get from this anything resembling intellectual life. So they say, classes have to be small, teachers have to know how to elicit discussion and make the subject matter interesting, the usual stuff. But this doesn't do the trick either.

The ironic thing is, that the four hundred seat arrangement *could* produce intellectual life if other things were in place. What things? A culture of conversation. A tradition that valued the exchange of ideas, the relationships that support that exchange, and the quality of experience that accompanies good talk.

The emotional dimensions of conversation—being together with another person, taking risks, becoming vulnerable, allowing oneself to be known, being willing to listen, to change one's mind, to be challenged without taking offense; the spiritual communion possible when the talk reaches a certain level of intimacy and depth; the social skills involved in knowing how to disagree without offending, how to hold one's ground without being stubborn, knowing when to give and when to press a point, when to keep silent; the intellectual skills required to articulate one's ideas, to distinguish them from others that seem similar but aren't, to find the exact point of disagreement, to discover the other person's hidden assumptions, to follow an alien train of thought for the fun of it, and so on—all of this, it seems to me necessitates a certain kind of *society.*

I think I'm about to say that we don't talk well because we're capitalists, materialists, militarists; that we don't talk well, as a culture, because we're too interested in money, power, and things. The skills I've just listed require time to cultivate, what some would call leisure time, but I regard these skills as so important in conducting the business of life that their acquisition should be regarded as work—it *is* work. It's social work, emotional work, spiritual, intellectual work—it builds character, refines the intellect, knits people together, generates energy and ideas, solves problems, entertains, satisfies.

Dear Jane,

I'm struck by the way you cut through the crap to get at the core of my point—"you have to build community and conversation into the *structure* of the education enterprise or they'll never happen, given that everyone is already maxed out."

Your rewriting of me makes me reflect that one of the most necessary things about a community—even just our little community of two here—is the opportunity it gives you to hear your own points played back to you in somebody else's terms. Arguably, we don't know our own thoughts until we hear them translated and altered by somebody else. Then, too, we who talk Academicspeak probably can't understand what we're saying until we hear it restated in colloquial terms (e.g., "maxed out"). It's always shocking to hear one's tortured academese reduced by our critics to the "bottom line," yet how can we know what we're talking about if we ourselves resist reducing it to the bottom line—out of a fear (really a copout) of being caught saying something "reductive."

I've long thought of my own writing career as a struggle in which the self that learned to write Academicspeak in graduate school has been groping to meet up with the self that learned to talk the "regular" way and still does when I'm not around academics and sometimes when I am. Maybe I've needed a collaborator like you to introduce these selves to each other.

In any case, I think one of the worst things about the structured isolation in which we academics work is that it closes down this process of hearing your own thoughts played back to you by others, and of hearing your Academicspeak translated into colloquial terms. I think this isolation also closes down the conversation between our emotional and intellectual selves, in ways that result in the impoverishment you describe in "the emotional dimensions of conversation" in the academy . . .

P.S. A lot more to say on this last theme, but I wanted to keep this short for now. You still seem to think that we need to create a climate of intimacy before we can realistically hope to produce a different structure, whereas I think it's only a different structure that can produce the climate of intimacy. But this perhaps is something best left for later on.

Dear Jerry,

I loved your reply. I'm writing right back before I lose the momentum.

I'm counting your postscript as part of the conversation. You say, "You still seem to think that we need to create a climate of intimacy before we can realistically hope to produce a different structure, whereas I think it's only a different structure that can produce the climate of intimacy." Part of me wants to say: this is chicken and egg stuff, let's forget which comes first and work on both at once, since obviously, both are needed—the climate of intimacy and the structure that nourishes it. But, the *other* part of me says unh-unh. In order for people to talk freely, they have to feel at least relatively safe. They need to know that they're not going to be ridiculed, put down, found wanting in any of a number of ways. When people feel safe, that's when they say what they really mean. That's when they talk about the things that mean the most to them. That's when true exchange occurs.

The question is, can a *structure* all by itself, produce this feeling? My guess is, no. Remember the conversation pits that were popular during the seventies? They *looked* good, they looked as if they might work. And at first, I thought they would. But I never sat in one that produced a good conversation. In fact, quite the reverse. There was something about them that actually stifled conversation. I'm not sure what it was. I think they were too *scripted* architecturally. Too rigid. The message they sent—come in here and talk—made people feel self-conscious. I know you're not recommending that universities establish conversation pits all over campus, but relying on structures has something of the same flavor. If the people involved aren't open, nonjudgmental, sensitive to other people's feelings, able to avoid defensiveness, and if they don't love talk for its own sake, if they don't know how to hang in there, what good will structures do?

I want to shift gears for a minute because there's something else that's been on my mind to say. Stan and I were talking the other day about who we thought were the real intellectuals among the people we knew. My answer was you, Barbara Herrnstein Smith, and Walter Michaels. My reason: you all have that rare and irreplaceable quality of knowing how to hang in there in an intellectual conversation. By which I mean, at that point in the conversation where most other people would give up, you refuse to pack it in. (In fact, though the other people don't realize it, you're just getting going.) Taking you as my major example, it's some kind of resilience that makes the difference, which is part nondefensiveness, part preparedness (you really know the arguments that support your position, *and* the arguments that can be used against it), and part sheer obstinacy. The other ingredient is the love of a certain kind of talk. All three of you come completely alive in this kind of conversation. You become animated and energized; it's almost like an athletic performance—you're fit, you've been practicing, and you're raring to go.

I like to engage in this kind of conversation too, and have done it with great zest from time to time, but I do it less easily than you. The reason, I think, is that I'm too thin-skinned. I become offended too easily, and lose heart. I start feeling bad about myself and then I have trouble articulating my ideas. That brings about the feeling that I'm losing in the competition for who's smartest, who's got the most watertight, best-thought-through position, and I end up feeling wounded and put down. I want to take my ball and go home.

I think there may be some gender differences lurking here. For instance, I would bet you a hundred dollars that women feel more comfortable in conversations that are cooperative than in conversations that are competitive. Men are probably more at ease than women are in the competitive kind, because they've been conditioned to be. Something I really think should be taught in school is how to talk noncompetitively, and how to talk competitively without getting your feelings hurt and without hurting the other person's feelings.

Well, I've strayed from the point about structure vs. climate. Maybe if you said more about what you mean by structure it would help clarify things.

Dear Jane,

I'm naturally very flattered to have made it into your honor roll of real intellectuals. But I suspect there are many more out there who crave more and better discussion, community, argument, debate, and not of the slash-and-burn kind. In any case, we may disagree over whether the psychological, personal, and emotional preconditions of intellectual community exist or not, but we'll never find out until we create structures that allow a conversation to begin. Granted, as you say, "structure, all by itself" won't produce genuine exchange, but such exchange can't occur while structures positively block them.

But "in order to talk freely," you say, "people have to feel at least relatively safe." That word "safe," I note, appears many times in your book, *A Life in School*. There's a certain circularity in this argument, isn't there?: if we can't have a conversation until we feel safe enough, when will we ever have a conversation? And if we never have a conversation because we don't yet feel safe enough, the sense of safety that might be created *through* the give-and-take of conversation can't emerge.

But maybe I can make this talk of structures a bit less abstract with a hypothetical case:

1. Literary Theorist X and Philosopher Y are young faculty members who

arrive in the same year at State Tech. Both are interested in speech act theory and the political implications of the concept of "performativity." Though they teach and have offices in the same complex, they don't meet until they've been at Tech for twelve years, at which time they rather shamefacedly realize that each could have profited greatly from the work of the other and could have had more fun besides. They make it a point to get together but what with being "maxed out" by their regular duties somehow never get around to it.

2. Professor A, in Linguistics, writes and teaches about how "women feel more comfortable than men in conversations that are cooperative than in those that are competitive." Professor B, who teaches Jane Austen, has heard about this theory of the gendered nature of human communication and rejects it incredulously. In their classes, both A and B make oblique ironic references to the obvious perversity of the opposing view. Undergraduates C, D, and E, who happen to be taking classes simultaneously from both A and B, find these oblique shafts of sarcasm intimidating. Though encouraged by both A and B to disagree with their professor's views, in their term papers these students end up shading them toward the opinions the professors seem to want to hear, for A siding with the gendered view of communication and for B either debunking this view or avoiding the issue.

A and B eventually cross swords antagonistically at a faculty meeting on a proposed gender studies program; both decide on the basis of their encounter that "it's no use trying to talk to those people." A goes away entrenched in her belief that men are inherently incapable of cooperation; B goes away hardened in his belief that feminist theory is nonsense.

3. At Utopia College, which is run by crazy visionaries, the curriculum is organized around the assumption that people can't really understand their own ideas until they hear the counterarguments against them. The college has appointed a special administrator whose job is to facilitate conversations across courses and other curricular divisions.

Thus within a year of their arrival at the college Literary Theorist X and Philosopher Y, who share an interest in speech act theory, not only meet but work out a way to connect their courses through a series of joint meetings based on common texts and issues. Linguist A and Jane Austen man B also link their courses around contested issues such as "Is Communication Gendered?" (with help from a colleague in cognitive science). Hostility and tension mark the first two or three exchanges between A and B, but after several meetings they begin to feel more comfortable with one another, and in their fourth meeting they concede some points to each other and start to feel some mutual respect. Students C, D, and E, who gradually enter into the exchanges (and even mediate between A and B, being less invested in the issues), feel illuminated by them; and since the communicative situation is balanced, they don't feel pressure to agree with one side or the other.

OK, I admit it, I stacked the deck here. The stories could easily be rewritten with different outcomes, with A and B in #3 even more viciously at one another's throats after linking their classes, and with their students even more confused; and with X and Y in #1 living happily ever after, their careers uncomplicated by any knowledge of each other. I think it's fair to assume, though, that a structure that isolates parties in walled-off classrooms (as in #1 and #2) promotes at best tension and paranoia and at worst miseducation and student intimidation; and that a structure that allows for conversations between courses (#3) makes a less hostile dialogue at least possible—to be sure, without guaranteeing it—and most important it begins to construct for students the conversations that the university expects them to join but that the conventional structure renders invisible. Not?

Dear Jerry,

Your proposal for how to get faculty talking to one another in the context of their teaching, thus letting students in on the real debates going on in the disciplines, is excellent. I think it should be done all the time in colleges and universities and believe that if it were, there would be better conversation both in and out of class. But I don't think that this outcome is automatic, or would result, even in the majority of cases, without some prior attention to the social and emotional dimensions of talk that I've been concerned about.

In order for the outcome you envision to occur most of the time, the participants would have to commit themselves both in spirit and in practice to a mode of exchange that supported good feelings among the participants. By this I mean: a commitment to cooperation rather than competition as the guiding principle of the debate. This would require, at first, an orientation program, a mini-course, some kind of formal preparation undertaken to insure that everyone—students and faculty alike—understood how to keep a discussion friendly, open, and focused.

When we were talking the other day, you said two things that impressed me a lot that are very much to the point. One is that you like to come out of a conversation with the feeling that you've neither won nor lost. This is absolutely key, I think, to a concept of conversation as cooperative rather than competitive. Winning and losing are the normal ego-centered modes of exchange that dominate academic discussion. I am identified with my position and you are identified with yours, so if you can make arguments that appear stronger than mine, I come out of the discussion feeling put down, hurt, and disinclined to want to debate with you again.

The problem is, everyone is identified with his or her ideas. So how do you ever discuss them, when people disagree, without someone's getting hurt? The answer, as far as I can see, and I'm taking this from Michael Kahn's book *The Tao of Conversation,* as well as from my own experience, is that participants in the conversation have to value their relationship to one another more than anything else. More than looking good, more than winning, more than the ideas themselves—for what we are talking about here is a real live situation, two or more people in a room who are behaving in a certain way toward each other. The reality of this situation needs to take precedence over the content of the ideas being discussed, no matter how earthshaking the content may seem, since otherwise, all too often, real damage will be done in the name of the weightiest matters and highest ideals. So, for example, if we're talking about the Holocaust, my way of treating you in the conversation is more important than what you or I believe about the fact that so many millions of people died. I'm in no way trying to diminish the importance of the Holocaust. But the moral gravity of a subject can't be an excuse for beating up on another person.

For people in academic life, putting respect for the other person *before* the sacredness of their opinions is a huge requirement, as difficult as it is alien, and it takes a generous and mature person to be equal to it. Often, as you've suggested, our students rise to the occasion better than we do because they've less invested in the arguments, and can see the social situation they're in more clearly. I've more to say about this privileging of process over content, but now I'd like to hear from you.

Dear Jane,

It's true: in debate situations there are two outcomes that leave me feeling lousy: winning and losing. The debates I come away from feeling best about are those that may begin antagonistically but somewhere along the way morph into a mutual exploration of the issues, with parties building on each other's contributions rather than trying to show each other up.

Having once been something of a polemical mugger myself, and having since been the muggee more times that I care to count, I know how painful and helpless it feels to be on the receiving end, especially when you feel you've been misrepresented or that your critic has ignored areas of agreement just to score points against you. So I agree completely that we should be working to replace such petty win/lose combats with collaborative discussions, and I applaud your efforts to create conditions in and out of academe in which this can happen.

That said, though, I have to ask this: in a fallen world, aren't there going to be conflicts in which a win/lose paradigm is unavoidable? If I think my government's policies are mean and destructive, I want my side to *win* the election—throw the rascals out. In the case you mention of the Holocaust (and you were brave not to pick an easy example for your argument), isn't it absolutely crucial to defeat those who claim the Holocaust is a "myth" that never occurred, and in doing so might one not be justified in "beating up" on them, at least rhetorically? Are there no positions that you and I would agree are so vicious that they could cancel the normal obligation to respect them?

It seems there may be situations where we don't have the luxury not to try to win, using every weapon in our rhetorical arsenal. And even in cases of less ultimacy, it seems hard to do away with all traces of win/lose aggression. You mention Michael Kahn's view in *The Tao of Conversation*, in which, as you say, we are to value our "relationship to one another" more "than looking good, more than winning, more than the ideas themselves." In my reading of his book, however, Kahn wants to *win* over those who like polarized debates, like the CNN *Crossfire* panel he cites as a bad example of win/lose debate. Kahn wants to make his own ideas "look good" over those who believe there can be virtue in slugging it out, and the effect of his remarks is to make them—i.e., me—feel guilty. Kahn can't avoid setting himself *against* something and risking making somebody feel bad. Who could and still write?

Deborah Tannen seems to me to improve on Kahn in her book, *The Argument Culture*. As I read her, what Tannen is against (at least some of the time) is not debate as such, but reductively *two-sided* debate that excludes the third and fourth positions that can mute antagonism and enable common ground to break out.

I do agree that it's important to try to reduce the amount of *needless* antagonism that our conflicts generate. But aren't conflicts in which somebody wins and loses and somebody gets hurt and put down part of the human condition? If so, then instead of trying to deny or eliminate the aggression that wells up in us when we fight for our beliefs, maybe it would be better to recognize the inevitability of this aggression, a recognition that might then help us control it better and be more respectful of opponents.

Dear Jerry,

I'm interested in your contention that "in a fallen world there are going to be conflicts in which a win/lose paradigm is inevitable." That seems to me to be giving in too soon. You say, and I believe you, that "a mutual exploration, with parties building on each other's contributions rather than trying to show each other up" is what you really want. So why are you so ready to insist that the reverse is inevitable? To me, that suggests that you don't really feel comfortable with what you say you want, and are trying to protect the old combat situation from becoming extinct.

My hunch is, there's something in all of us that feels this way. There's a dark side to this subject of conversation that you've been acknowledging and I've been pushing aside. A verbal argument is often a form of war in which one person tries to eliminate the other, or at least to beat the other down. The struggle is instinctual, reflexive, like putting up your hands to protect your face. Attack and counterattack occur involuntarily; something triggers the pattern and it plays itself out.

I know this happens to me all the time in conversation, even though I'm committed to being conscious of what's happening and not just reacting automatically. One example took place when I was at a lecture that Sacvan Bercovitch gave a few years back at UC Riverside. In the question period I dropped into the attack mode I had learned years ago at Johns Hopkins and asked a really mean question. I had an obscure sense at the time that I was doing something wrong but I plunged ahead. What was uppermost in the moment was a feeling that this famous critic, whom I both liked and admired, was unwittingly advocating a return to the New Criticism—a set of attitudes I had spent much of my professional life arguing against. In attacking him I felt I was rising once more to strike a blow for freedom from the oppressive regime. I certainly didn't see myself as attacking an innocent human being. It's this sense of righteous indignation, omnipresent in the PC wars, that covers over the other motivations at work when we attack another person's position, motivations such as: appearing to be smarter, better informed than the other person, more moral, more politically and socially aware, not identified with outmoded schools of thought.

You said in your last response something to the effect that, being human, we are bound to feel aggression when someone challenges our dearly held beliefs, and since our natural response is to fight for our beliefs, it's better to recognize our aggression so that we can control it rather than deny that it exists. Here is where I think there's an opportunity to move forward by bringing into consciousness the ways that these aggressive instincts play out in conversation, the ways people try to prop their egos up, score points, look good, one-up the other person, protect themselves, and so on. I believe that, through education, we can create a better environment for intellectual exchange. This is what Kahn and Tannen have done in their books, and this is what you and I can do also. I envision a consciousness-raising around the subject of conversation, in which we, you and I, would try to *practice* the thing we're aiming at—that mutual exploration of a subject where we build on each other's contributions.

I realized, when I made myself stop and try to see things from your point of view, that I believe there are very many positive things about conflict. In fact, there have been countless times when I've felt a little shiver of disappointment when I saw that a conversation was headed immediately toward agreement. Something in me wants to see a fight, just for the fun of it. If there's no contest, I think when I'm in this mood, there's no fun. The suspense and excitement generated by disagreement can be exhilarating. You have the sense of moving across vast territories in which each person is well in command of his or her position, articulates it confidently, and is well able to respond to objections from the other party.

As long as the contest stays good-natured, and there's no one-upmanship going on, argument is OK with me. In this kind of discussion, where the air remains clear and the atmosphere friendly, people can really learn from one another, and, if they're secure enough personally, even change their minds. Conflict can force people to see things about their own ideas they'd never seen before, get assumptions and biases out into the open, notice inconsistencies. I can get you to take your own position much further than you could have by yourself. People can even learn things about each other as human beings, if they're willing to go deep enough, and be honest about why they think the way they do. Conflict can actually bring people closer together, by making them say what they think more clearly and getting to the root of their position.

A question that remains open for me is: does the kind of depth it takes to get to that level require that one or both people get upset, or can it happen without anyone's being pushed into a corner?

I think that both of us could benefit by observing ourselves more closely when we get riled in the course of an exchange, and see if we can identify just which buttons are getting pushed and why. Usually, things happen much too fast and we can't get any purchase on the dynamics of what's going on. But it's worth a try. My sense is that most conversational hostility is driven by psychological factors that get automatically triggered but that don't really need to be in play. In the example I gave about myself, it was my long-standing identification with a certain intellectual cause that made me react negatively when I felt it being threatened, plus the opportunity to show off in front of some people I wanted to impress. In the event, I unconsciously wanted to make myself heard because I was living in an academic community where I had no official role and few people knew me. Or at least, that's what I thought. I needed to be seen and to feel that I mattered. Not coincidentally, this was exactly the situation I'd been in at Johns Hopkins when I'd learned to skewer a speaker with a question from the floor. It is of such exigencies and repetitions, I believe, that most arguments-that-hurt are made. The more conscious we can be of them, the better off we are.

Dear Jane,

You think I may be trying to protect "the old combat situation." Well, surely it doesn't need my protection—it's in no danger of "becoming extinct." But, yes, I *do* see creative possibilities in what you call "the old combat situation," and so think it's better and more realistic to try to "mend it, not end it."

But I like your response a lot this time around, especially the way you acknowledge the doubleness and ambivalence in our feelings about conflict. Maybe we can agree that we should acknowledge and maintain this doubleness and ambivalence rather than try to resolve them on "your" side or "mine."

I agree that "as long as the contest stays good-natured, and there's no one-upmanship going on, argument is OK," and that "conflict can actually bring people closer together, by making them say what they think more clearly and getting to the root of their position." But when you ask if that kind of depth can be reached without somebody having to "get upset" or feel "pushed into a corner," I answer (in the spirit of doubleness) yes and no. Yes, in our professional exchanges, we can and should try a lot harder to avoid the reflexive "attack mode" that you and I learned years ago and that you describe having unleashed on Bercovitch. We should establish a polemical Golden Rule—grant the same generosity to those you criticize that you'd have them grant you.

But no, good spiritual contention probably can't happen without somebody's getting upset and feeling pushed into a corner, and would we really want it otherwise? Dante's enemies must have felt upset and pushed into a corner when he depicted them in hell in *The Divine Comedy*, just as poor Thomas Shadwell and Pope's unlucky victims must have felt upset and cornered by the cruel lampooning they get in Dryden's *MacFlecknoe* and Pope's *Dunciad*. Think of Melville blowing Emerson out of the water in *Moby-Dick* and *The Confidence-Man*, Oscar Wilde's devastating attack on Lord Alfred Douglas in *De Profundis*, Lytton Strachey's demolition of his eminent Victorians, and (to establish that it's not just a male thing), Jane Austen's attacks on romantic sentimentalism in her novels and Virginia Woolf's on various patriarchs in *A Room of One's Own*. Plato writes against the Sophists, Sidney against the Puritans, Shelley against Thomas Love Peacock, and on and on. In fact, the more you list titles the harder it is to think of *any* significant work of art or criticism that isn't written against *somebody* who must have felt upset and pushed into a corner. The list could be extended to visual art, music, and even architecture, if not all human accomplishment.

This, I gather, is the message of Bakhtin, Harold Bloom, Saussure, Kenneth Burke, Derrida, and other recent thinkers who argue that difference, contrast, conflict, even violence according to Derrida, but in any case some kind of *againstness,* are structural conditions of communicating or being a person. In all this unavoidable againstness, there is always the risk of someone's feeling upset or pushed into a corner, so perhaps the best we can say is, get used to it!

And yet . . . none of this excuses the arbitrary cruelty, one-upping, and obnoxious self-promotion that, as you rightly say (and have been arguing in your work), marks so much of our intellectual and professional discourse. We probably would need to get down to specific cases: which acts of againstness are defensible and which inflict cruel and unnecessary pain?

Dear Jerry,

Oh, get used to it yourself (I hate that phrase).

But yes, there are different ways of disagreeing, and what we want is to cultivate a sense of which ways are harmless and which are not, and to practice the one rather than the other.

I think the part that taught me most in our conversation was the moment when I tried to see things from your point of view and discovered, somewhat to my surprise, the extent to which I shared it. I'm not sure exactly where this leaves us, but perhaps, as you say, we are both more ambivalent about conflict and its role in conversation than we thought, and that's a kind of common ground, isn't it?

I think this exchange has changed the way I will have to think about these issues.

Dear Jane,

One thing that strikes me is that the conversation with you made my writing considerably more relaxed, less stiff and guarded, than it usually sounds to me, which I take to be a point in favor of your ideal noncompetitive exchanges. I think our students and colleagues would probably write better if they wrote in dialogues with each other rather than in solo performances. It is also interesting to me that when we worked together for the first time on the final stage of this dialogue we started rewriting *the other's* sentences and suggesting things that would make the other's arguments stronger—the very opposite of the usual situation in which we try to make the other person look bad.

At the end, I like to think, we were more interested in the quality of our conversation than in getting the better of each other.

NOTE

This article started off as a conversation between the two of us on the question of why it's so difficult for academics to talk to each other about their work and other issues of serious concern. The conversation began one summer at meetings of the National Council of Teachers of English and the International Federation of Teachers of English and continued as an exchange of letters. After going back and forth several times, it lapsed. Then Jane moved to Chicago and the conversation began again in person, and continued in writing until we decided to bring it to a close.

2

Intellectual Work Today:
Some Trans-Atlantic Musings

John McGowan and Regenia Gagnier

LITERARY INTELLECTUALS FOR A DEMOCRATIC SOCIETY
John McGowan

I am an intellectual, not a scholar. The distinction is not meant to be invidious, nor to mark an absolute divide. My own work would be impossible without scholars, just as scholarly work always has some connection to current
affairs. Still, a rough distinction is useful, if only to suggest a continuum that
registers the relation of academic work to attempts to influence the polity right
now. Literature professors today often express a desire to speak to the "general public," a desire hardly shared by the chemist who writes for the fifty
people in the world able to understand his work, or by the traditional scholar
who is tracing the sources of Milton's Latin poetry. My musings on such desires will tack along a path my occasional changes in direction might obscure:
what I strive to identify are the goals and strategies of those literary intellectuals (including myself) who want their work to intervene in current political and cultural formations. My emphasis on the difficulties, even contradictions, this enterprise raises will justify (I hope) the tacking. Certainly there is
nothing pure nor simple about intellectual work, from its motives to its means
and its consequences, so I must often take back with one hand what I have given
with the other.

The political theorist John Dunn upbraids critics who "view the historical
character of texts with massive indifference, treating them, with varying degrees of attention and patience, simply as repositories of potential intellectual
stimulation for a contemporary reader, and permitting themselves to respond,
accordingly, just as fancy takes them" (*The History of Political Theory and Other*

Essays, 19). I cheerfully plead guilty as charged. Except, of course, Dunn rather overstates the freedom of the intellectual grasshopper as contrasted to the scholarly ant. The intellectual is rarely so footloose and fancy free; responsibility lies elsewhere for the intellectual, not nowhere. The intellectual, to venture a definition, articulates concepts, commitments, and visions that legitimate and/or contest the way that we live now. And working from such a commitment to present programs and constituencies, the intellectual might very well envy the freedom of the scholar whose pursuits are less guided by immediate pressures or the desire to address nonspecialist audiences. Certainly this work of intellectual articulation is eclectic. It requires, among other tasks, elucidation/elaboration/contestation of received and current ideas; the examination of prevailing practices, beliefs, and institutions in relation to stated principles and as indicators of unstated motivations; an engagement with the multiple traditions which traverse contemporary cultures and influence individual agents; and continuing efforts to bring intellectual discourse to bear within a polity which features a plurality of discourses.

To embark on these tasks would be difficult if the intellectual could not name for himself or herself the fundamental commitments that underwrite the work. To what do I feel responsible, to whom do I hold myself answerable? There have been various answers to this "what": art, economic justice, social equality, my ethnic group, my nation, my gender group. Intellectuals have been notoriously prone to opt for package deals that encompass a "what" to be committed to, an analysis of how that "what" has been maligned, and a program for correcting past and current wrongs. Think here of aestheticism, Marxism, nationalism, or whatever other "-ism" is your personal favorite or bête noire. Even when the intellectual eschews the rigidity which threatens the card-carrying adherent, intellectual positions are almost always charted by way of programmatic signposts. And such programs conveniently provide others with whom to converse and argue, thus offering an audience for the linguistic output that is the final product of almost all intellectual work.

But this audience only partly constitutes those to whom the intellectual feels answerable. There is almost always another group—a group figured as oppressed—who is to benefit from the intellectual's activities. This group isn't seen as directly connected (either through reading or other direct encounters) with the intellectual's work, but is to benefit nevertheless. At the very least, then, the intellectual's discourse is double-voiced, addressed to a peer audience which has similar concerns (and, very often, similar commitments) and to a more amorphous (often unlocatable) public.

And it is her allegiance to an "-ism" that provides both the significance and the agonies of the intellectual's efforts. At the current time, when the intellectual and her peers almost invariably hold university posts, work addressed solely to a peer audience would be entirely "academic." By way of the "-ism," the intellectual holds onto the aspiration of doing work that extends beyond the academy—and is ever aware of what few resources she has for successfully reaching nonacademics. While for the pure academic, a discipline may serve as the substitute for an "-ism," most intellectuals strive to subordinate academic work and academic disciplines to the service of their "larger" commitments. The intellectual struggles to make the university serve his or her program, not vice versa. Thus the intellectual's self-understanding usually includes an ironic relationship to academic usages and disciplines, a determination to keep things in perspective and to balance continuously "petty" academic concerns against the needs of the "wider" world. She dreams of being a "public intellectual."

Yet intellectuals are always vulnerable in their joint allegiance to a program and their relationship to the university. Every time they make careerist moves or win academic accolades, they can be accused of hypocrisy, of striving strenuously for honors they claim to despise. Even more pointedly, intellectual work seems to require a certain delusion of grandeur. Intellectuals could not do their work if they didn't project consequences wildly out of proportion to what they actually accomplish. A certain willful blindness is thus required. Called upon to explain how their work will effect the transformations it calls for, the intellectual has only feeble Rube Goldberg scenarios to offer, a voodoo politics replete with its own versions of "trickle down" theories. There are no palliatives for these vulnerabilities, certainly no a priori strategies to ensure scaling the academic walls and making an impact elsewhere. The intellectual is constantly bedeviled, no matter what she is doing, by the fear that she is doing the wrong work at the wrong time and, probably, in the wrong place.

There is no salvation from irony, double-voicedness, and double consciousness ("optimism of the will, pessimism of the intellect" in Gramsci's words), just as there is no escape from mixed motives, from writing manifestos with footnotes, from wanting to impress academic peers as we strive to better the world. All I would ask is that we intellectuals avoid fetishizing and cherishing our irony as we also eschew pronouncements of exceptional virtue, purity, and integrity. We are in the mix like everyone else, although in ways made distinctive by virtue of our specific institutional (academic) location. The too-frequent narcissism of intellectuals, their tendency to find their own ambiguous position in modern societies endlessly fascinating, bores me. "This is not about *us*," I want to yell.

It might help to think of the intellectual as an ideologue, as a public advocate for a particular set of arguments. The *American Heritage Dictionary* defines "ideology" as "the body of ideas reflecting the social needs and aspirations of an individual, group, or culture." Let's try, for a little while at least, to maintain the neutrality of the definition. The intellectual is someone who articulates publicly an ideology—and who makes no bones about her support of that ideology (and, often, refutation of rival ideologies). Thus my intellectual work involves struggling to articulate a position in such a way that I not only satisfy myself but that I think might persuade others. Certainly satisfying myself entails feeling that I have figured something out, have gotten things "right" in both expression and accuracy, and have been faithful to my primary commitments. But achievement of these satisfactions depends on the pointedness my thoughts only assume when they are articulated for a public airing.

And what does that articulation entail? Like many intellectuals today, I name my primary allegiance "democracy" and want my work to further the cause of democracy. Specifically, that aspiration entails regular and extensive elucidation of the term itself; advocating extension of democratic practices into social sites (the classroom, the workplace) where they are often deemed inappropriate; and considering how commitments to equality and autonomy can be negotiated in concrete situations involving differences and interdependencies (of various kinds) as well as complex, differentiated social structures/institutions. Even more specifically, then, I am a left democrat, one who thinks that the most vulnerable in society are those with the least economic resources and/or those who have historically (for whatever reason or for no reason whatsoever) been denied the full rights, benefits, and duties of citizenship. The rightist is more likely to think that the exceptional person (whether the writer of genius or the highly successful entrepreneur) is prone to the envy of the mediocre and/or the efforts of the state to rein him in, to regulate his activities. The rightist thus worries about the tyranny of the majority and about leveling effects that hamper excellence (either its achievement and/or its receiving due appreciation/reward). I have other worries.

What relation can the activities of literary intellectuals have to the project of left democracy? My answer is agnostic at the level of content, optimistic at the level of form. Intellectuals of every stripe make substantive arguments, content-laden interventions, which they publish in various venues, even as they know that there is absolutely no way to measure what, if any, impact is made. When the goal is as diffuse as influencing people (beyond an appeal directly made to a specific few), we can never know if the goal has been reached, or to what extent. This is as true for those relying on the indirect discourses of the arts as for those who employ a more direct, argumentative discourse. The ability of intellectual activity to generate further intellectual activity is palpable, but its ability to generate political conviction that results in political action is not.

And upon reflection, I wouldn't have it any other way. Despite postmodern critiques of autonomy and humanist individualism, most academics (even those who are, roughly speaking, postmodernist in their views) think it a fundamental violation of their students to tell them what to think and to require the regurgitation of that content on exams. A basic ethos of autonomy prevails. We can give people the materials for forming an opinion; we can expose them to strongly argued opinions on a topic; we can even express strongly our own opinion (although only carefully when our audience is subordinate to us in a hierarchical institution); but we cannot require others to adopt any particular opinion. Allowing individuals autonomy of belief seems fundamental to democracy. Critiques of autonomy usually aim at demonstrating that we shouldn't take the existence of autonomy for granted, and that individuals are continually influenced by forces that are invisible to them. Only rarely do such critiques argue that autonomy in opinion formation is not desirable. I strive mightily to overcome the gap between my enunciated beliefs and their adoption by my audience—and am relieved by my failure. The only thing worse than a world in which no one agreed with me about anything would be a world in which everyone agreed with me about everything.

This substantive failure is paired, however, with a formal success. The view of democracy which I am trying to enunciate here (democracy is a contested term, of course) highlights not only the individual determination of belief, but also transformative interaction. As we strive for a substantive agreement we never fully achieve, we engage others in a dialogic give-and-take that is potentially transformative. Admittedly, I am stressing (to the neglect of other elements for the moment) the rhetorical component of democracy. A democratic polity is marked by the continual efforts of various citizens to persuade their fellow citizens of something. Their relative failure at persuasion makes democracy look like cacophony. Yet, in my view, that cacophony is actually substantive. A democratic polity is not dependent on agreement; it depends on our continuing to talk to one another. A political community, a functioning public sphere, rests not on whom I agree with but on whom I keep talking to. And intellectual activity is precisely this continuing to talk, is it not?

Well, that solution is so simple that it makes me suspicious. For one thing, it smacks of the kind of "invisible hand" reasoning found in Adam Smith. Each of us just has to keep earnestly trying to persuade others and, behind our backs, our individual efforts will create the democratic public sphere we desire. How convenient! Literary intellectuals just need to do what they are paid to do—read books, then talk (with students) and write (for other intellectuals) about them—and they will be doing democracy's work.

What is missing if we simply celebrate existing public interactions (in the university or elsewhere) is any account of the risks, the costs, the context, of dialogue. For starters, the term democracy names a whole range of desires in the contemporary world; not all of those desires are compatible with the vision of enriching, transformative public interaction that I am gracing with the word democracy here. Furthermore, democracy (even in the most catholic uses of the term) hardly names the only desirable things in the world—and it is not compatible with many of those other desirable things. Finally, functioning public spheres are almost always parochial, that is, shielded from the power and resource inequities that afflict any but the smallest and most exclusive communities in the contemporary world. It is a pretty safe guess that anyone who has been privileged enough to experience democratic interaction is privileged in more obvious material ways as well.

The specific name for the privilege enjoyed by academics is "professionalization." George Bernard Shaw said that every profession was a conspiracy against the lay person, a statement true enough to bear repeating. Professions manage to create public spaces through gaining almost exclusive right to govern who can join the dialogue and who cannot. Long apprenticeships, peer review, and self-policing are just three of the mechanisms by which a profession controls membership. Such control is only won when the profession manages to gain consent (most crucially from the government, but also from professionals in other defined fields and from the general public) to its right (by virtue of expertise and competence) to monopolize a certain service of labor. The profession's monopoly covers both its exclusive right to provide the service or do the work *and* its exclusive right to determine (through credentials or licenses) which individuals belong. Professions do not possess absolute autonomy—they remain answerable (to varying degrees depending on the profession) to their clients and the government and the market—but they certainly enjoy a semi-autonomy that gives professionals a freedom in their work afforded no other laborers in today's economy.

That freedom, especially for academics, is intimately connected with job security. Tenure is a dinosaur. The kind of job security it provides has been lost by just about every other significant body of workers in contemporary society. When fighting to defend tenure, academics should recognize how privileged they are to still have that security, and (I believe) should argue on grounds that rest not on the uniqueness of what we do, but on the reasons for seeing job security as a basic right that should be available to all workers. The assault on tenure (especially the greatly expanded use of part-time or adjunct teachers where tenurable or tenured faculty previously were employed) is, in some cases, connected to efforts to combat professional monopolies. But such assaults are much more frequently connected with the contemporary economy's maximizing of productivity through use of a modified piecework system. Workers are only hired for the specific time and the specific tasks for which they are needed, and are not carried by the employer during slack times. This practice is not only cost-efficient and conducive to organizational "flexibility" in relation to demand and other economic fluctuations; it also drives down wages, since non-secure and temporary workers are much less able to hold out for decent pay. Contemporary assaults on tenure have very little to do with academic freedom, but are connected to new economic practices that have greatly lessened job security across the board in the United States (and elsewhere).

These questions of professional privilege and labor market practices are relevant to the left intellectual for reasons beyond the appalling job market for new Ph.D.s in English and related fields. (I do not mean to suggest that job market questions are unimportant; quite the contrary. But the specific factors involved in our particular job market would require an analysis that would supplement the more general musings on academic professionalization being offered here.) In regards to the professions, the leftist academic is in a bad spot somewhat similar to his position vis-à-vis the welfare state. Welfare does not work very well, if only because dignity and self-worth are so completely connected to having a job in our society, as any unemployed Ph.D. will testify. To defend welfare against abolishment is to argue for a flawed program against outright cruelty. Similarly, remembering Shaw, a full-scale justification of professionalism seems (to me at least) hardly the democratic route. At the present time, however, the work conditions afforded by academic professionals approach ones that would accord with various democratic ideals. In other words, it does not seem particularly productive to destroy professional privilege because it is enjoyed by so few, when many features of that professional privilege model the very conditions democrats want to see more fully available and practiced in our society.

In arguing that intellectual work in the contemporary academy models, in certain ways, the democratic interactions, I do not want to be hopelessly Pollyannaish about the academy. Our public space is also riven by inequities that are systematically produced and maintained. But I do believe that we have

more autonomy than is afforded most workers; that we participate in an agonistic give-and-take that both constitutes a public space of interaction and
serves to influence the ongoing formation of opinion by individual participants; and that such transformative interactions are a crucial component of
the kind of democracy I hope my work can foster and that I wish to inhabit. I
certainly believe that I've got the best job going, and that my ability to have
this job depends on the labor of many people (those who produce the necessities of life for starters) who do not get to work in conditions even remotely
comparable to mine. Therefore, it seems incumbent upon me to think about
how the freedom and security accorded me can stand as an example of the way
work can be (given a full recognition that the translation of freedom and security into other spheres of activity would result in very different institutional
arrangements. I am not aiming for a world transformed into so many campuses. God forbid.) In sum, I think our professional privileges are justified
partly by the work we do, but much more importantly by the example we provide of a democratic existence.

Which brings me to education. To think of myself as an example is to think
of myself as a teacher. If I influence my students, it is to a certain extent directly due to the things I say, the material I give them to read. But I also
influence them indirectly by striving to make the classroom a democratic space
of transformative interaction. As both a student and a teacher, the classroom
has been a magical space for me, a place where I am often most fully the person I would wish to be and in the type of society I would wish to inhabit. And
the classroom probably acquires its magic in large part through its immuni-
ties. Nothing momentous, nothing on which life hinges, is at stake in most class
meetings. But before we hasten to declare such immunity inevitably trivializ-
ing, let's think about security one last time. We can be more open to change,
to influence, to letting ourselves follow a thought or a whim where it goes,
precisely when nothing absolutely vital is at stake. Which suggests to me that
a democratic public sphere is dependent on a minimal material security that
cannot be jeopardized by one's activities in that sphere. If this is true, it is no
longer surprising that classrooms and other academic sites are our society's
closest approximations to such a democratic public sphere. Where else are the
stakes so carefully separately from economic consequences?[1]

A final thought or two about the "literary" in literary intellectuals and I will
be done. I take it as both necessary to my own democratic desires and as pedagogically required that I be as swayed by what happens in the classroom as I
hope my students are. That transformations occur over a semester is more
important than any particular transformation or conversion occur. And to take

this open-ended position is to get off the hook of directly (illegitimately) influencing a student's beliefs. Teaching literary texts goes well with such openness. What many English teachers want to convey to students about literature complicates the direct, simple, univocal notion of a message sent from speaker to hearer. The literary text works on its audience on a variety of levels and its messages cannot be easily unified or summarized. We want to make our students better able to become entangled in the miasma of emotions, thoughts, arguments, analogies, and associations that a literary work evokes.

But, I must admit, it would be ingenuous to claim that any and all transformations are equally prized. I think the teacher committed to democracy must cherish plurality. The thin and negative reed of tolerance is not enough to sustain democracy in the face of the difficult challenges it faces from those who pursue economic dominance and from those who find living in a pluralistic world a goad to violence. I prize the literary for its expansiveness of vision. Does this mean that everyone who reads literature—and especially those who do it for a life's work—gains an expanded vision? Surely not, we hasten to reply. We don't want to smugly claim moral superiority for ourselves. But the embarrassment of self-righteousness aside, don't we really believe, somewhere deep down, that a literary education is a moral education? I am uneasy with this thought, and don't fully know where or how to push it. But I think it leads toward the question of sensibility, toward considering whether democracy—insofar as it entails cherishing and enjoying the agonistic and potentially transformative interaction with those who think, feel, and believe differently from me—calls for a certain temperament, a certain sensibility. If a democratic education includes the effort to nourish this sensibility, I contend that time spent reading, discussing, and responding to literature has a specifically central role to play in that nourishing.

My final thought will return us now from the classroom to the written work of literary intellectuals. The combination of a commitment to democracy and to a vision of the literary as nonunivocal has, I have suggested, made it likely that literary intellectuals will have a taste for and want to champion a taste for plurality, for difference. The blatant, obsessive, and by now boring display of that taste forms the stereotypical image of the politically correct literary academic of our day. I am as wearied by politics worn on our sleeves and the public stagings of our own virtue (and everyone else's nefariousness) as the next guy. But I don't want to throw out the baby with the bathwater (at least not now and in this place—I think I have been guilty of such rash flingings in the past). It is not surprising that literary intellectuals often devote themselves to the practice of "cultural politics," intervening thereby in the basic categories of thought and the basic repertoire of representations circulating in the society. Of course, such practitioners tend to fluctuate wildly between proclaiming that the only true and effective political action must take place in the cultural realm *and* bemoaning their ineffectiveness because real politics happens elsewhere (in the halls of power, on the streets, or any place but the arts, the classroom, and the head). In similar fashion, educators tend to either wildly overstate the impact of education or to proclaim the complete impotence of schools in the face of all-determining influence of families, peers, and the wider culture.

But clearly, cultural politics, like education, is one kind of work; it is neither trivial nor omnipotent. I happen to think it is more likely to have an impact when its real limitations are acknowledged from the start, when the other sites of political action/intervention are also named, if not (at this moment) engaged. My point is that I do not think literary intellectuals should back down from their interest in how literary texts (in different instances) foreclose or enhance plurality in specific social realms. Similarly, attempts to make the classroom a utopian space must continually be tested against categorical and representational exclusions. An obsession with difference is salutary and is likely to remain so for any foreseeable future. But preaching to the converted and ritual displays of right beliefs are less useful, while believing that an engagement with prevalent forms of thought and representation is the be-all and end-all of democratic activism is to leave far too much of the field to those indifferent or hostile to democracy. My ideal intellectual, then, may work only in the field of cultural politics, but she keeps open the lines of communication with what is happening in other fields, and always reminds herself (and her readers and students) that important work is being done elsewhere, and that a richly plural democratic polity calls for these varieties of work. Finally, her work would be pitched in such a way that not only does it allow her dialogic interaction with those in her own specific field but it also provides an opening for those in other fields who want to maintain a sense of her field. In that way, in our written work as in our classrooms, we can strive to model the very forms of interaction that we want to claim are vitally important and desirable in a democracy.

EXPERTS AND INTELLECTUALS: OR COMMITMENT IN THE MARKETPLACE
Regenia Gagnier

John McGowan says above, "I am an intellectual, not a scholar." I am both a scholar and an intellectual. I love research in the archive and I love ideas for their own sake. I love to make fine distinctions between ideas that might appear similar or confused, and to articulate precisely the experience of the senses. I study what Adam Smith and J. S. Mill meant by the good life as well as what my current undergraduates mean when they reflect on that phrase. In the quality of attention I bring to historical scholarship and to our present life, I hope to burn with the same hard, gemlike flame.

In the problematic that John McGowan locates, I would make distinctions between the expert and the intellectual rather than the scholar and the intellectual. The departmental structures of universities today are very good at reproducing disciplines, which produce experts. An expert is thoroughly engaged with the questions, methods, and products of a narrowly circumscribed field and produces a body of work within that field. Experts—as in expert evidence or expert witnesses—are called population geneticists, moral philosophers, Victorianists, or labor economists. Their work is judged by other experts and, if they are respected within their field, they in turn spend a good deal of time judging the work of other experts in that field. They also train experts in the languages, conventions, practices, and behaviors of their discipline. This is why my more intellectual graduate students in Stanford's Program in Modern Thought and Literature used to grumble that they were being "disciplined." Many of them had hoped that university would be filled with intellectuals but instead they found rather narrow experts. It may be that the higher in the ranks of research a university ascends, the more likely it is that its faculty will be narrow experts. When I moved to Britain in 1996, my first impressions were of more intellectuals in British than in U.S. academia but also of more amateurs, for Britain is probably only beginning to be as "professionalized." Shaw's characterization of the professions as "conspiracies against the lay person," precisely to keep her out of the dialogue, represents a long history of resistance to professional exclusion in Britain. The professions were regularized by the nineteenth century to exercise monopolies (through professional associations and collegial control) over each profession's cognitive base (knowledge and techniques) and institutional training and licensing. Their relation to lay subjects or citizens was one of exclusion. In relation to professional expertise, the subjective attitude of the amateur toward the object of knowledge is less coercive or juridical and more affective. Professional expertise is intensely focused and territorial; amateurism is expansive, poaching, free. The price the amateur pays for her freedom is power, which in the modern world is linked to institutions rather than individuals.

For McGowan, being an intellectual is also a matter of commitment that is directed beyond expertise. "While for the pure academic, a discipline may serve as the substitute for an '-ism,' most intellectuals strive to subordinate academic

work and academic disciplines to the service of their 'larger' commitments."
This is why the theory of professional "interpretive communities" that Stanley
Fish developed in the 1980s seemed so narrow and alienating to so many of
us. When we entered the academy, our self-perception was at least as much
feminist or socialist as it was expert or professional. An intellectual within the
university must be an expert but she is also more: she is accustomed to reflect
upon her field and upon its relation to other kinds of knowledge. An expert
in the humanities knows how to interpret a literary, musical, artistic, or philosophical "object" within formal, chronological, or generic boundaries; but an
intellectual also knows how to reflect upon her interpretation and place it in a
larger context. Universities can so fetishize narrow forms of expertise that they
drive out intellectuals. This routing can occur through the regular processes
of peer review, in which we often ask narrow, limited experts to evaluate intellectuals and intellectuals duly come out wanting in the requisite narrowness.
It may have been ever thus, that experts and intellectuals have always been ri-
vals, the one calling for more discipline and the other for more latitude, with
the one tending toward myopia to anything outside of one's narrow special-
ism and the other toward megalomania. But it may also be that, after a century and a half of increasingly narrow experts, we need more intellectuals.

In the nineteenth century, intellectuals were explicitly distinguished from
experts for their willingness to discuss and take positions on *culture*. By "culture," I mean something like Hegel's definition in the *Lectures on Aesthetics*:
the ways that people represent themselves to themselves and thereby construct
identities. I have argued elsewhere that the expertise of literary and cultural
critics today lies in the study of cultures, including the study of cultural conflict
that leads to self-critical crises of expertise, as in the so-called culture wars, or
debates over whose cultures should be taught in universities. We represent the
critical study of language, literature, discourse, and other communicative
forms; of feeling, emotion, taste; and of cultural history. Personally, I would
not want to return to a nineteenth-century man-of-letters or "amateur" model
of transdisciplinarity so much as to defend the idea of an expert who is also
an intellectual, who uses her expertise in the service of larger social issues.
Elsewhere I have also outlined what these might include: recently cultural critics have had much to say about the cultural construction of taste and preference in consumer society, about nationalism, about gender and economic
development, about ethnic and racial conflict, about environmental justice and
affirmative action (in Britain, "positive discrimination"), about beauty in the
built environment. I have talked about the interventions of such scholars in
terms of "applied humanities," using the term "humanities" strictly in its dis-

ciplinary sense, to distinguish the role of the humanities from that of the sciences. What this means is that these scholars bring their expertise in the cultural construction of taste, nation, race, or beauty to the table where they and other experts can advise policy makers on matters of passionate concern to us all. The issue is not that academics must remain removed from politics or the affairs of the everyday, for scientists and social scientists, especially economists, have increasingly influenced policy. The only issue is whether other academic disciplines, specifically the humanities, ought also to exercise influence.

The departmental structure of universities reproduces disciplines, which reproduce experts. Is there a conflict between what the university reproduces and what the market demands? That is, as the social scientists say, an empirical question. Whether the taxpaying public wants more psychologists, economists, and historians or more intellectuals working on the causes of crime, the relation of economic growth to distribution, or the way that colonial history impacts development is something we actually have few reliable data about. Even if we had them, we would have to consider whether the university *ought* to respond to public demands. For even if the public and the university could achieve consensus on the narrowness of experts, it is likely that our estimation of intellectuals would differ. It could be that the public would want neither experts nor intellectuals but technicians.

If one were to take the case of what is called in Britain the "new feminism," one would see something surprising to intellectuals. The new feminism presents itself as activist, attacking the material bases and institutional supports of economic, social, and political inequality. It calls for a revolution in the organization of work, a national network of childcare, men taking on the same responsibilities as women at home, the elimination of poverty, and legislative and welfare support for women facing sexual and domestic violence. What it is against is precisely intellectuals, who allegedly overemphasize the cultural results of oppression rather than the primary need of equality. "We are burdened with knowledge. We must make sure that we can also act" (Walter, *The New Feminism*, 81). Old feminists, say the new, should stop telling young women how to act, what to wear, stop teaching them how to desire. For the new feminists, the overwhelmingly crucial element of the women's movement is women supporting women, networks of women, women as role models in every aspect of working life. For Natasha Walter, the women's movement is not a mass movement that marches to one drumbeat, but a large collection of single-issue organizations that press for "feminist aims," as Walter says because she is British, "in many different accents":

[S]ome hold parties with champagne and canapes, others hold demonstrations with banners, others hold drop-in sessions, some lobby government for changes in the legal system, others are trying to get into government, others are just trying to make life better for the women on their street. Some work with women who experience violence, such as Refuge. . . . Some provide a voice for professional women, such as Women in Journalism. . . . Some are composed of women in political and public life, such as the 300 Group or Labour Women's Network. Some foreground women's experience based on their race, such as Southall Black Sisters or Akina Mama wa Afrika, or based on their experiences of childbearing, such as the Abortion Law Reform Association, National Childbirth Trust and the Maternity Alliance, or their experience of specific health problems, such as the Hysterectomy Support Network and the Anorexia and Bulimia Nervosa Association. (*New Feminism*, 44–45)

Obviously an intellectual who tends toward systemic analyses would see the potential conflicts among these groups of women, each pursuing their own interests or happiness. Intellectuals will want women to be less positive, more critical and self-reflective with respect to their canapes and politics, that is, to the pursuit of self-interest when it is potentially at the expense of others. Yet to the extent that there is a feminist "movement" forward today, it is probably as Walter describes. As a senior academic who has over the years assumed my share of the administrative tasks that come with seniority, I find that feminism and the women's movement are less about "positions" per se than about a network of feminists who share the tasks, provide support when daily life is hectic or demoralizing, and who make demands on each other's behalf.

A few years ago Camille Paglia gave some lectures in England. Her visit was represented in the media as a struggle for the future of feminism: feminism as a movement would stand or fall depending on whether her interlocutors or Paglia won the debate. Ros Coward, however, pointed out in *The Guardian* that such absurdities come about when a visible women's movement is replaced by celebrity fetishism. To a generation who have known a women's movement, feminism and the women's movement have little to do with the pronouncements of media personalities. A feminist knows that the women's movement includes many different perspectives. The future of feminism hangs on none of them but on a sense of community among people who seek in their different ways to make the world better for women.

Again, a debate in the late 1990s between the novelist Fay Weldon and the columnist Polly Toynbee was billed "At issue, the future for feminism" (*Guardian*, 16 May 1998, sect. G2, p. 4). To Toynbee's credit, she rejected the sensational characterizations of feminists as either viragos (1970s or 1980s) or victims (1990s) with, "This is not what most feminism has been about. It has been about freeing humanity from socially enforced gender roles. It is not that men and women are the same, but gender has been allowed to dominate and destroy other more important character traits" (p. 5). In other words, feminism must deconstruct the binaries that have dominated both our theory (in the form of mind-forged manacles) and practice (in the division of labor). We in the actually existing women's movement can have parallel lives with media personalities without conflict; the damage will be done only if the next generation is not permitted to join—to get jobs in—the actually existing networks of solidarity and from the consequent exclusion comes to believe that solidarity stands or falls according to media representations. Thus the politics of solidarity (old feminism) and the economics of inclusion (new feminism) are a classic loop, each informing and enabling the other.

Here I shall take seriously the new feminist emphasis on economic conditions and the division of labor and say something more about the relation of the intellectual's politics to the next generation's economics. A few years ago I was invited to reply from the perspective of a social theorist to an MLA panel on what was then called, after a popular novel, Generation X. The panelists besides myself were all of Generation X, and they provided two distinct views of their generation. One view I would call political economic, and it was the typical view of Generation X represented, for example, by the joke, How many Gen Xers did it take to screw in a light bulb? Two—one to shoplift the bulb so the baby boomers had something to screw in and the other to screw it in for minimum wage. This was the view that represented Gen X as possessing a "no future" structure of feeling and a "post-consumption" ethos. The baby boomers consumed the goods and lived off the backs of the next generation. Jon Lewis, one of the panelists, provided a tropology of Gen X films. He concluded that the Generation's music was nostalgic; that its sex was post-AIDS, or always in the shadow of AIDS; that Gen Xers did not marry and that they did not have children; and that their work was characterized by overeducation, underemployment, and no advancement. If his characterization was accurate, we may postulate that three of the main ways that people have historically established their identities in communities—through leisure, through intimacy or family, and through the division of labor—no longer amounted to community. I shall return to how this lack of community relates to the "no future" structure of feeling, but we know from the work of Benedict Anderson and others that when successful communities imagine themselves, the master narratives that unite them do not narrate an "end of history" but rather project into the future.

After Lewis provided the tropology of film, another panelist, Leerom Medovoi, provided the considerable service of showing, through a number of different media, that the "no future" structure of feeling was shared across genders, classes, races, and ethnicities. His hope was that this very *sharedness* of the feeling of lack of future might function as a sort of Political Unconscious, eventually erupting into a collective demand for a future and end to the ethos of relative scarcity. That is, even a "no future" structure of feeling precisely as a "structure of feeling" is shared and therefore might provide the basis of a community and a politics.

The other two panelists, Cynthia Fuchs and Mike Pinsky, did not begin with a political view but with what I would call a performative view. They saw Generation X's misery as ironic, an attitude or a performance that, especially in its musical performance, provided possibilities of multicultural, multiracial, and multigender identification and sympathy. This is also, of course, a classic theory of subcultures.

Now in reflecting on these two representations of Generation X, as possessing a no-future structure of feeling based on the absence of the kinds of economic futures that had been available to their parents, and as *performing* a no-future structure of feeling, we might wonder whether the *actual* feeling of no future *and* the *performed* feeling of no future might both be the basis for a collective demand for a future. One way of putting this is, what is the relation of the political—the *demand*—to the economic? Politics requires community, or a shared structure of feeling. Economics, as most of Gen X (including the new feminists) know it, is different. Although its prehistory goes back at least two centuries, one of the striking ideological achievements of the 1980s was the *reification* of "The Economy"—the making people believe that the economy was a monolith out of their control. Bruce Springsteen expressed the passive structure of feeling that this reification contributed to when one of his unemployed builders said that there was no work "on account of the Economy."

At that time, we also heard repeatedly, "It's the Economy, stupid." I am reminded of the brilliant thumbnail analysis that said that "America has no politics—just an economics and a myth." The myth is presumably the myth of meritocratic, competitive individualism that ensures economic growth and precludes politics. And competitive individualism has historically been inextricably tied to consumption: individuals have mythically expressed their individuality by their consumption patterns.

Now if Gen X is actually or imaginatively post-consumption—if part of a generation could not or would not spend and thereby could not or would not assert its preferences as competitive individuals—then wouldn't the myth be jeopardized? If the myth of competitive individuals goes, then we might have a space for a politics—a collective demand for a future. But then we would still have the reification of the economy. Yet rather than a juggernaut that rolls over you, the economy was once imagined differently. Indeed, as late as the nineteenth century, it was imagined as that which provided for the needs and desires of the people. So the question, then, was, could a post-consumption, post-individualist, generation make a *political* demand that the economy *not* be driven by some reified "laws" of growth and productivity but rather by the provision of their needs and desires?

That question appears to be in abeyance for the moment. Since that MLA panel in the late 1990s the U.S.'s economic boom appears to have allayed the anxieties of Generation X and obviated the need for political solidarity.

But assume that Gen X really *were* post-consumption and post-individualist. Here we must confront the difference between a structure of feeling and a performance of a structure of feeling. If Gen X really had been incapable of competitive individualism then they might have been capable of political solidarity. But though they may have been economically incapable of competitive individualism, they still seemed imaginatively competitive and individualist. In this case, I think that the collective U.S. myth of competitive individualism, in conjunction with the structure of U.S. work, overshadowed the purely economic grounds for solidarity, until "The Economy" ostensibly improved and saved them.

I shall explain with a trans-Atlantic example. I have lived and taught in England for the past few years. If reports of prosperity in the United States during that time are accurate and its effects have trickled down, economic times are harder here than there. Yet the first term I taught here a huge majority of college and university faculty and staff staged two days of strikes that successfully raised wages across the board, that is, they expressed solidarity and voted for what they still, quaintly, call "industrial action." One reason that they act differently from their counterparts in the United States is that they are not in practice competitive individuals, at least not once they have secured a job. Salary scales are nationally set and until recently British academics have actively resisted star systems that lead to big differences, other than seniority, among them. That is, the structure of work has pushed them toward solidarity rather than competition. Just as significantly, due to a long history of socialism among the intelligentsia, many British academics still profess socialist sympathies. (In my department at Exeter, well over half the faculty do so profess. That is different from my colleagues of fourteen years at Stanford.)

Now I would think that the structures of feeling that push British academics toward solidarity and academics in the United States toward competitive individualism are largely historical, and both may well be undergoing considerable transformation. Yet the relevant histories—British left solidarity and the U.S. ideology of competitive individualism—are, for the time, determinative when added to the different structures of work. British academic solidarity, then, like the women's movement or any other kind of solidarity, is a structure of feeling that *precedes* political demand, and that working conditions can impede.

In reflecting on the relation of an old politics of solidarity to Generation X's and new feminism's neoliberal economics, I want to conclude with teaching and the relations between age and youth. I particularly appreciate McGowan's analogy between the limitations of cultural politics (the target of new feminists) and of education (the target of old feminists). He says, "cultural politics, like education, is one kind of work; it is neither trivial nor omnipotent." Education, an old feminist might say, is just one permeable ideological state apparatus (ISA) among others: the school, the church, the state, the family. I love teaching as much as I love scholarship and making links between scholarship and contemporary social life. By "teaching" I mean not the brain-deadening bureaucracy that currently passes for "quality assurance," but what happens in a good seminar, where the generations are increasingly interlocutors. I love teaching the Frankfurt School. To my mind few contemporary theorists come close to a Lukacs or a Benjamin in mental rigor or emotional power, or in the intricate thought patterns that inform their prose—even after the second half of the twentieth century revealed their conceptual limitations and blind spots. And students raised on Routledge paperback readers—which I assign—immediately sense the specialness of that Frankfurt generation's social analyses of commodification, exploitation, and domination. Sometimes I wonder, as I lead them into the labyrinthine wealth of Frankfurt cultural analysis, how long this quintessentially bookish critique will be accessible to young people raised on the Internet. But at this stage there is still dialogue, for their flexible minds respond more gaily (in Nietzsche's sense) to Frankfurt than mine to the Internet, through which they lead me with patience and tact. When I moved from the West Coast of the United States to the West of England, the thing that most worried me was teaching undergraduates. How would British twenty-year-olds respond to an American woman professor whose teaching experience had been primarily with graduate students and whose expertise in British culture was firmly rooted in the nineteenth century? But I need not have worried. The dialogue, the cultural contact, happened between the daughters of Albion and the American Revolution. I teach them cultural history and theory, they teach me what it is like to be a British subject (not, to be sure, a "citizen," the more American concept) today. I talk about race, ethnicity, and multiculturalism with a distinctly Californian perspective; they talk about the cosmopolitan consequences of a former empire, or the (post)colonial status of Wales and Cornwall. We read Frankfurt, we surf the Net.

English will increasingly appear to younger generations not as an island's literature but as complex and interactive anglophone cultures, in which the classics will be most eagerly read in relation to the hybrids they have "produced" in contact with other cultures and through a variety of historically specific media (e.g., film or the Internet). Seeing "English" as a language interacting with many diverse cultures, some of whom are making their voices heard at university for the first time, means that the teachers of that language are privileged to study the expression of a multicultural society's needs and desires. In principle, this remains very like Marx's project for critical theory, surely still the project of most intellectuals, as "the self-clarification of the wishes and struggles of the age" (letter to Arnold Ruge, in *The Marx-Engels Reader*, 15).

SOME FINAL THOUGHTS IN CONVERSATION BETWEEN REGENIA GAGNIER AND JOHN MCGOWAN

John McGowan: I spoke at length about my current interests in my essay, but I would still like to hear more about how you would characterize your work in relation to the positions we have been discussing.

Regenia Gagnier: I approach my work as problem solving. Each major project or book has begun as a question that I wanted to answer, at least to my own satisfaction. My first book, *Idylls of the Marketplace,* inquired into the nature of the artist in mass consumer society. The second, *Subjectivities,* asked about the relation of literary form to gender and social class. My recent book, *The Insatiability of Human Wants,* on the histories of economics and aesthetics in market society, began with a question I formulated in the 1980s: after Smith, Mill, Marx, and the Owenites, whose works I habitually taught, how had discourse about "The Economy" come to be so impoverished? In the academy economics had been largely reduced to a branch of mathematics; in public discourse it had been reduced to "growth." This question led me to the history of economics. As I began to understand the transition from classical political economy to marginalism, I saw that it had parallels in the history of aesthetics in the transition from productivist aesthetic models (Ruskin's or Morris's or Marx's) to models of taste, hedonics, and consumption in the fin de siècle. In order to guard against further reductionism, I then looked at how the dominant models in both aesthetics and economics were contested, which revealed the gendered valences of taste in both. My research for *Subjectivities* had frequently put me in contact with the social historians who had recovered working-class autobiographies and public- or boarding-school memoirs. Writing this new book put me in contact with economists and political theorists. I certainly read my Foucault or Judy Butler or anybody else who people are talking about, but my work is generated by the questions I want to answer and the community of experts and intellectuals who can help me answer them.

John McGowan: But do you ever worry about leaving a lit crit audience behind to do work that historians and economists may not read or may be dismissive about if they do read it? And to what extent can you take your research into the classroom if you are still teaching in a literature program?

Regenia Gagnier: I don't experience much anxiety about it. For me, interdisciplinarity is not "transdisciplinarity" on the part of one scholar who presumes to know everything, but rather a dialogue between disciplines that transforms each one. During my career I've worked closely with philosophers, historians, anthropologists, and political theorists, and even occasionally with natural scientists. This work has been based on common interests. For the past decade or so I've been in close contact with economists insofar as we've shared interest in concepts of production or creativity, consumption and taste, value, and the critique of the dominant neoclassical school of economics.

But the most successful interdisciplinarity, as a dialogue between disciplines, is through common commitments. When we founded the Feminist Studies program at Stanford it included faculty from history, economics, literature, law, sociology, and the rest who all from their different perspectives wanted to make the world better for women. I'm an associate editor of *Feminist Economics* because I share a commitment to feminism with the editor, Diana Strassmann, an economist, although my perspective is as a culturalist. I organize conferences with the group of economists who edit *Rethinking Marxism* because, despite our superficial differences, I share with them the desire to keep alive the possibility of socialism.

The Cultural Studies Group at Stanford included philosophers, classicists, anthropologists, several members from modern language and literature departments, historians, and law professors affiliated with the Critical Legal Studies movement. We initially came together over the politics of curriculum reform (crudely represented in the press as the "Culture Wars") and we continued working together against the reactionary policies of the State of California on immigration and affirmative action. At Exeter the philosopher John Dupré and I held a conference on Culture and Economics. For the final plenary session I asked Mark Blaug, the distinguished historian of economic thought, and Barry Barnes, the distinguished sociologist, to comment from their different professional perspectives on the papers they had heard and on the future of dialogue between the disciplines. In all these cases, each of us brings our different expertise to bear on a matter of common interest or commitment. Although it was never a primary concern, I've found that my published work has been well received among scholars in other disciplines, especially among those whom we've defined in our essays as "intellectuals."

What lags behind such interdisciplinary dialogue, unfortunately, is the just measurement of its research, which is typically evaluated, whether in tenure cases in the United States or the Research Assessment Exercises in Britain, within narrow conceptions of disciplinary expertise.

John McGowan: Certainly there is a growing number of academics who work from a similar model. Yet the university as an institution still seems largely incapable of fostering interdisciplinary work. What makes interdisciplinarity possible? How can we make it thrive?

Regenia Gagnier: Even at Stanford, which encouraged, even funded(!), dialogue across disciplines, every time new groups formed we met the same initial suspicions, the same prejudices, about each other's disciplines: literary critics were sexy but superficial, historians dull, sociologists were superficial without being sexy, and philosophers were arrogant but irrelevant. Each fledgling reading group or seminar has to work through such prejudice by listening to its members across the disciplines and by critiquing one's own discipline. If we are feminists at least as much as we are cultural critics, if we deplore the destruction of our environment as much as we deplore the methodology of economics, if we love the city even more than we hate sociologists, then we have reason to continue talking to each other. In my experience, patience, which amounts to listening to others at least as much as arguing for one's own perspective, has always been rewarding.

John McGowan: We need more—and diversified—models of collaborative work. The model in the humanities (it is, of course, strikingly different in the sciences) has been on individually produced work for so long that I almost think collaborative work should be mandated. And the same holds for collaborative work across disciplinary lines.

Regenia Gagnier: I was interested in the report of the commission sponsored by the Gulbenkian Foundation and chaired by Immanuel Wallerstein that recommended bringing together scholars from different disciplines to work on specific urgent themes for a fixed period of time (*Open the Social Sciences*). I do think that different disciplinary trainings yield different perspectives and insights. The most productive interdisciplinary work comes from dialogue and collaboration, not from individual efforts to be and know everything.

John McGowan: But for me, the question remains as to how all this connects to what we are trying to accomplish in graduate education? One of my recurring problems is that the work I do (say, for example, my current work on pragmatism and its contribution to democratic activism) is not very appropriate—in terms of professional training or preparation for the job market—for my graduate students. They need a more standard training, partly because the tight academic job market has made the discipline more conservative (the return of hiring by historical/national fields, more as a way to keep the number of applicants for any particular job down than as a result of any intellectual conviction or consensus that our work should be organized that way), partly because of a more general backlash against theory, cultural studies, and politically motivated English professors.

I must admit that I do, every third week or so, feel an old fogey twinge that tells me our grad students should learn the discipline of literary criticism the way I did; that, for example, the skills of close reading are valuable, and that we can't take it for granted that our students will possess those skills. They must be taught. But I also have no desire to teach those skills myself, and while I can be glad now, for various reasons, that I devoted twelve years or so of my life to literary scholarship, I want now to do the literary intellectual work that I discussed earlier. So I really don't know what graduate training should be at this point. I suspect that disciplinary training has good effects, but the discipline is currently so fragmented that it is hardly clear what disciplinary training would look like. And I offer no model at all for students, since I no longer do disciplinary work nor am I interested in strictly disciplinary questions.

Regenia Gagnier: I still feel very comfortable teaching students to read and interpret literature and other cultural media, and it may be that the kind of interdisciplinary work I've discussed can only come in the later stages of gradu-ate-level work and is not appropriate for undergraduates at all. If we train our students specifically to analyze cultural forms and aesthetic experience (in its widest sense), the world will push the best of them toward other disciplines as they need to learn about them. The best minds are rarely narrow, in the humanities or the sciences.

NOTE

1. My colleague Susan Bickford and the editor of this volume, Donald E. Hall, have sharply disagreed with my notion that nothing vital—either economic or political or intellectual—is at stake in the classroom. I seem committed to a very aestheticist no-tion of the classroom here, linking its separation from the "real" world to its ability to foster some fairly free play of the imagination, some fairly uncensored dialogues. On the level of practice, I fully admit that the classroom is hardly entirely untainted by power inequities or by the economic pressures that send many students to college, but I do want to believe (foolishly?) that these concerns are not utterly determining in the actual instance. On the level of theory, I am even more conflicted. To what extent am I committed to the positive effects of a semiautonomy for aesthetic? I don't know—and think that my indecision about the status of the aesthetic is pretty common among literary intellectuals of my generation and my (leftist) stripe, another indication of the confusion in the discipline of literary studies. My unwillingness to simply abandon a hankering for separate spaces is grounded on my intuition that democratic interac-tion is crippled where basic necessities like enough money to live are at stake in all interactions. Without some job and income security, democracy is a nonstarter.

3

What Do We Owe Texts?
Respect, Irreverence, or Nothing at All?

James Phelan and James R. Kincaid

James Phelan: With our choices framed this way, I'll go for what's behind door #3. Not even the most ardent ecopantheist would argue that we *owe* something to inanimate marks on paper—and I have deep doubts about Divinity of any kind. But the trouble with picking door #3 is, of course, that there's *nothing* behind it: no controversy, no debate, no interest. Of course we don't owe texts anything. Turn the page.

But there is something behind the question—a debate about how we should conduct and assess interpretations. What we need to avoid in this debate, though, is the assumption that there is *one true path*. Methods of interpretation are subordinate to the purposes of interpretation, and those purposes are multiple. If I want to know something about the structure, organization, and design of, say, *Middlemarch,* I will do one sort of analysis, whereas if I want to know how the novel's discourse about how a given cultural issue fits with or runs counter to the discourse about that issue in other arenas—the law, the popular press, government documents—I will do a very different kind of analysis. Furthermore, I may decide that in my own cultural circumstances the best approach to some literary icon is irreverence: enough already about Thomas Pynchon, what he needs is a good debunking. In all these cases, the purpose of the interpretation is the production of a certain kind of knowledge—of form, of culture, of what's wrong with our adulation—but the purposes of interpretation can also be political (Marxists, feminists, queer theorists, and others frequently invoke the goal of changing the world), aesthetic (the critical act as homage to the creative one), affective (the critical act as a way to touch the emotions generated by the creative one), and other things as well. And of course, these purposes are not mutually exclusive: some often overlap or get synthesized in a variety of ways.

I realize this endorsement of multiplicity may appear to be moving toward another door behind which lies no debate: not even Jim Kincaid (hereafter JK) is likely to argue against letting more than one kind of flower bloom, even though I'm sure I can count on him for some witty sallies against pluralism. And I also realize that in answering the initial question as "nothing" and in advocating multiplicity, I'm not fulfilling my prescribed role in this debate: defending *respect* for texts. But endorsing multiplicity is not the same as saying that "anything goes," and, in fact, I would argue that endorsing multiplicity makes both the conduct and the assessment of interpretation more difficult— and therefore, more interesting. Among other things, it raises questions about the identity and boundaries of "the text," questions which JK and I will no doubt get into before we're through. Furthermore, when I move from the meta-level of considering the relations among interpretive methods to the level of interpretive practice, I find myself especially drawn toward a rhetorical criticism that seeks to understand the interrelation of textual phenomena, authorial agency, and reader response. And this effort at understanding does require, among other things, what I am content to call respect for the text.

Let me illustrate briefly with a few remarks about Poe's "The Cask of Amontillado." Although I might start with questions about reader response (why am I both horrified and touched by Montresor's narrative?) or about authorial agency (why does Poe initially call attention to Montresor's narratee and then do nothing to characterize him or her?), I will start here with questions about textual phenomena. In the concluding paragraph of his narrative, Montresor reports that as he is on the verge of completing his revenge against Fortunato by walling him up in the catacombs, "My heart grew sick—on account of the dampness of the catacombs." Then, after reporting that he completed the job, he comments, "For the half century no mortal has disturbed [the spot]. *In pace requiescat!*" Respecting the text in this case means recognizing that (a) the last paragraph of the narrative is a place of great emphasis (see Rabinowitz on Rules of Notice); (b) Montresor's report of his heart sickness doesn't fit with most of the rest of his narration; (c) the revelation that he is telling the tale fifty years after the events demands explanation. Respecting the text also means seeking a coherent account of it, even as it means recognizing that some texts may be incoherent.

In this case, the two phenomena inform each other and, in turn, require us to reconfigure the whole story. Montresor's explanation of why his heart grows sick is unreliable, a case of denial on his part. It is not the dampness of the catacombs but his own instinctive revulsion at what he is doing to Fortunato that makes his heart grow sick. But his commitment to his code of revenge—announced in the first paragraph, another place of emphasis—means that he will not admit that revulsion to himself. On the verge of carrying out the dictates of the code—punishing Fortunato with impunity and with Fortunato's knowledge that he is the avenger—Montresor cannot stop. But the detail about Montresor's heart growing sick as he completed the revenge sheds light on why he is telling the tale fifty years later. The events are still vivid for him; he finds himself reliving the long-ago experience because he is not at peace with it. Thus, the point of his narrative is not to boast but to confess—or rather to confess under the guise of boasting. Once we recognize that, then we also must recognize that he has not been successful in following his code of revenge: he has not punished with impunity because he has not been at peace for these fifty years. His telling the story is a sign that his retribution for Fortunato's wrongs has "overtaken the redresser." The "requiescat," though in one way an ironic remark about Fortunato, is also an earnest wish for himself. Strikingly, though, this recognition of Montresor's failure to carry out the revenge works to humanize, although not redeem, him. It also doubles our attention, asking us to focus not only on Montresor the brilliant plotter who carried out the murder of Fortunato but also on Montresor the elderly narrator living with his uneasy knowledge of what he's done and no doubt contemplating his own death.

I could (frighteningly enough) say a lot more about all these things, but I'm already abusing the rules of turn-taking, so I'll yield the floor to JK.

James Kincaid: That Jim Phelan (hereafter JP) professes one thing and does another need not concern us. It's not that we—"we" here means me and *you,* who are on my side, cheering for me, not because you agree with what I say but because you are following your heart's dictates: I am the more comely of the two—it's not, I say, that we are after bigger game; we will, when it suits us, lay claim to the personal (JP does not, for instance, really know how to pronounce "Amontillado").

It's rather that it's fun to watch JP's duplicity, his Chicago shell game: JP begins with an enthusiastic double somersault onto the bandwagon of indeterminacy—we owe texts nothing at all—and then tells us just what it is we owe 'em. In the name of coherence (oh please!) he gives us Groucho Marx, which is, let me tell you, a lot more entertaining than the usual acts issuing from Chicago. You following me? (By "you" I mean all you readers, not Phelan, who will, of course, pretend to misunderstand.) JP first suggests we have nothing but marks on a page, then somehow assumes that our job is to "interpret" them, then says that we should honor multiple interpretations, then gives us, as an illustration of (get this!) multiplicity, a bullying bit of monism: "Thus, the point of his narrative is not to boast but to confess." As the layers peel off, Roland Barthes becomes Stanley Fish becomes ohmygod R. S. Crane.

Let's back up.

A Text is like God: the question is not "How Do We Approach Her?" but "Why Bother?" In the name of openhearted generosity—JP is the Mae West of neoformalists—we are offered "multiplicity," which is nice. All creeds, all religions are welcome. Goody. JP is like my dean who every year issues an ever-expanding list of religious holidays, urging us to respect each and every one and honor with stupefied silence and a slight bowing of the head students who ask for special consideration for one kind of woo-woo or another. Why? Why encourage superstition? Which, you see, is why I don't like starting this game inside JP's fences. If the issue is defined as ecumenical liberalism, it's like the Victorian notion of "doubt": it still assumes that the center of our world is God—or, in our more important dealings, the Text. Why take texts for granted? How about a bit of healthy atheism here?

Why grant the text independent authority? Why assume there are texts? Why assume, granting that there is some collective agreement on the illusion of texts, that texts are there to be interpreted? Whose interests are being served by such massive question-begging?

Why assume we are organized around a textual center, we being all of us in this game? I for one have no interest whatsoever in texts, and my interests should be your interests too.

I thought I'd try bullying, since it works so well for JP. Put it this way: what is the end of Phelan's practice? Why does he do it? Knowledge, he says. Hard to battle that, but what kind of "knowledge" is it if texts are dots on a page and interpretation simply the forceful application of interpretive codes that are entirely contingent, determined not by the dots but by professional, historical, cultural accident?

Why do this at all, then? Why produce one more interpretation of dots, when what's really at stake are the interpretive and professional discursive practices driving a master like JP. It's not what he produces but the machinery he puts in motion that should concern us. Let's say that JP's reading is fun, which it is, a lot of fun. It's fun because, I would say, he's so good at avoiding triviality in two directions: on one hand, reading the story as a mere bone-chiller (though, like you, I only pretend to sneer at mere bone-chillers), and, on the other, reading it as a dreary moralistic fable. JP's reading is balanced, judicious, nuanced, and zinging. It's an A reading. It's publishable. It's the best we can do. He's damn good. But all that, though true, has everything to do with the standards of professional discourse and nothing whatever to do with the dots on the page. We applaud JP's reading, find it in its way persuasive, because it is so in accord with professional practices we have been taught to honor, not because it has anything whatsoever to do with the dots. I leave it to you to produce the 747 other equally persuasive readings available within our current professional paradigm and to imagine the infinite number of readings available to other paradigms.

The text—this is not news—does not police what we say about it. It doesn't give a shit. That's because it has no will, no power, no being beyond what we can make of it. And we can make of it what we will.

(There's an opening, a gap, a piece of illogicality I invite JP to step into. Come on. Do it! I just said texts were just open possibilities constrained by history and culture and THEN I proceeded to say we were not constrained AT ALL. See the gap? Ask me about it. I dare you.)

So, even if we lapse into interpretation, it should be to explore the cultural and professional codes we have devised for reading and sense-making.

But, as you and I know very well, JP does not believe the dots are dots. He just says that to get us to like him. I like him myself—which says more about my open heart than his engaging qualities, but it's true. JP really thinks the dots are endowed with some sort of extra-historical, extra-cultural, extra-professional stability of some kind. Thus he refers for confirmation of some hunch of his or some feeling that he had better produce a subtle reading if he's going to command our admiration to the text. He confirms his view of the dots by asking the dots. The dots are mute, but he ventriloquizes the answers to his own questions and calls his voice "the text." It's only Charlie McCarthy all along. The frightening thing (or the stirring thing, depending on your point of view) is that JP thinks there's something there. He believes his own voice comes from somewhere else. He thinks there really is a text. Oh my. It's a matter of faith with him, I am afraid.

Anyhow, I'm not for multiplicity in interpretation; I'm for getting rid of interpretation altogether. Banning it. Anyone caught interpreting will be made an associate dean. I'm also against texts. We would be better off without them. They simply are no fun. That's what I don't like about them. They spoil the party. Like a cousin of mine who is ubiquitous and terrible at parties. JP is, though you'd never guess it, quite something to behold at parties. Why, there was one party at Ohio State honoring this departing drone, where JP . . . I guess I'll save that for next time.

James Phelan: Well, what a pleasant combination of the predictable and the surprising. I correctly anticipated that I'd end up playing the role of straight man in this dialogue and that I'd laugh out loud at JK's wit. I did not expect, however, that he would concede all my major points: texts are meant to be interpreted; there are multiple worthwhile ways of doing interpretations; one such way attends closely to the relation among authorial agency, reader response, and textual phenomena in order to offer knowledge of a text's rhetorical techniques, structure, effects, and purposes. JK's concession is great for me (and of course for him—it's always wonderful to have the scales fall from one's eyes) but perhaps not so good for our esteemed editor, Donald Hall, who was, I imagine, expecting more resistance from JK. But not to worry. JK and I can very profitably spend the rest of our allotted space illustrating—and celebrating—these very important, though generally underappreciated, points about interpretation, multiplicity, and rhetorical criticism.

[Pause]

By now, I expect that you and JK will have seen through the rather transparent strategy of the previous paragraph. If, as JK boldly claims, the text "has no will, no power, no being beyond what we can make of it. And we can make of it what we will," then I am free to read HIS text as a concession to my major points. But my very exercise of that freedom shows the radical inadequacy of his claim: he knows—and you and I also know—that his text disputes those points. Because we all know that much, we also recognize that my claim to have persuaded him disrespects his text. I, at least, believe that JK and his text deserve better. Or to put it another way, even if some of you are pro-dissing (either in general or in the case of JK's text), the very idea (and art) of the diss presupposes a text with enough of an identity to warrant such treatment. In short, JK's witty opposition to my case effectively undermines his claim about the lack of power in texts. This undermining, not surprisingly, also weakens his more radical claims that we should stop doing interpretation and stop organizing ourselves around texts. But before I turn to that issue, I would like to clarify the relation between my case for multiplicity and my treatment of "The Cask."

JK, I suspect, would seize on the previous paragraph to assert that once again it reveals a contradiction in my position: my objection to him shows that I do believe in the power of texts, yet my initial moves were to deny that we owe anything to texts and to affirm that there are multiple ways to analyze texts. There's a paradox here but no contradiction, and the paradox can be explained by attending to the difference in context for the initial question, "What do we owe texts?" and for the most recent question, "Does JK's text deserve my respect?" The context for the initial question includes, among other things, the general theoretical debate about the identity and stability of texts that has waxed and waned over the last thirty years or so. To answer the question is to stake out a general position about the ontological status of texts. And there aren't that many options: texts have fixed, immutable identities; texts have no identities in themselves but are written by our interpretive practices, which are themselves influenced by larger institutional forces (JK seems to be arguing for one version of this position but I await further elaboration); texts have fluid identities that shift as we bring different interpretive frameworks to them. My answer—we don't owe texts anything but we should recognize that there are multiple worthwhile ways of doing interpretation—is a version of the third position.

In my view, texts by themselves don't determine the purposes of our interpretation (we don't owe them one kind of reading or another). On that point, JK and I agree. In my view, unlike JK's, texts do have features independent of our interpretive methods but those features signify in different ways as our different purposes lead us to different interpretive methods. In my rhetorical frame, the sentences at the end of Poe's story demand interpretation because they signify new dimensions of Montresor's character and new dimensions of the relationship between his narration and his action. In a new historical frame emphasizing Poe's representations of Italy and Italian culture, these sentences would figure less prominently and may have different meanings—"*In pace requiescat!*" could be viewed as a mere coda—and other features of the story would move to the foreground. (This view of the relation between textual features and interpretive frames also underlies my brief remarks about *Middlemarch*.)

If texts don't determine the purposes for which they are used, and if there are multiple worthwhile purposes, why do I do rhetorical criticism? Because I find that it allows me to develop cognitive understanding of what I experience often intuitively and inchoately as I read. And because this relationship between cognition and experience becomes productively recursive. After I've puzzled through such phenomena as the sentences from "The Cask" that I quoted above, I get more out of my experience of the story—and of other first-person retrospective narratives. And as I get more experience in reading, I become a more resourceful analyst (however dull or unexciting by Kincaidian standards). I also practice rhetorical criticism because, like western civilization and communication between adults and adolescents, it's a good idea that is more frequently trashed or neglected than tried. Nevertheless, questions of rhetorical criticism are not the only ones I'm interested in, and I would be the first to denounce the move of judging others' work on "The Cask" according to its degree of agreement or disagreement with my rhetorical reading.

The context for the question, "Does JK's text deserve my respect?" is much more specific. His text is not just answering the question of our title but also responding to my opening statements, and if that response is to be at all effective, it needs, among other things, to demonstrate an adequate understanding of my text. And what holds for JK's response also holds for mine. We are, in other words, already in a rhetorical situation which induces us to read each other's texts for their probable intended meanings as they can be inferred from the words on the page, our knowledge of each other, including each other's work, and our understanding of the conventions of this dialogue. It's clear to me, as I trust it's clear to you, that as JK writes his text, he seeks to interpret what I have written in a way that does justice to my intended meaning, even as he tries—wittily, valiantly (and, dare I say it?, hopelessly)—to show that my text says one thing and does another. (All readers are cordially invited to a reception at the University of Southern California to honor JK on his appointment to the position of associate dean.) As I am writing this response, I am seeking to do justice to his intended meaning not only because I want to treat his text with the respect he has accorded mine but also because doing so is arguably the most effective way for this dialogue to be constructive. Acknowledging the power of each other's texts means that we can talk to rather than past each other. And if neither of us has a conversion experience, we should at least achieve a deeper understanding of what divides us and what's at stake in that division.

Could I lift JK's text out of this present context and read it differently? Sure. Had I world enough and time, I'd love to psychoanalyze it (what's going on in the psyche of some one who sees me as both Ronald Crane and Mae West?) or to read it as the product of discourses about theory and interpretation that have nothing to do with JK's individual agency and everything to do with the evolution of these discourses in the institution of literary studies over the past twenty-five years or so. But time's short, space is shorter, and I think we can make better—and certainly more efficient—progress by staying in our current context.

So, what does all this have to do with literary texts and their interpretation? Let's turn to JK's most direct complaint about my brief sketch of a rhetorical reading of the ending of "The Cask." "We applaud JP's reading, find it in its way persuasive, because it is so in accord with professional practices we have been taught to honor, not because it has anything whatsoever to do with the dots." JK goes on to assert with characteristic understatement that there are another "747 equally persuasive readings available" to us now and an infinite number potentially available. And all that because the text "has no will, no power, no being beyond what we can make of it."

I won't deny that my reading is in accord with professional practices; it needs to be in order to get a hearing by the audience I am addressing. But I will deny that the reading has nothing whatever to do with the text and that the text has no power beyond what I can make of it. The evidence is that the textual phenomena, considered within the rhetorical frame, resist some readings and conform to others. And once again JK provides useful support for my point. My reading, he says, "avoid[s] triviality" because it gets beyond an account of the story as "a mere bone-chiller" without reducing it to "a dreary moralistic fable." I'm grateful for the compliment, but I'd say that the test of the reading is not to be found by measuring it against JK's yardstick of triviality but against the capacity of the alternative readings to account for the textual phenomena fully, precisely, and coherently. Consider the bone-chiller reading: Montresor is an inhuman monster and the effect of the story is to leave the reader both appalled and horrified at the cold-blooded avenger who continues to revel in his sadistic revenge a half-century after its completion. This reading is weaker than the one I've sketched because it must gloss over Montresor's admission that his heart grew sick on account of the dampness of the catacombs. But if that admission were not part of the story, the bone-chiller reading would be more persuasive than mine (JK's charge of triviality could then be leveled at Poe rather than the critic). In short, to point out that a reading accords with professional practice is not to establish that the reading is unconstrained by the text. Furthermore, within a given interpretive frame, some readings will clearly be better than others because they will more fully, precisely, and coherently account for the textual phenomena. Because texts have features independent of our frameworks, cross-frame comparisons are also possible, though these are more difficult and inevitably more controversial.

JK may still want to suggest that we organize our activities around something other than literary texts. I'd be very interested to hear him develop that proposal. But if the proposal is based on the principle that texts are always only dots on a page, then I think he hasn't found a persuasive rationale. Furthermore, interpretation need not be simply a matter of making a text say what we will; instead, it can be an enlightening, difficult, and rigorous process that teaches us worthwhile knowledge about texts—and more rather than less fun for all that. Texts and interpretations need not spoil the party—but then again it depends on the kind of party you want to have.

Editorial Interruption: I think it would be instructive to whatever readers remain to reprint here the e-mail dialogue I had with one W. J. T. Mitchell (afterwards Widjit) at this point in the exchange between JP and JK. I turned, I will admit, to Widjit for help. I had read JK's second offering and was in need of help, so I turned, as I say, to Widjit at this point. (JK's second offering is withheld from you for a moment, for reasons that will become ever so clear.) Anyhow, I know that turning to another for help, much less reporting to you on that turn, is unusual; but the whole matter is, as I say, instructive, which counts for much. [DH]

DH: So you know both these people.
WIDJIT: Yes, friends with both, if you can believe it.
DH: Oh, I can. Phelan seems amiable.
WIDJIT: He is, very.
DH: Kincaid too?
WIDJIT: No, I wouldn't say that.
DH: Anyhow, you see my problem in this exchange.
WIDJIT: When are we going to start having fun?
DH: Something like that. There is something about the feel of all this, you know, the tone. It's . . .
WIDJIT: Fucking boring.
DH: Well, perhaps formal.
WIDJIT: Archaic fumblings, fussy pedantry, quadruple missings of the point, rhinocerine wit, convulsive belches.
DH: So what should I do?
WIDJIT: Edit Kincaid.
DH: He does seem to go on a bit in making his points.
WIDJIT: He doesn't by God get it. He never makes a point. I must say that even Phelan, weighted down with his 1930s-era theoretical clodhoppers, runs rings round him.
DH: So I should edit Kincaid.
WIDJIT: Yes. Rewrite him so he makes a point now and then.
DH: Actually meets head-on some of Phelan's claims, maybe refers to the Poe story?
WIDJIT: Jesus Christ, no. Don't get sucked into the Poe story. But yes, do pick

up some of Phelan's quite stunning propositions, seldom heard since the birth of Shirley Temple.

DH: Phelan makes some very clear claims. I admire his lucidity.

WIDJIT: Goody. Then focus on 'em. Kincaid never will. He can't recognize them, bull-elephant obvious as they are.

DH: But Kincaid is sure to notice that I'm writing it and not him.

WIDJIT: Nope. Count on it. He won't.

DH: I'll take that as a guarantee, you knowing him so well and all.

WIDJIT: One excuse for him, though. He has been through this mill before. Twice at least—and in my journal.

DH: No.

WIDJIT: Makes me shudder. You see where Phelan unloads that stuff about you can't diss a text without agreeing that texts have certain innate features?

DH: Yes. Kincaid's sure to unload on that nonsense.

WIDJIT: Already has, in his first rejoinder, you know. Easy to miss, of course, what with his prose. Phelan missed it anyhow. All that village atheist stuff where Kincaid says he isn't going to be drawn into assumptions that pre-suppose what is at issue.

DH: He did that twice before in your journal?

WIDJIT: No, not that. Something else. You see where Phelan argues that be-cause Kincaid's response seems to him intelligible—and because Phelan's opening statement must have been intelligible to Kincaid—that therefore Kincaid interprets texts just like Phelan, only he never noticed that's what he was doing?

DH: I don't follow you.

WIDJIT: How could you not? Phelan argues that Kincaid seeks to interpret Phelan's text "in a way that does justice to my intended meaning." Remem-ber that?

DH: Oh.

WIDJIT: Lot of leaps there, don't you think? A real hop, skip, and a jump to argue that because Kincaid submits to a discursive code (by which the dots seem to signal something) that he is demonstrating that there is not only a text but some kind of meaning *in the text,* even (Phelan most hilariously claims) in Phelan's "intentions," about which the less said the better.

DH: So what does this have to do with twice before in your journal.

WIDJIT: What Phelan is doing is the neo-Aristotelian shuffle, or, more prop-erly, Chicago-School Squirm #4: claim that the very fact that your post-structuralist opponent writes indicates that he is really an R. S. Crane wannabe.

DH: Kincaid met with that before?

WIDJIT: Twice, when some decades back M. H. Abrams tried exactly the same nyah-nyah with J. Hillis Miller (and Kincaid pointed out the fallacy) and then, later, when an otherwise brilliant and nice guy, Robert Denham, slipped into the same routine with him. I can't blame him for not responding over and over to the same knock-knock joke.

DH: So you're on Kincaid's side?

WIDJIT: God no! I read his second response. It's incoherent.

DH: He'd probably claim that as a virtue.

WIDJIT: I'm sure he would.

DH: OK. I think I'll rewrite Kincaid as elegantly simple, framing his remarks in the form of just a few questions or propositions—pointed ones. Only nobody'll think it's him doing it.

WIDJIT: Who gives a shit what they think? At least there'll be an argument.

DH: OK. Here goes:

1. What does JP mean by "a text"?
2. Does he really think texts have "no identities" but are written by our interpretive practices (which, surely, have no limit)?
3. If so, how on earth can texts have "independent features"?
4. What are some of those features?
5. What status do they have if they are, at once, written by interpretive practices and independent of them?
6. Platonic? Christian?
7. Does anybody but Phelan assume an innocent, "intuitive and inchoate" experience with a text that is prior to and uncorrupted by language?
8. Do those who do indeed assume just that figure that the later understanding that follows the raw experience, the understanding that arrives after dinner or maybe two weeks later, is the first time language enters the picture? Is Phelan's prior experience with what he thinks is a text pre-linguistic? What CAN such an experience be? And when Phelan later inserts language into his life with the text, is such an invasion nothing more than "understanding"? Doesn't language change the experience? I, of course, would say that there is no experience, textual or otherwise, without language, wouldn't you? I'd also say that what Phelan calls "understanding" is the experience and that it is not so primitive and visceral and universal as he suggests, Wordsworthian that he is, but a set of cultural and historical codes drawn up according to rules, rules that govern not only "understanding" but "experience." Correct me if I'm wrong here.
9. JP somewhat plaintively argues at the end that he likes what he does and that it likes him. I think that someone like JK (oops, me) who has written with scandalous tolerance of all kinds of deviance ought to respect pleasure where he finds it. If JP finds himself receiving bliss or promotion from imagining that he is illuminating "textual phenomena," then what harm is being done? He does teach and write, of course, and there is the question of influence. But, as Milton says, error must be protected.

10. It is only fair to ask me the following: What do we gain by dismissing "permanent features" of texts that are independent of interpretive practices?

    Does that do anything for us? That is the question.

11. In other words, JP, who has the most fun?

12. Now for something completely different: texts are to us a cowardly retreat, a way of ignoring everything we have been allowed to think about language, culture, and meaning in the last forty years. Paul de Man's collaborationist writings are used as a (preposterous) excuse to pretend that we needn't attend to the whole postmodern (much less poststructuralist) rumpus. We heave a huge sigh of relief and go back to finding meanings in texts, finding them with surprising ease.

13. "To account for the textual phenomena fully, precisely, and coherently": that seems to me a goal in life one might find admirable, in the same way one could admire all forms of double-entry bookkeeping, moth collecting, concordance compiling, and the honorable lot of scriveners. Everyone finds her or his bliss where she or he may. But there is such a thing as perversion!

14. In the name of common decency . . .

Kincaid's own submission, just to give you a taste, I attach below. Well, not all of it. In fact, you really don't need a full sentence.

James Kincaid: If that arrogant goddamn JP thinks he can come in here and throw around some old-hat—oh I'm sick of it!—Chicago tricks and a few evangelical remarks and Arnoldian repetitions and some—can you believe this is still around?—diddle about accounting for textual phenomena, why then he just should . . .

James Phelan: The thousand injuries of JK I have borne as I best could; but now that he has ventured upon insult—I laugh with pleasure and admiration. I love his wit. I'm impressed by his ability to take his jinks to ever-new heights (I might even feel complimented on being the occasion for this latest ascent if it weren't for my suspicion that ANY occasion could produce similar efforts). And of course there are insults and there are insults. The ones that sting or even inspire Montresorian thoughts of revenge make a palpable hit. It's hard to laugh while bleeding. But when the barbs go sailing harmlessly by, as JK's just have, it's easy to be jovial and admiring while waving them good-bye.

Yet there is one general aspect of the complaints voiced by Widjit that has been troubling me too. Is this a lost-in-the-seventies dialogue? JK's citing his *Critical Inquiry* essays (which, by the way, go back to the pre-Mitchell days when the journal was edited by Sheldon Sacks) and JK's been-there-done-that grousing about features of our exchange increase my doubt. We're all post-modern and poststructural now; indeed, we are even postmillennial. In such an era, there may be quicker ways to marginalize oneself than appearing to be stuck in the seventies—but not too many.

I've come to think, though, that this problem is more superficial than sub-stantive and that it arises largely from the way we've posed our question. Our initial focus on "texts" rather than "critical projects" or "cultural and literary studies" or "multicultural and postcolonial writing" or some other late-nine-ties' locutions and activities has led us back to issues in the seventies' debates. Once we ask what we owe to texts, we're off and running in a discussion about the nature of texts, the variety of interpretations, the relation of critical meth-ods to each other—and whether it is possible to escape interpretations. Al-though questions about culture and ideology have come to occupy criticism's collective attention more than the questions JK and I have been debating here, how critics do their work on culture and ideology is deeply dependent on their assumptions about texts, interpretations, and critical methods. If our discus-sion of these fundamental issues leads us to rehearse some of what was said in the seventies, so be it. Since the questions are neither new nor settled, we shouldn't be surprised to find ourselves thinking about them in ways that oth-ers—including our younger selves—sometimes did. That an idea has been thought before is no argument against it (despite JK's apparent belief to the contrary). But of course we need to do more than replay the earlier debates. Whether we succeed is a question best left to our readers.

To return to the specifics of JK's latest: underneath all his admirable but misguided wit, he is trying to press his case against both multiplicity and rhe-torical criticism, and that effort culminates this time in the questions he poses through HIS Charlie McCarthy, "DH." The only fair and decent thing to do is to respond to those questions.

1. *What does JP mean by "a text"?*

The first principle of my case for multiplicity is that a text is more than one thing. A text is a system of signs AND a multileveled communication between an author and audience AND a stimulus for reader response AND a site for revealing the ideological assumptions of its culture AND a link in a network of other texts, both literary and nonliterary, AND many other things as well, including syntheses of some of these definitions. In a particular act of inter-pretation, however, we typically take one definition as primary and go from there. Furthermore, not all definitions of a text are as useful or adequate as others. Yes, texts are dots on a page, but if that's all they are, there's not much else to say about them. And if that's all they are, JK and I are wasting our time trying to communicate with each other and with our readers. JK uses Widjit to object to my jumping from the fact that in our dialogue he "submits to a discursive code (by which the dots seem to signal something)" to the conclusion that "there is not only a text but some kind of meaning in the text." JK's objection makes sense only if one believes that the best definition of a text is that it is dots on a page. My point is that all our experience with texts, including the ones in this dialogue, argues for a different conclusion.

Finally, some definitions of texts contest other definitions. To say, for example, that a text is a centerless system of signs displaying its ultimate undecidability contests the view that texts are multilayered communications from author to audience (and vice versa). My own commitment to rhetorical criticism would lead me to argue that the deconstructive definition is less adequate than the rhetorical one, but the more important point here is that such contestation is both inevitable and not at all easy to resolve. (Texts, in my view, are not unique in possessing such multiplicity; the world itself is more than one thing—but the ontology of the world is beyond the scope of this dialogue.)

2–4. Does he really think texts have "no identities" but are written by our interpretive practices (which, surely, have no limit)? If so, how on earth can texts have "independent features"? What are some of those features?

The second principle of my case for multiplicity is that texts are not wholly written by our interpretive practices. Texts do contain features independent of our frameworks for viewing and analyzing them—and the fact of their independence means that not all interpretations are equal, as I tried to suggest when I presented JK's first contribution as conceding my points and when I found fault with the reading of "The Cask" seeing Montresor as pure evil. At the same time, independent textual features are not sufficient to give texts fixed identities. I once argued that Stephen Pepper's distinction between data and danda is a useful way to conceptualize this point. Data are the independent features of texts, danda are those features as construed within a given framework. The sentence, "My heart grew sick—on account of the dampness of the catacombs," exists as part of the textual data of "The Cask of Amontillado," but both its meaning and its salience can vary as one particular framework construes it in one way and another framework in a different way. From within my rhetorical frame, its salience is very high because it is the first explicit act of denial on the part of Montresor the narrator, and its meaning can be specified: Poe is revealing a new dimension of his character-narrator, one that leads to a reconfiguration of our understanding of him, his actions, and his narration. Within a psychoanalytic frame focusing on Poe, the sentence's salience would also be high, but its meaning would be different. The psychoanalytic critic would be interested in what Poe's representation of a character such as Montresor reveals about Poe himself. Within a new historical frame concerned with the story as one example of American attitudes toward Europe, the sentence is much less salient, and so the question of its meaning less significant, though the new historicist may, depending on other features of his project, agree with the rhetorical or the psychoanalytic critic or with neither.

5–6. What status do they have if they are, at once, written by interpretive practices and independent of them? Platonic? Christian?

Since, in my view, texts are neither wholly written by interpretive practices nor wholly independent of them (see above), I can't answer this question. But I'll seize the opportunity to speculate that this question—and at least some of JK's general resistance—stems from my not being clear enough about the difference between my metacritical stance and my interpretive practice. It's the difference between taking a position on all the positions interpreters might take on "The Cask" and taking a position on the story oneself. I'm located in one place and doing one kind of intellectual operation when answering such metacritical questions as what is a text and how are the multiple definitions related to each other. And I'm in a different place and doing a different kind of intellectual operation when answering such interpretive questions as how does the last paragraph of "The Cask" cause us to revise our understanding of Montresor and his relation to his storytelling and what does Poe gain by those moves. Within the metacritical location, I emphasize multiplicity; within the rhetorical location, I seek to characterize the specific communication from the author through the textual phenomena as precisely as possible. Of course the two locations are in the same critical hemisphere: the effort to understand critical difference is akin to the effort to understand authorial communication because in each case the intellectual task is to find an intelligible relation among disparate phenomena. Nevertheless, attending to the different locations and different intellectual operations should, I hope, clarify the relation between my claims about texts in general and my specific interpretations of Poe's and JK's texts.

7–8. Does anybody but Phelan assume an innocent, "intuitive and inchoate" experience with a text that is prior to and uncorrupted by language? Do those who do indeed assume just that figure that the later understanding that follows the raw experience, the understanding that arrives after dinner or maybe two weeks later, is the first time language enters the picture? Is Phelan's prior experience with what he thinks is a text pre-linguistic? What CAN such an experience be? And when Phelan later inserts language into his life with the text, is such an invasion nothing more than "understanding"? Doesn't language change the experience? I, of course, would say that there is no experience, textual or otherwise, without language, wouldn't you? I'd also say that what Phelan calls "understanding" is the experience and that it is not so primitive and visceral and universal as he suggests, Wordsworthian that he is, but a set of cultural and historical codes drawn up according to rules, rules that govern not only "understanding" but "experience." Correct me if I'm wrong here.

A horse is a horse of course of course. And of course language and cultural codes are mediating experience before, during, and after reading. (I would not agree that there is no experience without language—sudden, excruciating physical pain seems to me strong evidence of nonlinguistic experience—but I also think that that issue is beyond the scope of this dialogue.) My point about our always doing interpretation from within a certain frame is another version of JK's points about language and codes. But acknowledging their presence does not significantly alter my claim about the phenomenology of reading: as we read most literary texts, we don't have full cognitive understanding of the experience, even as that experience can powerfully affect us. And as we read, we sometimes are unsure of how to respond because the codes and the language of the text are not readily comprehensible either intuitively or consciously. Rhetorical criticism seeks cognitive knowledge of what we experience intuitively, and it seeks to transform the inchoate into the intelligible by looking for the causes of our affective response and illumination of our puzzlement in the textual phenomena understood as authorial communication. Yes, the articulation of the understanding does modify the experience, and that makes doing it well more rather than less important. And the whole process helps prepare us for experiences with new texts. I don't claim that my experience is universal. But I do assume that it is not just idiosyncratic (it has its causes in the textual phenomena), and it, therefore, has the potential to connect with other readers' efforts to understand their experiences.

9 & 13. JP somewhat plaintively argues at the end that he likes what he does and that it likes him. I think that some one like JK (oops, me) who has written with scandalous tolerance of all kinds of deviance ought to respect pleasure where he finds it. If JP finds himself receiving bliss or promotion from imagining that he is illuminating "textual phenomena," then what harm is being done? He does teach and write, of course, and there is the question of influence. But, as Milton says, error must be protected.

"To account for the textual phenomena fully, precisely, and coherently": that seems to me a goal in life one might find admirable, in the same way one could admire all forms of double-entry bookkeeping, moth collecting, concordance com-

*piling, and the honorable lot of scriveners. Everyone finds her or his bliss where
she or he may. But there is such a thing as perversion!*

I'm grinning and waving.

*10–11. It is only fair to ask JK the following: What do we gain by dismissing
"permanent features" of texts that are independent of interpretive practices? Does
that do anything for us? That is the question. In other words, JP, who has the most
fun?*

Easiest questions of the bunch: the dismissal licenses JK to do anything he
damn well pleases, and that does great things for him and us because his fancy
can fly unfettered and we get to see the results. He has the most fun but his
readers are a close second.

Though easy, these questions are also the cleverest. Almost anything I say
to counter (e.g., it's not ultimately about fun but about knowledge, persuasion, how we think and act) will leave me in the role of spoilsport. But what
the hell; I'm already the dullard of our duo. "It's only fair to ask JK" whether
he likes to play tennis without a net, without lines, without an opponent? In
other words, for me part of the fun of criticism comes from the challenge the
independent features of texts present to my efforts at understanding. (But I
also like being chair of an English department.)

*12. Now for something completely different: texts are to us a cowardly retreat,
a way of ignoring everything we have been allowed to think about language, culture, and meaning in the last forty years. Paul de Man's collaborationist writings
are used as a (preposterous) excuse to pretend that we needn't attend to the whole
postmodern (much less poststructuralist) rumpus. We heave a huge sigh of relief
and go back to finding meanings in texts, finding them with surprising ease.*

Just two brief comments: I never noticed that postmodernists or poststruc-
turalists had any trouble finding meanings in texts, though of course sometimes the meanings they found were about the undecidability of the text or
the fluidity of identity or the constructed nature of subjectivity. And aren't texts
the means by which everything we have been allowed to think about language,
culture, and meaning has come to us?

James Kincaid: Not that this is really JK, of course, since that wouldn't do. It's
close to JK, as close as reasonable people would want to get. What we've done
is sort of take over his e-mail sender, you see, which isn't as hard as it sounds,
since he has no idea how to operate it. I think it is fair to say that we have not
changed his sentiments, just redirected them into a channel where the sane
swim. Tone, of course, is another matter.

That JP is good, you're thinking. I am too. I believe I and the argument are best served by granting those parts of his argument which are important to him and which do not damage my case in the slightest, reserving my energy for those areas vital to my own position and salary. That would be gracious of me and would speed things along, which I must say JP does not seem good at doing. I'm faster. So, I'll do that, grant him, in fact, everything he says, everything (how do you like them apples?), every single point—ONCE YOU ACCEPT HIS PREMISES. If you start out by playing JP's particular version of hopscotch, you can't fault his hopping and picking up the stone without once falling on his nose or displaying his panties. So, for all I know, he is throwing all sorts of new light on that dreary Poe story.

But I don't think myself and neither do you that it's at all a question of throwing light ON something, as if something (or, as JP madly puts it, a part of something) is THERE. It all comes down to JP's Cartesian flummery. That's the meat of it. He asserts that "Data are the independent features of texts." (You can always tell a serious thinker by the fact that he knows right off that *data* is plural.) Not that texts have nothing inside them but "data," though. Oh no. JP thinks it's sort of this and sort of that, kinda independent and kinda well like ye gods you know determined by what we bring to it. These last non-data, which JP still mashes inside texts, are "danda." There's a word that comes lolloping off the tongue. I'm a danda man and JP is data. He says *tomato* and I don't know how to spell it. Danda "are those features that are construed within a given framework."

So JP, knowing danda when he sees them but also knowing enough to keep his distance, hones in on the data, which have nothing whatever to do with his constructions but which sit there forever the same, for the smart and the dim, from China to Peru, for the Greek astronomer and the late Marlin Perkins, for Albertus Magnus and Catherine MacKinnon, for Jesus and Janet Reno, for . . . (JK goes on for some time here, but who wants to follow him?)

That's it in a nutshell. Don't you think? No need to read any more. If you think texts exist (or parts of them do) in some way wholly independent of culture, history, perspective, then good luck to you. I don't wish you ill.

If, on the other hand, you think texts are brought into being in symbiotic relation with the modes of seeing, then we can proceed. But not too far for now. I submit that this symbiotic model renders boring the question of whether texts exist, since their existence is obvious, but not independent of the way we have of cooperating in that existence. And, as the modes of seeing texts are without limit, so are the things we might see in and do with texts.

And we might do a lot more with them than go on forever demonstrating that the ways of seeing them are without limit, controlled at any one time only by the rhetorical and institutional models that give us our lenses. JP's way of doing business, I submit, gives us a miraculously redundant demonstration of this principle: there's potentially no end to the ways in which we can read texts. I think his manufacturing would be harmless, but for the fact that it directs our energies to one enterprise alone and seems to distract us from other duties. For instance, how is discourse (not texts, mind you) generated? How is it distributed? What are the conventions by which it is read? Why has interpretation seized on us like mad cow disease? Why is it not a single reader has ever been persuaded by another's interpretation? Put another way, how is it that no interpretation has ever failed to be persuasive?

These are good questions. But we neglect them. Among the brilliant, completely persuasive points JP makes is this one: "How critics do their work on culture and ideology is deeply dependent on their assumptions about texts . . ." How true. And how sad. We all remember how deconstruction was softened and pablumized so as to make it edible over here. It became not a radical playground for cultural and ideological activity but another means oh lord help us of reading texts. We were told that texts deconstructed themselves, that it was all somehow inside them. Well it isn't and it wasn't and it shouldn't be.

One last thing: The Big Guy in the Sky isn't Power. There is no metaphysical center. Power's just a word. Paranoid question-begging arguments should have no particular force except with the paranoid. Why not assume that things are held together by habit and sloth, not mysterious, super-brilliant agencies of—gasp when you say this—POWER? We can then whistle while we work. Even JP.

James Phelan: JK will grant me "every single point." Wow. I'm whistling as I write. Them apples taste very sweet, thank you kindly. And the sweetness for me, believe it or not, involves more than just JK's concession. His move restores my faith in our form. Despite earlier appearances, we can't justifiably title this dialogue, "The Dogged Dullard v. the Whimsical Wit; or Dueling Testosterone." One of us at least is capable of listening to the other and moving from his initial position.

To be sure, I'm aware that there's a catch to JK's concession, a catch embedded in the uppercase letters of "ONCE YOU ACCEPT HIS PREMISES." Although JK will grant those premises, he can't stop regarding their consequences as deplorable: they will keep us doing such boring things as interpreting "The Cask of Amontillado," when we could—and should—be asking an allegedly richer set of questions: "how is discourse (not texts, mind you) generated? How is it distributed? What are the conventions by which it is read? Why has interpretation seized on us like mad cow disease? Why is it not a single reader has ever been persuaded by another's interpretation? Put another way, how is it that no interpretation has ever failed to be persuasive?" I translate the catch in JK's concession this way: "JP has premises to keep; don't they put us all to sleep?"

What I'm happy to grant is the richness of JK's first four questions: yes, let's ask and answer them, let's go beyond what Foucault, Bakhtin, and others have taught us about the generation and distribution of discourse; let's go beyond the standard histories of twentieth-century criticism that chronicle the institution's turn toward interpretation and get at its underlying causes and its staying power. These matters are worth inquiring into because they promise to tell us, in the first case, a lot about language and culture (and even habit and sloth) and, in the second, a lot about the bedrock assumptions, anxieties, and obsessions of our profession (not to mention more about habit and sloth). I'm also happy to grant that these questions are richer than interpretive questions about a single text such as "how does the ending of 'The Cask' alter the configuration of both the events and the narrative situation?" But I can't grant that they're richer because they escape my premises about texts and interpretations. They're richer because they're more ambitious and significant than one question about a single text. They have more at stake, and they score higher on the degree-of-difficulty scale. A question with comparable scope, arising out of assumptions about the importance of texts and interpretation, can be equally rich. Asking "how does the use of a character-narrator affect the ethical dimension of reading narrative?" promises to tell us a lot about an activity that many people in our culture value (not to mention all those writers and readers of past cultures). Nothing dreary, deplorable, or easy here that I can see. Why not welcome both kinds of questions? Why assume that there's only one hierarchy of value and that as a profession we should choose one kind of question over the other?

JK's implicit answer perhaps can be found in the assumption behind his last two questions: "Why is it not a single reader has ever been persuaded by another's interpretation? Put another way, how is it that no interpretation has ever failed to be persuasive?" The assumption is that we have so many ways to do interpretation (somewhere in the neighborhood of 748) and have been doing it so obsessively (it's like mad cow disease) that we've reached a paradoxical situation: any one interpretation will be utterly persuasive and utterly resistible. If that assumption is warranted, then JK's hierarchy of value is also warranted: why continue doing interpretation under such conditions? But I don't see the warrant for the assumption—and what's more, if JK meant what he said about granting my premises, he shouldn't be able to see it anymore either. The warrant is located in a view of interpretation as any institutionally sanctioned story about a text—something accountable not to textual phenomena (which tend to disappear as we move from institutionally sanctioned way #1 to institutionally sanctioned way #748) but to "professional practices." I've already argued that we can distinguish better and worse interpretations within any given interpretive framework and that we can also make cross-framework comparisons. And JK has now said that he will grant this point (along with all the others). Thus, neither he nor the rest of us need to accept JK's implicit hierarchy of value that privileges questions about discourse over questions about interpretation. Thus, we can recognize the worth of both kinds of questions. Although JK and I are not likely ever to become workers in each other's vineyards, there's no reason we can't enjoy each other's wine—and no reason for either of us to call for a boycott of the other's products.

James Kincaid: JP ends his characteristically gracious-yet-obstinate (I really expected to convert him) entry with an allusion to vineyards, no doubt one last game try at hooking the attentive among you back into the wretched Poe story he wanted so much to worry. Before reading JP's last, I had counted it among my triumphs that I had artfully sucked us away from text-talk. Now I am sort of sorry I did. It wouldn't have cost me that much to play his game and let him beat me up some. I can take it. Makes me come off looking a lot like Bob Eubanks, the game-show-host-as-bully, a little sleazy. I wish now I had agreed to participate in JP's Old-Timers Game. It means so much to him.

If only there were any other games going on. JP talks about working in vineyards, probably thinking of his favorite wineries. I happen to know from colleagues of his that he has direct ties to several noted Ohio wineries (two in Cleveland, one in Akron) and supplies department parties quite handsomely at a price you wouldn't believe if I told you. I think I'll tell you. Last year, the total wine budget—for a retreat, a Christmas party, seventeen retirements, a Wouldn't-You-Like-To-Be-An-English-Major? Get Together, a Staff Recognition, two speakers, and miscellaneous—was (hold onto your garters) $47 and change. And that includes three bottles barely used that JP has recorked for service again this fall. One note: the department sponsors more than two speakers but only serves wine for some of them. Not all. I gave a talk there myself a few years back. No wine in sight. Anyhow, when I think of wine, which I do all the time, I think not of manufactures but of the parable of the vineyard. It's a beauty: the last shall be first. A comic parable written by Jesus or one of his ventriloquists, the antic one. It's an absurdist celebration of nonlogic, that parable, a text worth swimming in. He who argues most weakly shall be crowned with laurels. That's how it applies here. I win.

JP says it isn't really a contest we've been having, but a kind of reluctant airing, an embarrassed and unplanned meeting during exercise time in the Yard. How'd this happen, two academics exchanging views? JP says we now mumble a few polite words, hurry back to our separate cells, and hope to hell this never happens again. We agree to disagree. We agree to ignore the other. That's hardly fair to JP. He's argued vigorously and with unswerving devotion to the principles that animate him. I grant him that. More than you can say for me, too. I admit it.

But, put it this way: what's it cost him to be generous anyhow? Huh? I know that's rude, but holy hell. I mean he has everybody already on his side. There are now, I would say, about 43,214 people, of all genders, who are in something like English departments and who think of themselves as teaching texts. There are seven people, all queer, who are also (for now) in English departments and who try very hard never to teach a text. Talk about carrying coals to Newcastle!

JP says, sweetly sweetly, that we should oh yes certainly do those things I do, they are after all ever so important. And he knows all the time that the vast armies of lit and comp teachers will be back at it next semester teaching oh jesus damn it shit Intro to the Short Story, Am Lit 1790–1890, and Marxist Approaches to Lit.

Anyhow, it's been a contest all along between JP and me. I submit that I came in dead last, and therefore, if Jesus is the judge, I shall be first. Jesus doesn't say exactly when I'll be first, of course, and that bothers me a little, as he is given to postponing things a lot—maybe until I'm dead or something. Still, I'll take what I can get.

And what I have to admit is that I am not a pluralist, nor do I think interpreting texts is an innocent activity. It is stained, deeply stained. In order to ask questions of texts, you have to assume there's something there to answer. For me, texts are like little people under the leaves: one can, like JP, hold conversations with them. Most folks do. The question for the sane slim minority (me and my few friends, very few) is: what institutional climate, what mental state, would lead people to kneel and jabber into blank space?

But people also believe in alien abductions, Satanic abuse, the fairness of deans, the Second Coming, Clarence Thomas, and a quick Elvis. JP is arguing for honoring every private lunacy and I suppose that's hard to counter without sounding churlish. I am no churl. I have known churls, and I'm not one.

In conclusion, then, still believing this to be a contest and in the interests of complete fairness, I submitted the manuscript to my students (Intro to the

Short Story) and asked them to judge—without my final entry. That gave JP four shots to my three, but never mind. You'll think my students represent a biased sample, but not so. For one thing, I was not present during the administration of this little questioning. For another, they used a No. 2 pencil. Finally, it's not as if they like me or something. I give here a representative sampling of the results:

> While JP is the more focused (duh!) of the two, he has to spend a lot of time repeating himself in an attempt to get JK to attend to the subject. That's what struck me.

> I thought both were very good.

> I was wondering when the midterms were due.

> This exchange helps me to understand better what we're doing in this class which, up to now wasn't all that clear since I thought we'd be talking about stories and novels.

> JK is the best professor I've ever had and I'm sure glad I don't have JP.

> JP shines through all the smog like a ray of sunshine. He also seems very nice—much younger than JK, obviously and more in touch with the feelings and needs of his students, for sure. What's his phone number?

> I think this is a important issue as these things go and that there's a lot to be said on both sides and they said it.

Well, that pretty well sums it up. I suggested to DH that he allow us more space. He was very rude. I suggested to JP that we continue on our own time, as it were. He wasn't rude, of course. He said oh sure great we'll do that—after I tend to a few (thousand) other things. I can read between the lines, not as well as JP perhaps but I know those text games too and can tell pretty well when yes means no. He means no clear enough. You don't have to be a graduate of old U of Chicago to see that. So, good-bye. I recommend, though, that readers interested in extending or deepening this discussion contact JP or, even better, DH, who deserves it. Don't bother me. I'm going to go read "The Cask of Amontillado."

PART TWO

Changing Applications

4

A Dialogue on Evaluation in Poetry

Marjorie Perloff and Robert von Hallberg

Robert von Hallberg: I thought we would pursue our dialogue by assessing various evaluative criteria that are in play now among poet-critics, since they are the writers who most forthrightly make evaluative arguments. Readers find all sorts of reasons to admire a particular poem, poet, or even school of poets, but critics of poetry are often asked to state their standards abstractly, exactly because they traditionally assert on principle that poetry is not just another discourse but a specially authoritative use of language. I know we can both speak abstractly about particular criteria; probably neither of us has the old aspiration of advocating some universal or permanent criterion for assessing poetry. I want to leave open the possibility of invoking different criteria for different poems, and even of invoking different criteria at different moments. You probably want the same latitude, so focusing on particular critical arguments now current makes sense to me.

Marjorie Perloff: Well, no, actually I do still have that "old aspiration." And in a way my definition of poetry is quite conventional and classical. I believe a poem differs from routine or normal discourse (like this statement, for instance) by being the art form that foregrounds language, in its complexity, intensity, and, especially, *relatedness*. My criterion here is what Aristotle called *to prepon* or fitness. In the poetic text, everything is related to everything else— or should be—the whole being a construct of sameness and difference in pleasing proportions. What makes something "pleasing" can of course not be said outright and depends on the reader, the historical moment, and the cultural milieu. But we can say what poetry isn't: it is not straightforward, expository discourse (as in a chemistry textbook), whose aim is to convey information. I go back to Wittgenstein's proposition (#160) in *Zettel,* "Do not forget that a poem, even though it is composed in the language of information, is not used in the language-game of giving information."

Poetry must meet the criterion of re-readability. If a poem can be absorbed at one reading (as the typical poetry reading demands—i.e., at one hearing), then it's not much of a poem. Poetry is news that stays news; it is "language charged with meaning" (Ezra Pound). And here Pound's aphorisms accord with Russian Formalism and the notion of defamiliarization, making strange, the orientation toward the neighboring word. But neither Pound's nor the Russian Formalist notion is new: one finds the same formula in Sidney's *Defense of Poetry* or in Johnson's *Preface to Shakespeare,* where we read "Nothing can please many, and please long, but just representations of general nature." I take Johnson's "just" to mean the Aristotelian "fitting" (the *prepon* again), the implication being that representations (whether in lyric, drama, or fiction) must strike us not just as plausible according to some outside norm but internally consistent and coherent.

"Language charged with meaning" suggests that poetry can never be a matter of "lovely" or "elegant" language but that it must be meaningful; on the other hand, "meaning" that is external to or prior to language, as in much contemporary writing that passes for "poetry," is not poetry either.

Robert von Hallberg: You have surprised me already. When you say that "everything is related to everything else" in the poetic text, I wonder how you experience the reading of Pound's *Cantos* or Susan Howe's *Articulations of Sound Forms in Time.* No one sees how all words, phrases, and sentences in these texts are related to all the others there; no poem is all coherence. When the sounds of adjacent syllables or the feel of proximate rhythms leads one to sense a relatedness beyond what can be fully articulated, that is the deep charm of poetry that underwrites the sense that poetry and religion are somehow neighbors—as well as the suspicion that poetry is a game of smoke and mirrors, of illusory relatedness. As critics we tell all about the relatedness we can explicate, and frequently imply that we might tell more, had we world enough and time. But much of the contemporary poetry I love is frankly mysterious to me, which means that I cannot go very far with the coherence criterion.

Coherence, as you describe it, is bound implicitly to a notion of economy: your point is not the simple one that there is much coherence in poetry but that there is no incoherence in poetry. I constantly try to read past incoherence in poetry, but I accept this effort as my lot. You seem to want poetry that appears to be very highly coherent, which means highly economical. The poets I admire most are those who, on the one hand, condense their work so that its coherence is palpable, stony; Turner Cassity and Philip Larkin might be useful examples because their formality expresses that condensation so boldly, but Louise Glück and her onetime mentor George Oppen can also serve as examples, and they are not metrical poets. Reading these poets, one knows that one cannot account for each word and syntactic turn in terms of relatedness to other words and turns, but one does feel, line by line, that a strenuous process of selection for coherence has pruned the words down to remarkably few. On the other hand are those poets, whom I also admire, like Pound, Olson, and Ashbery, who accept the inevitability of incoherence and let economy be damned. For these writers, a principle of coherence is negatively involved; one admires their work despite its moments of apparent incoherence, despite its lack of economy. In fact, incoherence and extravagance are signs that a poem is working at the edges of convention, straining for beauty and meaning that come without coherence. I expected you to speak more for the avant-garde range of the latter, capacious, Whitmanesque approach to poetry. So, as I said, you surprise me.

Marjorie Perloff: I think we're talking about two different kinds of "coherence" or "relatedness" here. *The Cantos,* to take one of your examples, exhibit precisely the re-readability I was talking about. I opened at random to this passage in Canto LXXIV:

> One day were clouds banked on Taishan
>> Or in glory of sunset
>>> And tovarish blessed without aim
> Wept in the rainditch at evening
>> Sunt lumina
> That the drama is wholly subjective
> Stone knowing the form which the carver imparts it
> The stone knows the form
> Sia Cythera, sia Ixotta, sia in Santa Maria dei Miracoli
>> Where Pietro Romano had fashioned the bases
> OU TIS
> A man on whom the sun has gone down

Here in the first of the Pisan Cantos is a recharging of the sacred images we know from the earlier cantos: Mount Taishan, the light from the great crystal, Cythera (Venus), Ixotta degli Atti (Malatesta's adored mistress), the church of Santa Maria dei Miracoli, the reference to "OU TIS" (Odysseus in the Cyclops's cave calling himself "no man"), a "man on whom the sun has gone down" who is obviously the poet himself. The reference to himself as "tovarish" ("comrade"), on the other hand, reminds us of the actual political situation in 1945, a situation tragically at odds with those images of Mount Taishan and Cythera. And the wonderful chiming of "tovarish"/"rainditch" reinforces that harsh note. And yet another kind of relatedness is that of linguistic registers: we shift from the "glory of sunset" (line 1) to "sunt lumina" (line 5), so that light itself is refracted in complex ways, "sunt lumina," taken from Ovid, having been used earlier in the poem.

So I would say that here everything is "related" with great finesse, both to neighboring words and images and to cantos written thirty years earlier. True, there are places in the cantos where Pound rants on and on in his didactic, Douglasite, paranoid, anti-Semitic way, and clearly those parts are not as effective poetically, quite aside from the noxious "ideas" conveyed.

So far I've been focusing on universals. But now: if certain basic poetic principles remain intact across time, clearly other features change. Metrical and generic forms, for example, are often historically and culturally generated and conditioned. The Petrarchan sonnet, we know, originated in a particular court culture in fourteenth-century Italy; there are no Roman sonnets. The Pindaric ode, originally a war poem and adapted in various ways by Renaissance and eighteenth-century poets, no longer plays a significant role in poetry. Yet many critics persist in arguing, as has Helen Vendler, that the poet at any time has the choice of using any verse form he or she likes.

Robert von Hallberg: Well, certainly contemporary poetry presents a special case, exactly because contemporaneity is one widely used evaluative criterion. It may be a mistake, as many critics have claimed, to evaluate art in terms of its special purchase on a historical moment. But the pressure to evaluate the art of our own moment in terms of its responsiveness to the immediate energies we recognize is very great. Eliot said that the poetry of our contemporaries has special pleasure for us, and this is what I mean. Contemporary poetry engages with this special moment of community, and this is where the accumulated interpretation of our predecessors is minimal. The burden of the past is negligible, and the future is open. A critic of the present feels that this or that quality in art is in short supply, a little more of something or other seems the prescription for the art just now.

Marjorie Perloff: Now it's my turn to be surprised. I would have thought you believed that the "burden of the past" is never negligible, that it's always *there.*

Perhaps we can discuss this a bit with respect to Susan Howe, perhaps beginning with *The Birth-mark* (1993).

Robert von Hallberg: Susan Howe's work rightly enjoys a great deal of currency among writers and readers committed to experimental poetry. *My Emily Dickinson* (1985) and *The Birth-mark* raise issues that pertain particularly but not exclusively to current avant-garde writing. She is not concerned in her critical prose, though, with contemporary writing, so our construal of her criticism in relation to contemporary poetry may become a little unfair. The evaluative criteria at work in these prose books may not be quite the ones she would invoke in assessing contemporary poetry. All the same, the authority of her very engaging criticism does bring into prominence among her readers certain ways of assessing poetry that I want to discuss with you.

Generally, she has an ambitious antiformal understanding of poetry—ambitious because she asks antiformality to do a lot of work. Dickinson's "formlessness"—her syntactic and orthographical idiosyncrasies—has been understood by her editors as "lawlessness" that has to be disciplined into regularity, conformity (*Birth-mark*, 1), and Howe accepts this view of Dickinson as anarchist transgressor. The opening of *My Emily Dickinson* says that "In prose and in poetry she explored the implications of breaking the law just short of breaking off communication with a reader" (11). Howe charts the American antinomian tradition as a subterranean vein of wildness. She cites Thoreau, you remember, to the effect that "in literature it is only the wild that attracts us" (*Birth-mark*, 18). This recent book suggests not that such wildness is one among many resources for American writers, but rather that the best writers, like Dickinson, set themselves completely apart from the normative social institutions that attempt to govern the art and imaginative life of America. She cites Pierre Macherey with approval when he says, arguing for a kind of autonomy of literary texts, that "the work has its beginnings in a break from the usual ways of speaking and writing—a break which sets it apart from all other forms of ideological expression" (*Birth-mark*, 46). What she prizes in Dickinson and American literature generally is a standing apart from the dominant social institutions whose authority is implied by conventions of spelling, syntax, prosody, and publication. For W. S. Merwin, Philip Levine, and any number of her contemporaries, free verse has no such grand significance, and few of her contemporaries are seriously engaged in syntactic experimentation. Howe's antiformality is a throwback to that of Williams, Pound, and other modernists, who strove to discover new systems of order—the variable foot, the ideogrammic method. More than once she speaks of Dickinson asserting "a new grammar"—of the heart, of humility (*My Emily,* 21, 13). Howe, after Derrida, sees the slippage of signification as systemic to language (*My Emily,* 13), but it is the systemic orders of language that structure her expectations of meaning in matters.

Marjorie Perloff: First of all, I don't agree that *My Emily Dickinson* and *Birth-mark* are "not concerned . . . with contemporary writing." They *are* contemporary writing, and most readers, I would guess, are much more interested in what Howe's take on Dickinson tells us about Howe's own poetry rather than what it can teach us about Dickinson. Also both books have poetic passages and she is consciously trying to produce a new genre, loosely based on Charles Olson's *Call Me Ishmael,* Williams's *In the American Grain,* and so on. These books are, so to speak, borderworks—part poetry, part critique, part autobiography. As for specifics, although I don't care much for Macherey and for Howe's habit of throwing in "big name" critics—a sign of her insecurity, I would say, since she was, for so long, a marginalized poet—I think this particular Macherey quote serves Howe well. For her, poetry is always *oppositional,* always a form of calling into question the dominant culture. As for "wildness," by the way, I don't think Howe means free verse. Free verse, after all, is now the norm, the staple especially of the poetry of the sixties and seventies, like Merwin's and Levine's. Her deconstructions of linearity are more radical than theirs.

But let's turn to the larger question of poetry/theory. Howe and such poets as Charles Bernstein have been accused of being "too theoretical," too programmatic rather than naturally lyrical. Yet surely Louise Glück or Frank Bidart or Robert Pinsky also have a "theory," a poetics that informs their work, even if they don't write the sort of essays or manifestos one finds in Bernstein's *Content's Dream* or Howe's *Birth-mark.* Can poetry ignore theory? (We know theory can ignore poetry, don't we?)

Robert von Hallberg: You ask whether poetry can ignore theory. The answer is plainly yes, and that is disturbing. The fact seems to be that many estimable contemporary poets do not attend closely to the discourse known as literary theory. I tried in 1990 to assemble a collection of essays on this subject. I gave up the project because so few poets I asked wished to address the issue at all. Literary theory in the United States is a professional academic discourse that competes for readers, authority, and prestige with the traditional genres of literary production. My colleague W. J. T. Mitchell has said that we live in a golden age of theory, and that the traditional literary genres are not so distinguished now. The academic discipline of literary studies is hierarchically structured, and this is the view from the upper regions of the structure. The yield of literary theory for what I recognize as literary issues is often so slender that the principal significance of the field seems to be the construction and distribution of professional authority. When theorists engage with contemporary poetry, as Jameson does with Bob Perelman's "China," the results are unimpressive. Poetry seems to resist theory.

Marjorie Perloff: I would argue slightly differently. It's true that, within academe and its leading journals, poetry plays a slight role, but then so do fiction and drama. The most egregious instance of this is *American Literary History,* where poetry seems all but nonexistent, unless it can be construed as a cultural symptom. But *ALH* does not focus on theory either and neither does *Critical Inquiry* in its recent incarnation. These journals focus on cultural studies and the articles printed recall the pre–New Critical 1930s in their zeal to establish "context" and cultural discourse, never mind the poem or novel in question. At the same time—and here's the irony—poet-theorists like Howe, Bernstein, and Steve McCaffery have found that their essays are in great demand in these journals: *Critical Inquiry* publishes work by Susan Stewart, *ALH* published Bernstein, and so on. And I notice these essays are not written in conventional academic prose; Stewart, for example, writes very personally and collages things together. It's as if the editors have no "use" for poetry as such but *are* genuinely interested in larger discussions of the poetic and its place among other discourses and so on. So when you say that "poetry" is of no interest to theory, I'd respond, true, if you're talking about conventional poetry à la Pinsky and Hass but not true where the poetry itself is a little more challenging.

Robert von Hallberg: Well, I have to admit that I resist Howe's antiformality partly because it's so much the poetic doctrine of the 1960s—long since discredited for me—fortified by later academic literary theory; and yet I very much share her commitment to a concept of literary autonomy. The academic understanding of autonomy that Macherey goes on to argue for, beyond the passage Howe cites, is not, however, the independence as I would have it, because the literary text, for him, is always secondary to other ideological uses of language. Literary language parodies ordinary language. This is a common way of seeing literary language once formality has become a sign for social conformity. I've learned from East German writers that the concept of literary autonomy, despite the critiques of western writers and scholars, is a precious and powerful thing. As Ernst Bloch suggests, poems express a wish to speak and live otherwise. It is not just that a community poet, like Tom McGrath, adheres to a mirror image of a capitalist economy and society, and surely not that East German poets meant to articulate some capitalist imaginary in a communist society. A long aesthetic tradition, however compromised and maligned, holds out the possibility, as anarchism does too, of unaffiliated opposition, a rare and indefinite alternative. "Mystery is the content," Howe says. "Intractable expression" (*Birth-mark*, 143). "Poems and poets of the first rank," she had earlier said, "remain mysterious" (*My Emily*, 27). Howe is less politically predictable than Macherey in this regard, because she will not restrict the literary text to a parodic, secondary relation to ordinary language.

Marjorie Perloff: I like that Ernst Bloch quote very much and I agree with what you say about autonomy. And Macherey's old-line Marxism now seems quite beside the point.

Robert von Hallberg: One problem with Howe's advocacy, however, is that it settles too patly on the side of so-called formlessness, or mutilation, glaring across at the stodgy repressive patriarchs of Order. The unacceptable axiom is that conventional forms of syntax and prosody stand for established social orders. I join Howe in insisting on the literary and political resources of a tradition of poetic autonomy, but without wanting always to read those resources simplified by some inversion of conventional form. Rigorously formal poets like Turner Cassity and Philip Larkin are staunchly resistant to the norms of literary and social institutions, despite the familiar analogies drawn between metrical order and political authority. Howe tends to describe conventional form as merely shallow or referential in a stable way to societal order. When she speaks of Anne Bradstreet's poems wearing "a mask of civility, domesticity, and perfect submission to contemporary dogmatism" (*Birth-mark*, 113), I remember that the civility of art often implies a critique of the brutality of the society outside the poem. Resistance to the symmetries of conventional forms is commonly thought of as particularly honest, and formality as duplicitous. I have been reading a lot of Paul Celan lately and see in him too a commitment to an art that indicates formally—principally in terms of diction—a historical rupture or wound in postwar poetry. Celan lost his family, as you know, to the Nazis and his native culture to Stalinism. In a sense, his historical experience is everyone's; the significance of the Holocaust and of Stalinism is global, and for that reason the case for imitative form here seem especially strong. But most

American readers of poetry witness that rupture in Celan from a historical distance. The familiar argument that contemporaneity is post-prosody (a development of the axiomatic equation of conventional form and established social order that Howe does not pursue)—that there can be no lyricism after Auschwitz, to modify Adorno—finds support here because of an American willingness to borrow trouble. I feel no right to claim that my culture, which has shown remarkable coherence in the past half-century, needs to display a relation to cataclysms of any kind; nor do I see that an attack on syntax or prosody is a particularly acute way of criticizing social order. Although I can be persuaded by Howe that Dickinson's resistance to political and social order shows up in her orthography, my generation cannot be so easily charmed by assertions of necessary relations between form and political allegiance.

Marjorie Perloff: Now here is where we really do disagree. If you believe, as I do, that form can never be separated from something called "content," then of course the choice of form is itself a statement. Take the heroic couplet. It was a marvelous form for Pope and Swift and they did wonders with it. But today, the very appearance of heroic couplets, say, in the *TLS,* is a signifier of "light verse," something fun and parodic, not meant to be taken too seriously. In France, as Jacques Roubaud argues in *The Death of Alexander,* the alexandrine was the straitjacket that controlled all verse until the mid-nineteenth century when Baudelaire wrote *Les Petits poèmes en prose* and Rimbaud tried both prose poetry and "free verse." And now there's no going back. You won't find a single French poet, I don't think, writing regularly in alexandrines. And if they did, there would have to be a good reason, the desire to deconstruct some other form, for example.

But in the case of Larkin, whom we mentioned earlier, it occurs to me that actually his "form" *is* appropriate to his meanings: both are quite retrograde. One thing his form "says" is that English poetry took the wrong turn when it welcomed Pound and Eliot and Williams and that it's time to return to the good old stanzas of Hardy and Houseman. And that goes nicely with his dislike of strangers, immigrants, Americans, Jews, new social measures, and so on. It's true that, say, John Ashbery experiments with pantoums, villanelles, and other obscure forms. But he is playing with those forms, and his standard rhythmic contours, as many critics have pointed out, is the purposely unmusical, ungainly, "scratchy" rhythm we find in "Houseboat Days" as well as in his so-called pantoums. These are gaming frameworks.

Two further points. I am confused by your reference to the sixties—hardly a very "experimental" time in poetry when you scratch the surface. Allen

Ginsberg didn't write especially "experimental" poetry; he adapted the Whitman line to a wonderfully exuberant, baroque performance mode. The poetry is often very good but no more radical than his ideas and sentiments. But I also want to say— and this is my second point—that experimentation is not ipso facto a good thing. There are plenty of "experiments" that are merely boring: for example, Richard Kostelanetz's many texts using generative structures. But I'm saying that real poets inevitably and even unconsciously *will* create new forms so as to represent the world they live in. John Cage is the great example of this. He doesn't set out to "experiment"; he's really quite empirical—trying to capture the noises and images we actually live with.

Robert von Hallberg: I do not mean to be enforcing a content/form bifurcation. My claim is that Cassity and Larkin are formally and thematically resistant to the literary culture in which their books circulate. My understanding is that the Anglo-American literary culture is predominantly academic and liberal or left-center in its political affiliations. These two poets often express frankly illiberal views, and they do so in strenuously metrical verse that violates the dominant literary taste for free verse. My point is less that Larkin and Cassity attack certain social institutions than that they demonstrate by their work that fine art is producible from their point of view, from their position, politically and poetically. The quality of their poems underwrites their ideological and aesthetic views. This is what Eliot called an "aesthetic sanction."

Too often resistance in the literary culture is understood as being something that comes from the left, that seeks freedom from convention, but there is no reason to think of the center of American literary opinion as that of the Republican Party. Larkin and Cassity are oppositional poets in that they oppose not the rightist drift of the state's political center but instead the center of the literary culture that actually reads them. In this sense, they are confrontational. Most of the poets spoken of as oppositional are actually not terribly far from the left-liberal center of the academic literary culture, however far they are from the right-center of American politics, that is, from the audiences that are indifferent to poetry.

Marjorie Perloff: Here you have a good point—but I think it also proves my point. Cassity and Larkin, as you note, return to strict metrical forms that accord with their opposition to the dominant left-liberal orthodoxy of the Academy. But another way of saying this would be that they're retrograde both formally and thematically!

Then, too, Cassity and Larkin represent different things. Cassity may be positioning himself against the left-wing academic orthodoxy, as you note, but that in itself seems like a fairly trivial pursuit (i.e., taking on the left-wing English department!) And perhaps it accounts for Cassity's near-total obscurity. I doubt whether ten people reading this dialogue have ever heard of him. The case of Larkin is more complicated because he was hardly writing with an eye to the left-literary culture of the British universities but for what was still a literary culture—of the *TLS, New Statesman,* and so on—where in fact he was immediately successful. In the Britain of his time where only 7 percent of 18-year-olds went to university, it was hardly the university that valorized (or rejected) new poetry. No, Larkin was picked up by middle-brow culture and the professors came on board only afterward.

Robert von Hallberg: Well, let's agree to disagree there and return to the issue of formalism in contemporary poetic evaluation. It seems odd to me that Howe expresses so little appreciation for the pleasures of formal fulfillment, because her own writing is exceptional among avant-gardists particularly because she has an extraordinary ear for the recurrences of sound and stress that fortify sense. She says, in Hopkins-like prose, that "A lyric poet hunts after some still unmutilated musical wild of the Mind's world" (*My Emily,* 105). Her access to the traditional lushness of language distinguishes her writing from that of most other avant-gardists. Here I don't mean those tight, tough passages that conform to her expressed poetics but rather passages like the one that closes the first section of *The Nonconformist's Memorial* (1993):

> Half thought thought otherwise
> loveless and sleepless the sea
> where you are where I would be
> half thought thought otherwise
> Loveless and sleepless the sea

This little strophe formally concludes a lyric of twelve additional lines that I won't quote, because here I want only to show that Howe uses the resources of formal symmetry to resolve matters that arise in her less formal explorations. There are the echoes of syllables such as "thought," "-less," and "where" that give shape to these lines, and the syntactic structures too echo each other. But the prosody of the strophe is especially worth remarking. The first line has a rhythmic structure—two dactyls—that does not quite conform to the syntactic structure, with its pause after the first two syllables. The second line adheres to a dactylic rhythm, but with an extra stress concluding the line. The third line gives up on the falling rhythm altogether, but builds on the pattern in the previous line of two trisyllabic feet plus a concluding stress: x/x x/x/. And the third line resembles the first in exemplifying a shift of pace after the caesura: both lines effectively speed up after their pauses, as though fitting more syllables into their second "halves." It is remarkable that a poet who insists vigorously on the mutilation of form is so drawn to a pastiche of the narcotic lyricism of nineteenth-century British poetry. I always feel the allure of such an ear's working, line by line, but after hearing such song I obviously listen skeptically to the antiformal rhetoric of her prose. The best objection to imitative form is strengthened by the example of passages like this one from Howe: conventional forms do much else beyond imitating social structure; a too reductive allegorization of form reduces the resources of the art.

Although resistance to conventional form is a prominent feature of the literature that she esteems, Howe's more interesting evaluative criterion is intensity. Much of *The Birth-mark* is devoted to writing about forceful experiences and feelings. In *My Emily* she doubts that before World War II "any work of European imagining" exceeded "the rough-hewn intensity" of Mary Rowlandson's narrative. (The *Iliad,* the *Medea,* and *Lear* are presumably not rough-hewn; it took fascism and the Holocaust to roughen up European literature.) The frontier experience itself obviously provided writers a highly charged subject matter, and that is a large part of the intensity Howe admires. Yet at the heart of her sense of poetic intensity is not just the deprivations and brutality of the frontier but the rivalry of poetry and religion. American poets, to their credit, are drawn to "Divinity's sovereign source" (*My Emily,* 55). The particular poetic intensity she analyzes is inconceivable in strictly secular poetry. Her own poems, and those of Michael Palmer too, draw often on Christian aspirations to a language comprehending divinity. Is contemporary academic criticism ready to return to the connections between poetry and faith that engaged American critics from the 1920s to the 1950s? Probably not: our academic intellectual climate is insistently secular and ironic. On the evidence of Howe's project, though, the modernist view that secularization diminishes poetic resources is far from passé.

But beyond the resources of particular subject matter, she treasures still more intellectual intensity. Her account of American literature might be extended to explain the Americanness of writers like Louise Glück and Frank Bidart, as well as Dickinson and Rowlandson; the scope of her assessment is grand beyond the immediate terms of her narrative. The assessment of poetry in terms of intensity is uncontroversial insofar as strong feeling is what is most commonly expected of poetry; but even a veteran reader of poetry feels the appeal of a prophylactic against the mediocrity one witnesses inevitably as one follows an art season by season. The worst charge against contemporary poetry is that it is merely industrial product.

There is of course a hazard in the ardent pursuit of intensity: it has been too easy for critics of the last thirty-five years to mistake forceful subject matter for emotional, intellectual, or linguistic intensity. There are some poems, like Bishop's villanelle "One Art," in which the intensity of the language seems to derive from the force of the subject—in this case, loss. The formal resources of the villanelle concentrate her force and dramatize the speaker's willfulness, which is the poem's subject too. In a poem like "One Art" the distinction between subject and treatment seems tenuous. But James Merrill's work, for example, rarely has patently forceful subject matter, though the pressure he puts on his syntax and prosody in some poems produces an intensity less obvious than that of, say, Anne Sexton's poems. One can distinguish clearly between form and content in Merrill's and Sexton's poems. And for one the intensity is all in the style, and for the other in the content. Howe herself is drawn to extreme scenes, that is, to the power of subject matter itself, such as the eating of raw horse liver (*Birth-mark*, 125–26), and she recognizes this as a problem: "I am concerned that so much of my work carries violence in it. I don't want to be of Ahab's party. I want to find peace. Anyway, you balance on the edge in poetry" (*Birth-mark*, 177). But her work gets its more important intensity from the pressure on her style. Her diction, syntactic patterns, and sound structures forge a "terse, tense, sometimes violent" style—"Chaos cast cold intellect back" (*Singularities*, 34)—suitable to the intellectual ambitions she most admires (*My Emily*, 84). In many of her poems an austere refusal of eloquence, fluency, or formality acts as a structure of concentration comparable to that of the villanelle for Bishop. It is important when reading with Howe for intensity to remember that extreme subject matter is only one part of the intensity that matters most in poetry; often it only feeds a prurient appetite for violence.

Although I do often read as Howe does, looking for nodes of intensity, a line or a poem, this evaluative criterion is for me dialectically involved with its contrary: range. I cannot imagine a steady diet of Plath's "Lady Lazarus," "Daddy," and Bidart's "Ellen West," though these are exceptional poems that belong in any anthology of postwar poetry. To some extent the issue is whether one assesses poems one by one, in which case intensity counts a great deal, or whether poets are measured by their overall work. Eliot argued that minor poets are adequately represented by a small number of poems but major poets must be understood in terms of their entire work. Coleridge similarly says that "Our genuine admiration of a great poet is a continuous *under-current* of feeling; it is everywhere present, but seldom anywhere as a separate excitement" (*Biographia Literaria*, ed. Engell, vol. 1, 23). Coleridge does not stipulate the quality of that feeling, but if among the qualities one seeks are flexibility, proportion, judgment, variety, one is unlikely to be at peace with the results of an assessment in terms of intensity alone. Much of the poetry I appreciate is not of the first intensity in terms of subject or style, and most of Bishop's is not either. There are pleasures to be had from the fluency and elegance of poems that deliberately avoid extremity and intensity. How can we justly account for the Horatian pleasures of, say, Robert Pinsky's recent poem "Impossible to Tell"? Not with Howe's evaluative criteria alone. I use an intensity criterion often in sorting out the poems to read to friends, to study with students, or to discuss in an essay. But I long for ways of talking about the humaneness of poetry that moves away from the strains of intensity and force in order to express an appreciation for a more normal or ordinary life. Howe cites Thoreau as saying that poetry is "exaggerated history" (*Birth-mark*, 96). Exaggeration isn't satisfying in the long run.

Marjorie Perloff: Your commentary on intensity interests me a great deal because I almost wrote my Ph.D. dissertation on the history of the meaning of "intensity" as poetic criterion. Before the nineteenth century, "intensity" was NOT especially valued; it's very much a Romantic invention (Blake, Keats, Baudelaire, Poe) and often comes down to the moderns in the form of the privileged moment, the epiphany. "Can you recommend some novels of the first intensity?" Yeats wrote to Dorothy Wellesley. In this sense Howe is most certainly a Romantic. But intensity needn't mean "strong feeling"—it can mean, as for Eliot, "intensity" of the poetic process, the making. I think this is also what Keats meant when he said "The excellence of every art is in its intensity" or what Poe had in mind when he declared that one should excise those parts of *Paradise Lost* that lacked intensity. It's not a matter of feeling but a matter of language. And here I can't see how you can invoke Frank Bidart. To me his language is generally quite slack, as is Pinsky's—and I'll return to this. As for Louise Glück, that's "intensity" on the surface level—a breathless invocatory lyric that doesn't seem to have much substance. Not enough difference, always the same note of High Seriousness. Also I would never describe Bishop's "One Art" as having "intensity of language." It's too reasonable, rational, crafted, and willed.

Robert von Hallberg: Even after we have agreed that intensity of language or style is the proper goal of poetry, we are going to disagree greatly as to what constitutes intensity of language in particular poems. In many poems we recognize intense language by its appearance of being *worked* by the poet; Lowell's style in *Lord Weary's Castle* might be an instance of this. The intensity of language characteristic of seventeenth-century English poetry is reasonable, rational, crafted, and willed, isn't it? I don't sense any necessary conflict between these qualities and what I recognize as intensity of language. But in other sorts of poems intensity seems the result of strenuous selection, of an austerity that was not part of Lowell's, Donne's, or Marvell's intention; Bidart's poems seem intense to me in just that way. Perhaps, though, we can agree that the common notion that language becomes intense when its style imitates its sense is mistaken.

Marjorie Perloff: Well, here I'd like to come back to the notion of relatedness, fitness, making every word count—which is, of course, another form of "intensity." One of my favorite seventeenth-century poems is George Herbert's "The Windows," which begins:

> Lord, how can Man preach thy eternall word?
>   He is a brittle crazie glasse;
> Yet in thy temple thou dost him afford
>   This glorious and transcendent place,
>   To be a window through thy grace.

And the poem then develops the metaphor of priest = stained glass window, both worthless unless "illuminated" by "light" (the grace of God). One of the great feats of this poem is that when the tenor and vehicle of the metaphor fuse in the last stanza, they do so phonemically as well as semantically, with the words "in," "Mingle," "bring," "flaring," with the final rhyme "flaring thing"/"ring" bringing the point home with great finesse. It's the sort of effect Robert Lowell can only strain for in *Lord Weary's Castle* because—and here is a topic we have barely touched on—the sort of correspondence between the natural and the spiritual ("Doctrine and life, colours and light, in one"). What Herbert took as a given can't be willed by a secular poet of Lowell's day without a good deal of strain.

Robert von Hallberg: Well, certainly today Pope's principle ("The sound must seem an echo to the sense") presides over most critical discussion of poetic style: prosody is appreciated most often as an imitation of sense. But this is a way of rendering the sound of poetry servile to the ideas that critics specialize in explicating. It is consoling to a reader to find some neat parallel between the sound structure of a poem and what one wants to think of as its point. But sounds provide other pleasures that do not fall into line so obediently. Sound is a sense experience, and it has its own being beyond its instrumentality. The sensuality of poetry, generally speaking, is greater than that of prose. This is often part of the mysteriousness of poems: their sensual shapeliness, altogether aside from their paraphrasable sense. This side of poetry sometimes seems just unknowable, in the sense that it can't be reduced to paraphrase.

Marjorie Perloff: I agree, but do you really think most critics today talk about sound at all? Or about syntax and diction? The typical discussion of, say, Ashbery (where there has been a great deal of criticism) is about meaning, voice, larger structure (or lack thereof) of specific poems, and so on, but critics (Harold Bloom is a case in point) rarely stop to so much as mention that *Three Poems* is in prose, not verse, or to ask what that might mean. So we have to look more closely at the materiality of poetry and here I want to have a closer look at a poet you've praised as especially "humane"—Robert Pinsky.

Pinsky's poems are barely poems at all. Or at best, to use Coleridge's distinction, works of fancy, not imagination. Take the celebrated "History of My Heart":

> One Christmastime Fats Waller in a fur coat
> Rolled beaming from a taxicab with two pretty girls
> Each at an arm as he led them in a thick downy snowfall
>
> Across Thirty-Fourth Street into the busy crowd
> Shopping at Macy's: perfume, holly, snowflake displays.
> Chimes rang for change. In Toys, where my mother worked
>
> Over her school vacation, the crowd swelled and stood
> Filling the aisles, whispered at the fringes. . . .

"Do not retell in mediocre verse," Pound said, "what has already been done in good prose." Let's first of all transfer Pinsky's loose blank verse into prose:

> One Christmastime Fats Waller in a fur coat rolled beaming from a taxicab with two pretty girls each at an arm as he led them in a thick downy snowfall across Thirty-Fourth Street into the busy crowd shopping at Macy's, with its perfume, holly and snowflake displays. Chimes rang for change. In Toys, where my mother worked over her school vacation, the crowd swelled and stood filling the aisles and whispered at the fringes. . . .

What have I lost here? I've added nothing except that in line 5 I got rid of the colon and made it syntactically smooth with "with its" and in the case of line

8 I added an "and." I wouldn't even have had to do that. So: what does Pinsky gain by lineating his text and by using tercets? Now, my objection to Pinsky is not at all that he uses traditional "form" but that he doesn't do anything with the form. Just as, say, Ferlinghetti doesn't do anything with "formlessness." I think—forgive me for being cynical—that what he does gain is that his reader processes the work as a "poem," which is to say that the tercet form is meant as a signpost whereby the reader is prompted to related "History of My Heart" to great poems of the past. But I actually think the cited text looks/sounds/reads better as prose because that's what it *is* internally. If Pinsky were writing short stories, though, the audience would be more stringent. I honestly believe that he couldn't get away with a lot of his flatness if he admitted he were writing prose. Short-story audiences are, in fact, more demanding than poetry audiences even if they're bigger.

Let me specify: "One Christmastime": why not "One Christmas"? The "Once upon a time" note is merely cute. Fats Waller "rolled beaming...": no defamiliarization there. Wouldn't it have been interesting if Fats Waller were scowling? Or something else that might arrest our attention. "Thick downy snowfall"—what else? What do you now know about December on Thirty-fourth Street you didn't know before? "The busy crowd." Are crowds usually "unbusy"? If not, why not just "crowd," as Hemingway might have put it? "The crowd swelled and stood / Filling the aisles"—again, what else? All this is, of course, part of Mother's Tales for Young Bob, "romance of Joy, / Co-authored by her and the movies, like her others." But you know what: it's not credible because if it were really a scene co-authored with the movies, it would be more graphic, more striking—more interesting. And the words do nothing to character their purported speaker. I think immediately of Frank O'Hara's great New York poems like "A Step Away from Them"—poems that make us "see" Times Square (same locale!) as if for the first time, what with the blond chorus girl clicking and the "Negro" who is "languorously agitating."

So when you and others tell me Pinsky is "humane," I honestly don't know what this means. He just seems like everyone else—a very nice guy, maybe a little more sensitive and articulate than other nice guys, but why should I be interested in this story about his mother, a story that is not much more than a *New Yorker* profile? What Pinsky lacks here is "le mot juste"—language that is memorable, graphic, precise.

Robert von Hallberg: Your questions about the opening of "History of My Heart" revolve around the issue of ordinary language: what is the function of ordinary diction and syntax in poetry? Some poets invest highly in striking diction and surprising syntax, but Pinsky puts more in story than many of his contemporaries do. In order to carry stories, I think, his style is well suited to a plausible narrator who speaks in sentences—not just syllables—that can be articulated easily. One recognizes such a style as familiar, more fluent than intense or startling. Only in the sixth line, beginning with the second sentence—"Chimes rang for change. In Toys, where my mother worked . . ."— does the diction indicate any flight. "Change" might be capitalized to indicate a season of transformation, and "toys" might be lowercased to suggest Mother Hubbard more than Mother Pinsky. That is, when the diction becomes most obviously a mouthful, with the "Chi"/"cha" echo, the fantastic quality of even ordinary discourse surfaces for a moment. The poet is not taking credit for the figurative potentiality of the language here, as Merrill often does; ordinary life at Macy's every Christmas season is about transformation and play. But the syntax moves one's mouth and attention through an abrupt change, with a crisp four-word sentence following the forty-four-word opening sentence. Pinsky is not displaying virtuosity, but the form of the poem is giving sensual shape to the movement of attention through the story. As for Fats Waller, he is the black man bringing sumptuous, sexy excess to the white world.

Part of your objection to Pinsky's language, I take it, is its conventionality, which truly is a prominent feature of the style here, and this has everything to do with the claim that his work exhibits an unusual degree of what I called humaneness. He does not try to make everything graphic or particular. The "two pretty girls," say, are adequately represented, it seems, by this abstract, conventional phrase. And similarly he tells of his father punching an "enraged gambler," in a corny scene fit for the movies, as he suggests. The poem affirms the occasional adequacy of conventional categories of expression and representation: "Shepherds and shepherdesses in the grass"; "the back room of Carly's parents' shop." That's a fit. He presents this conformity with some amusement or irony—"To see eyes 'melting' so I could think *This is it, / They're melting!* Mutual arousal of suddenly feeling / Desired: *This is it: 'desire'!*"—but it is nonetheless a match: conventional language will serve in some instances. And in just these moments the ordinary, conventional structures in which speakers of this language live are affirmed. The implication of the poems then is that the ways that we have found as groups to live together are significantly humane.

And not just any groups. The term "humane" is obviously slippery, exactly because it is meant to be inclusive above all; hence the continuing currency of the Latin tag from Terence—"nothing human is alien to me." The relevant counter-term is less "inhumane" than "partisan." Poets like Whitman and

Williams attempt to elude the exclusions of partisan analysis, though of course they do not always avoid partisanship: they represent themselves as poets who wish to refuse certain kinds of partisanship; they claim a measure of inclusiveness that runs against the dividing lines of camps that their readers are expected to recognize. This is not a strictly thematic issue. The refusal of encampment that I am talking about can certainly be expressed through features of style or theme; the important thing is the aspiration toward some inclusive ground of affiliation—humaneness, which can mean an attitude toward a political issue or a style that is not devoted to a narrow range of effect. The esteem for the humaneness of certain poetry rests ultimately on rhetorical properties, not on a claim about the nature of a particular poet as person.

You say that Pinsky just isn't sufficiently interesting, but I think this poem is quite rich. The richness I appreciate is not in the graphic language of the poem (and you would surely agree that elsewhere in the poem there are teeth-marks on the railing, etc.—enough graphic particularity to satisfy me), but rather in the overlap of various representations of the production of desire, the elaboration of some ornament, and the communication of a sense of identity. Is there another poet who can so nicely account for the mix of selfishness and mother love?

> She wanted to have made the whole world up,
>
> So that it could be hers to give. So she opened
> A letter I wrote to my sister, who was having trouble
> Getting on with her, and read some things about herself
>
> That made her go to the telephone and call me up:
> "You shouldn't open other people's letters," I said
> And she said "Yes—*who taught you that?*"
>
> —As is she owned the copyright on good and bad,
> Or having followed pain inside she owned her children
> From the inside out, or made us when she named us,
>
> III
>
> Made me Robert.

I think it is quite interesting that a predictable, ordinary moment can be transformed by someone like Fats Waller emerging out of nowhere. Why should he wish to transform the moment for the crowd of strangers, since he has surely had lots of adulation already? The answer suggested by the poem is that it pleases one to give gifts, to make someone else feel lucky. It is erotic to give pleasure, to make someone else feel desire. And yes, it is selfish too to want to see oneself desired in the eyes of others, to read one's name everywhere in the world. What we commonly take to be the type of selfless devotion is a mother's love. Pinsky relates how his mother's intelligence is bent to pursuing her claim on the identity of her children.

Marjorie Perloff: Bob, you make the most eloquent case possible for Pinsky's "History of My Heart" but it does leave me with some questions.

First, "ordinary language." I've written a whole book (*Wittgenstein's Ladder*) on Wittgenstein's theory that "ordinary language is alright," showing how "poetic" ordinary language can be. But Pinsky's is patently not ordinary language—that is *the language that we actually use*—but calculated to "seem" ordinary. In ordinary conversation we don't in fact talk about people "beaming from a taxicab" or "the crowd . . . whispered at the fringes." It's not at all what Wittgenstein had in mind when he cautioned us to see how fascinating our ordinary sentences (e.g., "The rose is red") can be when we try to understand their uses. You then say Pinsky's language is conventional, and intentionally so. Well, which is it, ordinary or conventional? Because once something is conventionalized, it's not really ordinary.

But, finally, a few words about your discussion of the passage about mother love. If I understand you correctly, you find the passage effective because you feel that this *is* what mother love is like, that it nicely embodies the tension between a mother's "selfless devotion" and her urge to pursue "her claim on the identity of her children." You argument here is, of course, extra-literary: you are praising Pinsky for presenting what you take to be a psychological truth about motherhood.

But suppose I don't agree that this is a "just" representation of what you call the "mix of selfishness and mother love"? Perhaps our difference here is gendered. From my perspective (and since we're being extra-literary, I write as myself a mother and grandmother), Pinsky's representation is that of the slightly patronizing successful poet-son, who is here imputing motives to his middle-class nonprofessional mother. The lines "She wanted to have made the whole world up, / So that it could be hers to give," imply that she really has nothing of her own to give anyone, that she lives vicariously through her children (the Jewish mother cliché)—a statement that may or may not have been true of the poet's mother but that doesn't quite ring true poetically (fictionally) because the reader senses that there's more involved here than the poet admits, that he is casting his mother in a role. Then, too, I find, the passage irritating because the poet claims to *know* what it is that makes his mother tick, *knows*

that she wanted "copyright on good and bad," wanted "to own her children /
From the inside out." But the reader is given no alternative: we have to take
Pinsky's representation on faith, even though, for all we know, the real Mrs.
Pinsky had a secret love and a rich sex life in middle age!

But, isn't this by definition what lyric is: a subjective representation of events,
the expression of the first person? Romantic lyric, yes, but not all lyric and the
voice is the problem here. For even if we don't subscribe, as I don't, to the
current orthodoxy about the cultural construction of the subject, with its concomitant axioms about the end of individualism, the "waning of affect," and
"new depthlessness" (Fredric Jameson), it seems problematic, at the beginning
of the twenty-first century to give the individual voice so much *authority,* so
much *knowingness.* The facility of interpretation ("Or having followed pain
inside, she owned her children / From the inside out") flies in the face of the
ethos of today, however one chooses to construct it.

I don't mean to beat up on Pinsky: God knows he is a much more accom-
plished poet than many now writing, and he is a sensitive and interesting es-
sayist and commentator. But I would conclude—and here I do think we differ—by suggesting that if one takes Pinsky as a paradigmatic contemporary
poet, one is bound to have the feeling, which you said you have, that poetry
just isn't a very vital part of the culture any more. I think the reason you may
feel this way is that what you suggest Pinsky does "well" is really done equally
well in essays, short stories, and especially in film. So to come back to Pound's
caveat: "Do not retell in mediocre verse what has already been done in good
prose!"

And here I come back to my original proposition that poetry is the language
art. Readers continue to come to poetry because, unlike film, or the personal
essay, or video, or even the novel, it contains *language charged with meaning.*
The pleasure of the text, in, say, Susan Howe's *Frame Structures,* is that the word
"mark," which appears and reappears in the first of Howe's four books in that
collection, "History of the Dividing Line," without registering fully on the
reader's consciousness, is now charged by the knowledge provided in the new
title piece, the autobiographical memoir "Frame Structures," that "Mark" is
the name of Howe's father as well as of her son. Mark deWolfe Howe is central to her story, for the quest for paternity stands behind the poet's obsession
with the New England and Ireland of her parents, her documentary history
of Buffalo and Boston, her vignettes of Beacon Hill ancestors and friends. After
a while, every "mark" provided begins to fit into the puzzle.

I find that students are thrilled when they begin to "see" these connections,
not because Howe has anything unique to "say" about paternity or ancestry

but because her poems enact such amazing labyrinthine paths that allow for exploration of the issue. On the "flat" documentary surface, the poet's very real pain appears at the interstices of the text, and the reader experiences what Aristotle called the pleasure of recognition. It's a pleasure, in any case, that is currently very widespread as a large alternate poetry culture is making itself heard through reading series, Internet projects, Web sites, conferences, festivals, and so on. A poetry world literally humming and with which I can hardly keep up!

5

Negotiating Constituencies: Some Thoughts on Diaspora and the Past, Present, and Future of African American Studies

Judith Jackson Fossett and Kevin Gaines

I should begin by saying that African American studies is an enormous field, and due to the limitations of my training and interests, I will inescapably slight vast areas of it.
—*Kevin Gaines*

We both come out of the humanities/social sciences wing of the field, and we both tend to focus on literature, history, and culture more than political science, sociology, or psychology. But even as we both establish our credentials (and realize the importance of this move), I want to think about "why?" Given the political and cultural tendency in U.S. race relations to see the black community as a monolith—a kind of unthinking automaton—I continually resist the urge to speak for the race, the field. But might we not also read an impulse to "spokesperson-ship" as itself revelatory of the status of African American studies as a field? Perhaps some joint thoughts on the history of African American studies and the legacies of that genealogy in the current moment may begin to offer answers here . . .
—*Judith Jackson Fossett*

African American studies today enjoys an unprecedented vitality and diversity; there are few limits to the questions that can be asked or the issues that can be explored. At the same time, correspondingly, the parameters of the field are being contested along many lines. There's spirited debate over the contours and content of "African American studies" on political, geographical, methodological, and generational grounds. This contestation is to be expected, and in many respects, it's healthy. Yet it is also the product of the waning historical memory of the political origins of African American scholarship and Black studies. We're in the process of forgetting a moment of black solidarity dating from the convergence of the civil rights and African liberation movements, a moment defined by the attempt to bring African and African-descended peoples together politically and culturally, to redefine black consciousness. It might be useful then to open our conversation by tracing briefly the current situation in African American studies to the field's antecedents in black social sciences and literary discourse from the 1930s onward.

If we consider the early prominence of scholars such as W. E. B. Du Bois, Charles S. Johnson, Carter G. Woodson, E. Franklin Frazier, Oliver C. Cox, St. Clair Drake, and others, we might ask ourselves why social scientists so dominated the field's beginnings. Perhaps history and social science marked the terrain of early intellectual and political struggles because of the heavy weight of academic and popular racism in those disciplines. Certainly such social science research—on the urban experience of social disorganization following the initial one marked by slavery, on questions of assimilation or its lack, on the status of the family—presupposed a vindicationist outlook that explained racial and social inequality in environmentalist rather than innate terms. Indeed, these sociological concerns soon informed literature, too, including Richard Wright's fiction, most notably *Native Son,* and Ann Petry's novel, *The Street.*

Yet the internationalism of World War II also fostered some very different interests among some black scholars—in the wider black world. The anthropologist and choreographer Katherine Dunham studied the expressive cultures of Haiti and Jamaica. The predominantly U.S.-centered concerns of black social science scholarship were challenged, as well, with postwar sponsorship of national character studies and academic research on race in an international context. The growing interest in a larger black diasporic identity among black writers, musicians, and visual and performing artists soon informed literary and artistic protests against American imperial moves as they affected the black world.

But ours is no simple narrative of expansion, for just as internationalism became an enabling intellectual and creative outlook for black intellectuals, the cold war came to exert a policing effect on the terms of that internationalism. In the early 1950s, Dunham was dropped from State Department sponsorship for portraying lynching during her troupe's tour of Latin America. James Baldwin's critique of Wright's protest fiction may seem warranted with the passage of time, but even it was serviceable to the cold war's apolitical vision of literature and the discrediting of black dissenters. With the emergence of Ralph Ellison, U.S. reviewers and critics began to view black writers and literature through the prism of a fetishized, false universalism. At stake was the assertion of a cold war canon whose evaluative criteria privileged artistic freedom over political engagement, and imposed presumably universal, elite standards on black writers. Of course, this served also as one prong in the larger critical project of the institutionalization of American literature in the postwar period.

Amidst the exiles of Wright, Baldwin, and others from McCarthyite repression, the persecution and abandonment of Du Bois and Paul Robeson, and the rise of African anticolonialism and nationalism, cultural dissenters like E. Franklin Frazier and LeRoi Jones came to decry conformist tendencies among the "black bourgeoisie." Their dissent helped launch the Black studies movement, which was heavily influenced, as well, by such black radicals as Malcolm X and the Black Panthers. Indeed, Black studies built upon the dual heritage of social science scholarship and literary criticism. Central to Black studies was a critique of liberal social science on race and also a demystification of the ideological content of academic "objectivity." Equally important to the work of Black studies was the cultivation of a black cultural aesthetic and the quest for a black literary criticism, projects that were also concerned with unmasking the nature of "universalism" as applied to black literature. Black studies was international, as well, in its receptivity to African and black diaspora radicals such as Walter Rodney, Amilcar Cabral, Frantz Fanon, et cetera. And fundamentally, as Black studies was an outgrowth of political struggles in its analyses of internal colonialism and institutional racism, it was also, in its original constitution, a masculinist discourse that needed to be challenged by a discourse of black feminism responding to the sexism of the black liberation movement.

This (very) brief account of the emergence of Black studies as foundational for African American studies points to certain conflicts that continue to this day. The burning question has long been, "What is the relation of black scholarship (and cultural production) to the interests of black communities?" Such a question, or rather an injunction, led in the past to political litmus tests for black scholarship and literature that highlighted conflicts over gender and sexuality, as black women and gay and lesbian writers were accused of betraying their blackness. Of course, within the past ten years or so, African American studies has become a haven for explorations of race, gender, and sexuality. Marlon Riggs's work is a testament to an inclusiveness, a breaking of silences, on issues that, unfortunately, remain taboo within much of black political culture. Indeed, with the achievement of one of the Black studies movement's goals, namely, the institutionalization of the field within the academy, the question of the political role of black intellectuals and the field remains particularly urgent. While we wouldn't want to reduce the field in crude utilitarian fashion to its perceived political benefit to black communities, its relative acceptance is certainly belied by the legal and political attacks against African Americans and people of color through challenges to affirmative action and the wider crisis in civil liberties, criminal justice, and public health facing blacks and other communities of color.

Of course, tension between activists and intellectuals is hardly new. But if the current contestation over the parameters and content of the field is to avoid becoming an irrelevant luxury in the face of the plight of communities of color, then it strikes us that a continuing historical perspective is needed. Take, for example, the question of the geographical scope of the field, as it relates to popular black consciousness, a question sparked by Paul Gilroy's *The Black Atlantic.* Gilroy's critique of the hegemony of a U.S.-centered, African American cultural nationalism raises the question of how the field's geographical boundaries have been constructed, and whether the very notion of "African American studies" might itself be complicit in a kind of exclusion of diasporic voices and perspectives from Latin America and the Caribbean. One way to resolve this question would be the accumulation of historical, empirical work documenting a long history of cross-cultural collaboration and exchange between black world intellectuals. If we look at what Earl Lewis has called the "histories of overlapping diasporas," we will go a long way toward an enriched understanding of the African diaspora that will provide a model for solidarities across differences of culture or country of origin, rather than demonstrating a reliance on fixed, essentializing identities.

We also find troubling a generational aspect to the current divide over the scope and content of the field. This generational schism is a legacy of Black studies, which often seemed to be defined by a suspicion of elders, of black bourgeois leaders or institutions seen as compromising with the establishment. The conflict within the black freedom movement around the slogan "Black Power" was one such generational dispute. Starting with Frazier, Black studies discourse often dwelled on the political failures and compromises of previous generations. There was little spirit of generosity or respect for elder statesmen, though Baraka and Stokely Carmichael certainly learned something from Frazier, Sterling Brown, and others at Howard University. It was common for black militants to denounce black writers identified with the establishment, such as Baldwin, Ellison, and Lorraine Hansberry, even as Baldwin had criticized Wright in his own youth.

Today, one encounters among the generation of scholars who came of age at the moment of Black studies (or women's studies, for that matter) expressions of deep anxiety about the extent to which junior scholars do not mirror their political assumptions and intellectual concerns. With the shift from materialist social science or historical approaches rooted in the experiences of oppressed groups to the "linguistic turn" of poststructuralist theoretical approaches to language, discourse, and power, rightly or wrongly younger scholars are perceived as betraying radical ideals. Perhaps this generational dispute is inflamed by those who believe theoretical approaches or issues of gender and sexuality are not sufficiently grounded within a "black perspective." Certainly there is a sense among many older scholars that a trendy cultural studies approach has taken hold that aestheticizes black consciousness and politics, and ultimately reflects a historical amnesia about the very subjects it purports to study.

And a final well-known and aggravating factor in some of the current conflicts arises from faculty development in the field today. A reverse musical chairs scenario awaits new black Ph.D.s, for whom there is more demand than supply. Nellie McKay, in a perceptive column in the *PMLA,* has spoken forcefully about the evolution of this crisis of scarcity, as severe today as it was in the 1960s: "Perhaps the most frustrating is the thirty-year interdisciplinary shortage of African American faculty members, a shortfall that negatively affects almost every white college and university across the country. Students protest, administrators mumble, and liberals wring their hands. . . . [But] the same institutions grapple over the tiny pool of star scholars, and many positions go unfulfilled." In practical terms, the seemingly commensurate goals of diversification across the entire faculty and the staffing of African American studies programs or departments may, in fact, clash. African American programs function as the primary conduit of African American faculty into the university. But given the shortfall of Ph.D.s, it might be years before a position is filled. Conversely, as African American studies remains the focus for minority faculty recruitment, other departments may fail to make diversification a goal, and consequently, make little or no effort to identify candidates and, ironically, compound these personnel pressures. And throughout these struggles African American studies programs themselves exist as fragile bubbles on the heads of straight pins: beautiful to behold, but always in danger of popping. The departure of one, two, or three faculty members in a year can lay waste to many years of careful planning.

In this attempt to sketch the condition of the field today, a double-edged situation of expansion becomes apparent, of a hundred flowers blooming, as it were, but a situation which carries a downside of decentering, of a tendency toward abstraction from social, political, and historical realities. The problem is that African American studies is often both everywhere and nowhere in terms of both location and historical memory. Certainly there remains a great deal of work to be done, but decentering is always an obstacle to doing that work in a way that makes connections among overlapping diasporas. The construction and existence of canons within African American literature and scholarship remains a primary concern of this decentering impulse as old standards are replaced with newer texts and newer approaches. Yet there are consequences to continuously replacing old canons with new ones. Our African American students, many of whom already feel unwelcome and under siege on campuses, can feel deeply frustrated in their legitimate quest for knowledge about black historical agency and cultural practices. From their perspective, it makes no sense to deconstruct a past that they've hardly been taught. Furthermore if too many African Americanists and African diasporists get bogged down in intellectual turf battles over canons, then the field will only become further marginalized vis-à-vis the disciplines.

And this exacerbates a problem found in many of those disciplines: it is much easier to promote the selective recuperation of representative black writers or scholars than to do the difficult empirical work of grounding them in complicated historical processes and movements. In the recent past we found an explosion of scholarly interest in Zora Neale Hurston and black women writers, but one which prompted Hazel Carby's observation that black women writers have come to stand for black female subjectivity within predominantly white academic settings where the actual black presence in terms of faculty or students is minuscule at best. And then there have been the academic vogues surrounding the "rediscovery" of radical black intellectuals like Du Bois, or C. L. R. James, or Fanon, which has been accompanied by a spate of scholarship that treats them in somewhat individualistic fashion, abstracted out of a world of political movements and collaborations with others.

A few years ago, an incident at the American Studies Association annual meeting reflected this apparent resistance to a more rigorous approach historicizing such figures. At a session devoted to situating W. E. B. Du Bois within an international framework, a member of the audience asked the panelists to discuss Du Bois's relationship with C. L. R. James. One of the speakers dismissed the question, claiming that the session was about Du Bois, and not James! While the question of a relationship between Du Bois and James probably would not have disclosed any actual collaboration, Du Bois and James both produced scholarship during the 1930s that placed black and African peoples at the center of movements for revolutionary social change. Du Bois's *Black Reconstruction* and James's *Black Jacobins* were published within three years of each other. Perhaps their contemporary George Padmore, the Trinidadian Pan-Africanist and revolutionary, served as the link between the two. But the hostility to the question sparked a nasty argument which ended with people angrily storming out of the room.

African American studies might benefit tremendously from making these kinds of connections, from seeing black writers or leaders within a global or diasporic historical framework rather than in an attenuated African American or U.S. context. To do only the latter would be to forget how enabling and transgressive the international context was for black intellectuals and struggles for freedom, dating from David Walker and the black abolitionists to Denmark Vesey and other insurrectionists. Internationalism helped define black modernism and its political and cultural aesthetics during the twentieth century, from Garveyism to Negritude, to Wright, Fanon, Malcolm X, and even Maya Angelou. Manthia Diawara, in his recent memoir on the problematic legacy of independence in Guinea, has championed Richard Wright as an exemplary and prophetic commentator on Africa at the moment of independence. Diawara contends that Wright's argument that new African states needed to embrace modernization, although it was unpopular at the time, represented an important and still relevant challenge to what he sees as the detrimental inertia of tradition and ancestor worship. An international framework is equally essential for understanding that quintessential black nationalist icon, Malcolm X. Jan Carew, the black radical writer from Guyana, has written a beautiful and moving book on Malcolm, which describes him as tragically cut off from the West Indian cultural heritage of his mother, Louise Little, who was born in Grenada. Carew observes that had Malcolm allowed himself more time by remaining in exile, and thus granting himself the opportunity to connect with his mother's West Indian culture and its ancestral "spirit protectors," he might have availed himself of a birthright of spiritual resources that could have healed the alienation caused by his rejection of the bankrupt ideology of the Nation of Islam. Malcolm, in Carew's account, might thereby have fortified himself to continue living for the struggle. Carew's book on Malcolm, *Ghosts in Our Blood,* is a wonderful illustration of the agenda mapped out in Gilroy's *Black Atlantic.*

Carew's work is inspiring because it grounds Malcolm politically and demonstrates the complexity of his identity, showing how identity is not just the product of elective choices but also of paths not taken by virtue of repression and historical amnesia. At his death, Malcolm was struggling to transcend a narrow black nationalism and sexism that repressed the memory of his mother's influence and the wisdom of his Caribbean cultural heritage. In this sense, Malcolm could be seen as a metaphor for the field, which could continue to thrive if its practitioners remain in touch with the political nature of its origins, and commit themselves to integrating cross-cultural, diverse, and diasporic historical experiences and literatures.

SOME ELABORATIONS IN CONVERSATION

Kevin Gaines: Although we commented earlier on the vitality and diversity that currently characterize African American studies, that same vitality and diversity may partially account for a general state of uneasiness, if not an actual sense of crisis, in public discussions of African American studies and black public intellectualism. Within the black community and the wider black intelligentsia of activists and leaders this often arises from concerns over the possible irrelevance of African American studies to the needs and interests of the African American community.

Yet it also seems that within the academy itself, African American studies has more than its share of detractors. There's a general nonrecognition of the contributions of the field, as well as an argument that African American studies or Black studies has now been made obsolete by a supposedly more sophisticated approach embodied in "cultural studies." Wahneema Lubiano wrote an article in *Callaloo* a couple of years ago that addressed a phenomenon of cultural studies actually taking the credit for critical contributions made by African American studies and Black studies. According to Lubiano, and also Mae Henderson, there's a perception among, but not limited to, practitioners of cultural studies that African American studies is somehow intellectually or methodologically unsophisticated or traffics in identity politics or racial essentialism. Lubiano challenges this view very strongly and I am sympathetic to her critique. But further evidence of a continuing conflict between cultural studies and African American studies was provided in a recent article in the *Chronicle of Higher Education* that advertised a virtual cottage industry of recent work dealing with racial and gender border crossings.

Judith Jackson Fossett: Is that the piece featuring Ann duCille?

Kevin Gaines: Yes. And Ann was quite rightly arguing that all this work on passing and border crossing in terms of race and gender is very fashionable now, but what it really represents is a lot of nonblack scholars getting recognition for work that's been done within the field of African American studies for quite some time. Another aspect of this same problem was experienced by David Roediger. He recently published a book, *Black on White: Black Writers on Whiteness,* which explicitly reframes the new field of "whiteness studies" to acknowledge the pioneering contributions of African American writers who have long been concerned with demystifying white identity. For example, in 1947, Chester Himes wrote of whiteness in *If He Hollers Let Him Go* as a public performance resorted to by whites threatened by black assertiveness. Roediger's book contests a view that credits Roediger himself with discovering the field of whiteness studies, which is something Roediger himself, for all his pathbreaking work, has been at pains to dissociate himself from. At a talk at the American Studies meeting a couple years ago, he spoke of being mortified to have people coming up to him saying, "Thank you, man, for doing this work," when in fact a multitude of African American writers including Himes on back to Ida B. Wells, and later, James Baldwin and Toni Morrison, have been looking critically at this problem of whiteness.

Judith Jackson Fossett: Yes, exactly. Ellison, James Weldon Johnson, Du Bois, and so on.

Kevin Gaines: So it might be useful for us to emphasize the real contributions and wide influence of African American studies. I guess we are addressing those contributions already.

Judith Jackson Fossett: Yes, and what you have sketched out is right on target. But in some respects what you have pointed to in terms of crisis is really *external,* how people view the field from the outside, whether they are other scholars in the academy or other black people in the community who look *on* African American studies. I also want to think about what's actually going on in African American studies now, with work being done by not just African American scholars (though certainly primarily by them). What critical or theoretical litmus test defines what we think of as African American studies? And let me be more specific, does the inquiry into questions of race and its construction in various literary and cultural settings that may or may not be created by black writers count as African American studies?

Kevin Gaines: Oh, absolutely.

Judith Jackson Fossett: Well, I would agree with that, too, but some folks have the impression that people are drifting away from the black experience as a

central focus, by looking at white writers or at other kinds of phenomena beyond what the parameters around black experience were ten, fifteen, or twenty
years ago. But ours is really a trajectory which moves from documenting what
black women writers of the Harlem Renaissance produced to considering the
racial, intellectual, gendered, and commercial context that, itself, produced
Nella Larsen and, say, Marianne Moore.

Kevin Gaines: Yes, and that's important. You can't analyze black experience with
a mindset that replicates segregation. You have to look at Nella Larsen within
the prevailing literary tendencies of her time. Thadious Davis's recent biography of Larsen demonstrates methodologically the wealth of understanding that
comes from situating Larsen, black women writers, and the Harlem Renaissance
as cultural movement within the broader currents of American literature.

Judith Jackson Fossett: Yes, but imagine the kind of debate that would generate internally with an Afrocentric colleague who might respond, "That's not
black enough." Or those who would complain that scholars are too fluent with
white writers, cite and engage with them too much, thereby slighting black
writers.

Kevin Gaines: And I think that's a real problem. There *are* so many important
but neglected African American writers. But then there was that unnecessary
furor during the 1980s over black women writers supposedly usurping all the
attention at the expense of black men. Internal and external processes of can-
onization and neglect are a given. That said, I think the issue you've quite
rightly identified suggests a generational fault line within African American
studies. You have people who entered the academy as a result of political
struggles and see academic work as being inherently political, but perhaps only
in a narrow sense not unlike Carter G. Woodson's project (quite necessary in
its time and still necessary) of being grounded within the black experience,
recovering the contributions of black or African-descended peoples to American life. But it doesn't have to be an either/or proposition. To regard it as such
seems to be a habit of thinking that endures from the 1960s, you know, that
there's one authentic revolutionary path, or ideology, or leader, instead of a
multiplicity of possibilities. So we might well be witnessing a generational
schism between those folks who see Black studies as a strictly black enterprise
and those of us who are certainly interested in black culture and history, but
are also more broadly interested in the problems of race and the intersections
between African American discourses on race and dominant discourses on

race. We want to look outward from the black experience, pointing out where it also intersects inevitably with American history and culture.

Judith Jackson Fossett: And toward the black diaspora . . .

Kevin Gaines: An approach popularized by Paul Gilroy, one that looks toward an international context for the formulation and reformulation of black consciousness. And when I say black consciousness, I assume that means interactions between African American and Afro-Caribbean peoples. That produces a much more nuanced reading of what constitutes black culture and consciousness. And we have to see the extent to which what is "black" in black culture and black experience might actually derive from somewhere else, and how African Americans have had allies with other oppressed peoples, such as Native Americans, or Filipino Americans in the Brotherhood of Sleeping Car Porters. In addition, it's a commonplace that, for better or worse, African American culture has been the compelling model for many nonblack groups in terms of their own identity. So we are interested in African American culture and experience, but we are interested in it because ultimately it is essential to understanding American experience. For every American, whether they know it or not, or whether they are willing to admit it or not, is black, culturally speaking. And what some of us would like to do is make a compelling case for that. I see the best work in African American studies as being tremendously enabling for scholars of all backgrounds to do critical work and ultimately train a new generation of Americanists who will reconceptualize American history and literature.

Judith Jackson Fossett: But given your paradigm, how do we situate Proposition 209 in California and the Hopwood decision in Texas regarding affirmative action, in terms of what they will mean for African American studies?

Kevin Gaines: I see a connection between attacks on affirmative action and the disregard for African American studies in that they seem to be attempts to eliminate a black presence in higher education, particularly among undergraduate and graduate populations. For me it's eerily reminiscent of the late nineteenth-century emphasis on industrial education at the expense of higher education for blacks. Obviously the implications of that, in its current phase, are ominous for the perpetual struggle of African American educators to reproduce themselves, for African American studies programs and the traditional disciplines to train the next generation of students of color.

And the attacks on affirmative action also create a climate in which the standard for black undergraduates to be perceived as "qualified" is elevated unfairly. You have a situation in which students of color, who by dint of effort and ambition have managed to overcome the lack of social privileges that many white students enjoy—material and cultural resources and first-rate educational opportunities—who have to prove yet again that they are worthy. The suspicion created by attacks on affirmative action means that they are doubly penalized. And this growing hostility to affirmative action certainly has a counterpart in terms of how African American studies is itself perceived. At elite institutions there is a very insidious star system that creates an impossible standard for many practitioners of African American studies: they have to walk on water. They have to be Cornel West.

Judith Jackson Fossett: They have to be Skip Gates.

Kevin Gaines: Yes, "successful" in ways that sometimes have little to do with intellectual contributions. They have to be highly visible entrepreneurs or celebrities. This is a pernicious double standard. Most white scholars, even at the top institutions, are not required to be megastars.

Judith Jackson Fossett: I don't know if I ever told you this joke while we were at Princeton: Princeton is indeed firmly committed to affirmative action. All faculty of color who also happen to be MacArthur Fellows, Nobel laureates, Pulitzer Prize and National Book Award winners will be gladly accepted!

Kevin Gaines: That's great! And, seriously, I think this reflects a political battle. Universities are in retrenchment mode. There's some real disinvestment in African American studies programs. And along with this financial retrenchment comes a sort of political retrenchment in which members of related disciplines like English and history departments are skeptical of an African American studies program, unless it is associated with Nobel laureates and MacArthur Fellows and extremely charismatic figures who make us feel good by their very presence. It's a serious problem. And inevitably, African American studies has to be assessed today in relation to how it responds to this crisis, how well or how badly.

Yet while I know that we have to deal with these kinds of grim realities, I do not want us to forget what the very important contributions of the African American studies project have been. And in my view, one of its most significant contributions would have to be to gender studies. African American studies has spoken to gender studies work in many different disciplines, certainly to that in U.S. women's history. But within a black academic and community context, this contribution is not widely recognized because African American public culture seems so deeply invested in male-dominated, masculinist politics. But internal nonrecognition of the contributions of black feminist studies is still part of a general nonrecognition of African American studies. I am thinking of the lack of recognition of the work of Nell Irvin Painter, Darlene Clark Hine, of Mary Helen Washington in literary studies, of Paula Giddings, of Thadious Davis's fantastic biography of Nella Larsen. The implications of that last book for both African American studies and American literature are just tremendous. But it's a book that hasn't received the recognition it deserves.

Judith Jackson Fossett: And I would also add to this list: Hortense Spillers, Hazel Carby, and Evelyn Brooks Higginbotham.

Kevin Gaines: Look at the purported crisis of the Negro intellectual as described by Harold Cruse, that African American intellectuals were seduced by the "white left," away from the interests and needs of black communities and were not engaged in the perpetual struggle over the control and reconstruction of African American culture and institutions. If anything the contributions of black feminist studies within an African American studies project have done more than any other area of intellectual production to work toward healing divisions within the black community. I should add that black gay and lesbian studies have made vital contributions as well, particularly the work of Barbara Smith and the late Marlon Riggs.

Judith Jackson Fossett: I wanted to get back to this notion of contributions in terms of disciplinary effect and influence. I would certainly say that the field of American literature has changed enormously as a consequence of African American studies. I am thinking here just of the impact in the classroom of three or four figures, including Frederick Douglass, Zora Neale Hurston, Toni Morrison, and Alice Walker. I've seen the texts by them produce life-changing effects on many undergraduates, but particularly white students, who have never to that point known a way to get into black culture (despite the continual African Americanizing of so much of American culture, from music—R&B to hip hop—to clothes, to speech, etc.). Some works are now required reading, alongside Hawthorne or Emerson. In one of my upper-level undergraduate seminars, everyone in the class had already read Douglass's 1845 narrative, which I found astounding.

Kevin Gaines: They had read it in high school or college?

Judith Jackson Fossett: Some in high school, but most of them had read it in college. And the ways in which they engaged with it give them entrée to consider the slave experience in a primarily discursive mode that facilitated new kinds of discussion. It was no longer solely a question of thinking about the material violence of slavery. If you ask them to read other kinds of slave narratives that don't conform to Douglass's model of rhetorical sophistication and masculinist discourse, they get impatient and frustrated (say, with Juan Francisco Manzano's *Autobiography of a Slave* [1839] from Cuba or Nat Turner's confession [1831]). I would say the same thing about *Their Eyes Were Watching God, The Bluest Eye, The Color Purple, Sula,* or *Beloved;* these are life-changing texts for students that are now "safe" for a lot of white literary folks to put on their syllabi. These books are rotated into the pedagogical canon; they are in the regular cycle of the "survey." There are now even competing editions available—a far cry from a decade or so ago when many of the few available editions were either out of stock or out of print. Of course there are other texts that are equally revelatory for students—ones by Ellison or Wright or Baldwin—that unfortunately don't get taught nearly as much. I would like to think of *Invisible Man* crossing that barrier, but its length often precludes its inclusion, and, as a consequence, it doesn't get taught as much.

Kevin Gaines: Besides the length and time constraints, it's also pretty complicated. Think of *Huckleberry Finn.* At the high school level, at least, many teachers don't have the patience or the training to deal with its complexity.

Judith Jackson Fossett: There's an article I would like to write about how to teach *Invisible Man* by teaching the first half of the book. It is the blues, with all the requisite repetition! If we as teachers can get students to the paint factory (about the novel's midpoint), they can probably read on themselves. And half of Ellison is infinitely preferable to none at all. Still, it is no longer simply a question of one poem by Langston Hughes on the syllabus, though there are also so many important authors that have not attained this privileged status: Frances Harper, Charles Chesnutt, Claude McKay, Nella Larsen, Ann Petry, Gayl Jones, James Alan MacPherson, John Edgar Wideman, and others.

Kevin Gaines: Speaking as a historian, the contributions of African American literature are so crucial that you can't even do African American history without literature. Leon Litwack's study of the black experience of Jim Crow relies heavily on African American autobiographies to describe the psychological terror of segregation. In fact, I always assign literature in my history surveys and seminars. The last time I taught my introductory survey to African American history, I used *Beloved* to teach the history of slavery. And my students were initially quite disconcerted by this. Many of them were first-year students who brought with them a limited sense of history as just "facts," actual events, so the idea of reading a work of historical fiction was really unsettling to their assumptions about history as *truth*. But, of course, I was able to communicate to them that everything in *Beloved* has a historical significance, and it is, in fact, based on an actual occurrence. So I'm going to continue to use it. I am also looking at black expatriate writers and the literature that came out of the black expatriate experience. And it's all historical; they're fundamentally political writings. From reading Wright's fiction, Baldwin's essays, a couple of Maya Angelou's memoirs, or even John A. Williams, you get insights into the so-called civil rights era largely undisclosed in much scholarship on the movement. I have found these to be very powerful texts in history courses.

Judith Jackson Fossett: These changes seem palpable to me. Imagine all of your students having read Douglass's *Narrative*! And not just having read it, but being conversant about it. And we should remember the interest and facility that have consequently been developed among non–African American colleagues in order to teach this text and others.

Kevin Gaines: We'd love to see that kind of entry of African American studies texts into the social science disciplines, for Anne Moody to be part of every twentieth-century U.S. history course. It's very encouraging to hear you talk about how students have read Frederick Douglass.

But I also don't think we should lose sight of the sobering fact that, in many ways, African American literature is not taught as much as it once was a few short years ago, specifically in high school curricula. I say this having lived and worked in Texas and having seen how controversial some of the texts within the African American studies canon are for some conservative school boards. Maya Angelou and Toni Morrison are routinely being banned by high school districts in Texas and elsewhere. And they are being banned on the pretext that they deal with sexually explicit themes, though in fact I think the impetus behind this censorship is that these works deal with African American history and black realities in general. These are books that were part of our high school training, texts that were not controversial then, but now are being taken out of school libraries. Despite what you say about your students, I now tend to see a fair number of students who don't have any grounding in African American literature and history.

Judith Jackson Fossett: Part of my optimism may stem from teaching such a diverse group of students in southern California. And even as my students and faculty colleagues seem open to some texts and ideas and motifs of African American studies, I still encounter a myriad of obstacles. When I taught an undergraduate seminar on slavery, I felt a real sense of students' anger much of the time. They felt like they had been denied "real history" in high school that would have been meaningful or significant to them. It's unclear to me whether or not they had been fed the myth of slavery as a benevolent, benign institution in their high school history courses, but the details of the brutality of the institution generally and of the sexual exploitation of female slaves particularly riveted them. They peppered me with questions about the dissemination of knowledge: "Why didn't I learn this in high school?" and about the gatekeepers of that knowledge: "Why was this kept from me?" I got these questions not so much in the sense that there was a conspiracy but with a sense of frustration that only now were they able to discern the importance of this history and the issues surrounding slavery. Feeling galvanized by this material, they wondered why the college classroom was their first scene of instruction on these issues. This, I think, makes the question of affirmative action even more important. The environment of higher education is often the only space in which you actually have access to this material, now that in some places, this material has been effectively barred from secondary schools. What does that mean when you have assaults on affirmative action? And when there are fewer students of color admitted who might be interested in this material? African American studies then has no effective means of being disseminated.

Kevin Gaines: It's a chilling prospect.

Judith Jackson Fossett: What is some of the other work that you think should galvanize us today and in the future?

Kevin Gaines: I think particularly of work in African American history that focuses on that controversial period, Reconstruction. Our coming to terms with the history of slavery and the moment of emancipation is crucial both for the field and for the nation's cultural memory. Reconstruction is such a significant period because it foregrounds questions of citizenship. In fact, I think what's really at stake in the critique of racial essentialism within African American studies or Afrocentrism is the issue of citizenship and equal rights, one that often is completely sacrificed in a more cultural-nationalist view of black consciousness and identity. Reconstruction provides a vital case study for looking at such questions, foregrounding African Americans' struggles to define freedom in terms of their new status of citizenship. It's deeply relevant because the struggle for freedom, full citizenship, and economic and cultural independence were all linked. These goals weren't perceived in terms of a false dichotomy between nationalism and integration, according to contemporary common sense. Reconstruction as a movement animated by black struggle sought to transform and democratize the nation; that's quite different from today's more inward-looking, if not reactionary, cultural nationalism with its imperative to reconstruct black communities in the narrowest sense of restoring patriarchal authority. I think that strong demands of citizenship are virtually extinct, and what we have with mass media spectacles like the Million Man March is a double-edged phenomenon of a deep desire to revitalize black communities and to mobilize ourselves politically, but one being carried out in a reactionary way that betrays the legacy of the freedpeople's struggle to give concrete meaning to their citizenship. So I think that current and future scholarship on the Reconstruction era is absolutely crucial, particularly the work of Du Bois, Nell Painter, and Eric Foner and a host of other scholars, including the Freedom Project out of the University of Maryland under Ira Berlin. I consider that the sort of project where African American studies is going to help us reconceptualize American history more broadly. It has crucial implications for African American public culture particularly within a contemporary moment in which black conservative politics seems to be visible out of proportion to its actual following within black communities.

Judith Jackson Fossett: And I would offer a literary counterpart related to something you mentioned earlier. If, as you suggested, African American culture constitutes a compelling model for many nonblack groups in terms of their identity, how do we intellectually and pedagogically deal with the issue of fungibility and identity? In other words, might we consider the ways in which African American literature foregrounds questions of identity, questions which are often highly compelling to college readers? When I teach *Invisible Man*, the narrator's quest to make sense of his grandfather's cryptic deathbed statements—about the duplicitous nature of supposed black acquiescence—functions as a threshold for broader understandings of identity and identification. Does African American experience become a kind of handmaiden? How do we help our students recognize and avoid the pitfalls of identification and sentiment? Recent work like Saidiya Hartman's book on slavery, sentiment, and performance and Hortense Spiller's essays generally are key here. We also need to look to Toni Morrison's critical essays (from "Unspeakable Things Unspoken" to *Playing in the Dark*) on the central but shadowlike Africanist presence in American culture. This process of white or American identity formation is one in which a black presence functions as a "ghost in the machine" of American political and racial identity formations. These are critical and theoretical models that will be applicable in many other fields as scholars explore both individual and group identity. In essence, the movement of African Americans from the status of chattel to secondary citizenship to full citizenship foregrounds for all Americans the broader category of identity and its varied trajectories. And I think it may account for why this process is one to which students really respond.

Kevin Gaines: To explore this complicated process of identity formation as treated in a particular text or within a particular moment of U.S. history is ultimately to suggest a broader framework for identity formation that translates to other experiences, other racialized and ethnic groups. That's why looking at the phenomenon of exile and migration and its relevance for the black experience generally in terms of social and intellectual history offers a chance to look at the struggle of black intellectuals to function within a hostile American environment with severely restricted resources and opportunities. And the migration experience is crucial for reshaping black collective consciousness. For intellectuals, exile, escaping the constraints of American racism, was tremendously important for their understanding of their relationship to the larger world, not only to Europe but also to black communities throughout the diaspora and to African peoples on the continent. I should add that I don't see travel, or exile, as a universalizing move, in which one necessarily sheds one's previous identity for something "more universal." When black expatriates considered themselves "citizens of the world," they refined and reaffirmed their radical black sensibility. So I think we need to come up with alternative frameworks (and much of the valuable scholarship you mentioned earlier does this) to look at identity and the process of identity formation. Ways that speak to the experiences of others without losing sight of being fundamentally grounded in a black cultural identity and experience . . .

But before we finish here, I want to mention a worry that I have: about the dismal state of mass-mediated public culture that in its demand for celebrity, controversy, and sensation is steadily diminishing what little authority black intellectuals may have had. It strikes me that in middlebrow magazines, there is a tendency to deny or debunk affirmations of black cultural identity. There was that piece by Randall Kennedy in the *Atlantic Monthly* about how black solidarity is a thing of the past, and how he renounces favoritism toward his black students. This is absurd on many levels, the most important revolving around the demographics of Kennedy's classroom. Probably 95 percent of his students are not black. So for him to claim that he agonizes over the choice to mentor his black students or treat everyone "equally" is just plain grandstanding! You have occasional statements by Henry Louis Gates in the *New Yorker* making loaded contrasts between declarations of black solidarity (as being passé and less sophisticated) and more ironic approaches to black identity. He said this in an article on the new black British intelligentsia and how it seems to have matured, forsaking a more oppositional posture against Thatcherism to achieve a successful entry into mainstream British cultural institutions. Gates even appropriates Stuart Hall, who led the black British intellectual challenge to Thatcherism, to ratify his view of this rhetorical shift. Then you have Keith Richberg's book that made such a big splash. Richberg covered Africa for the *Washington Post* in the early 1990s, and his beat coincided with the catastrophes of Somalia and Rwanda. And so he publishes *Out of America,* in which he debunks what he sees as this hopelessly romantic notion of black American solidarity with African peoples. And his whole account was suffused with a horror and disillusionment that was understandable, perhaps, but ultimately one-sided and misleading. His Afro-pessimism reduces postcolonial Africa to chaos, disorder, corruption, and genocide.

And we are still witnessing occasional broadsides against African American writers whose work has been generative for subsequent generations of writers—James Baldwin, for example. There was an article in the *New Yorker* by Hilton Als which was yet another attack on Baldwin's reputation. And in what has long been something of a cliché, Gates argued in the *New Republic* in the early 1990s that James Baldwin failed to live up to his promise as a writer. In the *New Yorker,* Gates also reported Albert Murray's somewhat resentful dismissal of Toni Morrison. It appears that the posture increasingly adopted by black critics and writers tapped for mainstream publications is to denigrate the reputation of estimable African American writers. In doing so, they function as gatekeepers for voyeuristic white audiences who are probably confirmed in their suspicion that these acclaimed black writers must be the beneficiaries of some literary version of affirmative action. It all amounts to a not-so-subtle attack on black cultural identity, and in many cases this attack is waged by African American writers, perhaps at the behest of white editors. For a black critic to appear in these magazines, must he engage in this oedipal game of trashing black writers and their legacy of struggle? What a waste of talent, given the number of neglected black writers one might discuss instead.

Some people would say that the mainstreaming of African American studies as represented by Gates's department at Harvard represents success. But it does seem to have its costs. It seems to perpetuate the very thing that Gates claims to be opposing—that is, the "one nigger syndrome."

Judith Jackson Fossett: Yes, the "head-nigger-in-charge (HNIC) syndrome." And just as I worry about the larger American perception of a "monolith" politically or culturally in the black community and am concerned about Frederick Douglass functioning as not merely the preeminent but the sole (and universal) black literary figure in the average American literature survey, so too do I worry about the perception of the HNIC phenomenon. Gates's facility to be representative in his exemplariness is a case in point. The current "Dream Team" model of Harvard's Afro-American studies department represents an institutional approach that simply cannot be duplicated: Skip Gates, Cornel West, William Julius Wilson, Evelyn Brooks Higginbotham, Larry Bobo all on the same faculty. And if this department exists as the new flagship for U.S. colleges and universities, what message does this model send across the country? Can African American studies only flourish in this star-type atmosphere? In fact, what is the relation between faculty and students in a "Dream Team" environment? Or are there perhaps other more productive models, like Yale's department with its thriving M.A. and now Ph.D. programs in African American studies?

Kevin Gaines: And with those questions perhaps it is a good time to summarize and conclude here. It's clear that what we have been saying about the challenges facing African American studies, and to a lesser extent, the contributions of the field, is deeply influenced by the places we currently work, and frankly, the privileged places we've been. I suspect that those scholars working at large state universities or historically black colleges, and nonblack scholars, for that matter, will have entirely different opinions on the question of African American studies, but nevertheless I hope our conversation will be of some value.

Judith Jackson Fossett: Perhaps some will observe that we haven't had much to say regarding the view that scholarship needs to question and revise the black/white paradigm for race relations. For my part, I concur with this view, just as

I would support the view that scholarship on race must integrate categories of gender, class, and sexuality. I fully recognize that our multiracial future, which has already arrived in California, Texas, New York, and Florida, if not almost everywhere else, demands it. But I am concerned that such calls to move beyond the black/white model might reflect in part a certain naivete about the continuing salience of antiblack racism as the litmus test for the inclusion of racialized immigrant groups. In that regard, as a society, we clearly haven't forsaken the black/white paradigm and show little signs of doing so. The calls to move beyond the black/white model echo loudly in a California context. But that din has only solidified my commitment to the elaboration of African American studies in an otherwise "rainbow" society. As Cornel West observes, it is not as if moving beyond black and white ensures the overthrow of white supremacy. Quite the opposite in fact. A case in point concerns the affirmative action debate in my state. While Governor Pete Wilson and Rev. Jesse Jackson lined up on opposite sides of the issue and ostensibly cast the debate in white and black terms, the heart of the issue concerned the relative success of Asian American students and white female students in comparison to their white male peers in admissions to the University of California. In other words, the black/white model (with Wilson and Ward Connerly on one side and Jackson and others on the other) obfuscated the complexity of racial and gender-based differences in standardized scores and grades. But without a more comprehensive sense of the pervasiveness and the *power* of that model, voters allowed themselves to be led astray, thinking that the issue was a battle between black and white high school students, and not the more complicated matter of multiracial and gender diversity in higher education.

So, against the grain of a postmodern marginalization of the legacy of black struggles, my project remains the elaboration of black subjectivities and their changing definitions of freedom and democracy in national and global contexts. It continues to center upon how American literary culture has been shaped by the codifying institutions of slavery and Jim Crow, and how constructions of blackness, whiteness, and otherness *evolve* through the nation's multiracial and multicultural history.

Kevin Gaines: So what we have said, on the whole, reflects our experiences in states that are on the front line in the battle over affirmative action. It seems our lot, as black people, to be challenged by a hostile environment in such a way that complacency seems an outrageously inappropriate response. And yet, it is also important to catch our breath and reflect on contributions, on what has been achieved, not in any superficial sense but through the production of new and enduring knowledge. It's my hope that such knowledge will continue to resonate and transform lives and give inspiration the way that the work of Cornel West, Toni Morrison, James Baldwin, and others made me want to write about African American intellectuals and work in the field of African American Studies.

6

Star Search:
Psychoanalysis and Marxism in
Lesbian and Gay Studies

Dennis W. Allen and Judith Roof

*One small but central moment discussed in the following dialogue is the an-
nouncement near the end of 1998 that Ellen DeGeneres would appear at a public
rally in response to the murder of Matthew Shepard. Now, DeGeneres was undoubtedly asked to speak on this occasion because she is both a celebrity and a
lesbian (in fact, as we will discuss below, because she is a celebrity she may well
serve as America's notion of* the *lesbian), and the linking of her name to this
planned rally invokes a familiar logic of representation in both the semiotic and
political senses of the term. Standing on that platform, DeGeneres would embody
not only the identity category "lesbian" but, through a slight extension, the larger,
combined category of the "queer," and this embodiment, the literal incarnation
of a collective identity and of an abstraction ("lesbianism," "queerness") in the
person of an individual, is not only the basis of our political system ("the senator
from Kansas") but also an unexamined premise of much of the work done in identity studies in general and "queer theory" in particular. As such, in our attempts
to analyze the relative merits of psychoanalytic and Marxist approaches in lesbian and gay studies, it became apparent to us very early on that this dialogue
might best proceed by both invoking and analyzing this logic of representation.
Thus, we begin by discussing three exemplary instances (the murder of Matthew
Shepard, the coming-out of Ellen DeGeneres, and the rise of the academic star
system in lesbigay studies) in order to illustrate the strengths and limitations of
the two methodologies but also, finally, to provide the basis for a critique of the
very idea of the exemplary individual, a critique that leads us in turn to an in-
terrogation of the nature and function of methodology itself.*

*Yet Ellen's speech is also important for another, related reason. Because she
would stand on the platform as a representative of the same identity category*

("queer") to which Matthew Shepard himself belonged, when Ellen speaks about Matthew she is also, in a sense, understood to be speaking for him, and, writing as a lesbian and a gay man, our own dialogue places us in a similar position. To speak about lesbian and gay studies in this instance will, in a sense, be implicitly understood as speaking for it or for lesbian and gay scholars in general. Since one of our goals, as we've already suggested, will be to interrogate the logic that operates here, to call into question this notion of the exemplary instance and of the individual's "representative" identity, we have decided not to label our "individual" contributions to this dialogue by name. Similarly, after some consideration, we have decided not to use pseudonyms, and not simply because, having settled on "Sluggo" and "Nancy," we couldn't agree over which one of us would get to be "Sluggo." While pseudonyms may veil, albeit only slightly, individual identities, they nonetheless leave the underlying belief in the representative individual in place. Instead, as the closest we could come to calling this ideal of exemplarity into question while still fulfilling the insistence on it that is mandated by the profession (by annual reviews of faculty performance, if nothing else), we have marked the dialogue by three different fonts (one each for the "individual" contributions and a third for the jointly written sections) as yet another way of suggesting one of our points: that it may ultimately be less important to focus on who says something than to focus on what it is that "s/he" may happen to say.

"A DIMINUTIVE MAN. . . ."

Tied to a wooden fence along an old dirt road, the weight of his small body sagging against the cheap utility cord, Matthew Shepard begged for his life as his attackers pistol-whipped him, according to allegations read in court Friday. But the assailants kept hitting the 21-year-old gay college student with the butt of a .357 Magnum until they believed he was dead. They broke his skull. Then they took his wallet, his patent leather shoes and took off to burglarize his house. Albany County Judge Robert Castor read the allegations against Russell Arthur Henderson, 21, and Aaron James McKinney, age unknown [22], on Friday during the pair's initial court appearance.
—Jim Hughes, "Beating Victim Begged for Life," Denver Post, *Oct. 10, 1998*

Perhaps as a result of the shocking brutality of the incident, any attempt to explain Matthew Shepard's murder would seem to insist on a psychoanalytic reading, to direct us toward the psyches of Henderson and McKinney in order to understand what happened and why it happened. And, more generally, the current interpretive paradigm of "queer theory" would tend to see this event in a psychoanalytically inflected way, as an incident that is precisely about processes of projection and (dis)identification, about desire and its repudiation. Yet, while such an analysis can be instructive, as I hope to show, it is also incomplete. To understand fully the "meaning" of Matthew Shepard's murder, we will thus need to interrogate the reporting of the event itself: in other words, we will need to see how Matthew Shepard functions within media culture as an object of another operation: the process of representation and commodification.

To begin a psychoanalytic interpretation of this event as a story about identity and desire, it is difficult to think of a better example of homographesis, Lee Edelman's term for the heterosexual fantasy that the gay body is always marked visually, clearly set off and distinguished from the straight male body, a fantasy that serves to ward off the unsettling awareness that desire does not in fact write itself on the body, that anyone can turn out to be gay (*Homographesis*, 12). Homographesis thus insists on clear lines of demarcation, on an inside and an outside, between the straight male self and the gay man, between the (heterosexual) desire within and the (homosexual) desire of the other.

> Matthew Shepard, a 5-foot-2, 105-pound gay college student . . .
>
> . . . a diminutive man who wanted to dedicate his life to the fight for human rights . . .
>
> . . . Shepard, barely 5-ft. 2-in. tall and on a good day 105 lbs . . .
>
> Matthew Shepard was 21. He was tiny, stood 5'2", only weighed 105 pounds, and he was also unabashedly gay.
> —*Various news sources*

It is not then surprising that, in all the news coverage of this incident, the press has relentlessly focused on Matt's physical characteristics: his height, weight, and appearance. What it is easy to miss, however, is that, in all the print media at least, there are no corresponding physical descriptions of his assailants. Henderson and McKinney consistently remain undescribed. They might be 4'9" and 95 pounds or 6' and 215. In a sense, Shepard is the only one in these reports who has a body, however small and inadequate; the straight man, by contrast, is incorporeal, a transcendental principle.

> . . . Shepard, a slight 5-foot, 2-inch man who wore braces on his teeth . . .
> —*James Brooke, "Gay Man Beaten and Left for Dead; Two Are Charged," New York Times, Oct. 10, 1998*

Nor is this just any body. Even if one were to miss the relentless insistence on Shepard's "slightness" or his diminutive stature, the synecdochic detail that returns again and again in descriptions of Matt is these braces. This is, then, the flawed body: immature, imperfect, incomplete, deficient, a gay body visibly marked by its failure even to approximate the ontological fullness of the masculine, straight (and masculine because it is straight) male body.

> According to the local police and prosecutors, the two men lured Shepard out of a bar by saying they were gay.
> —James Brooke, "After Beating of Gay Man, Town Looks at Its Attitudes," New York Times, Oct. 12, 1998

The homographic fantasy unravels, of course. If Shepard himself was fatally unable to tell, by looking, who was gay and who was not, then the gay body is not marked after all, which is why it must be marked by violence. And it is precisely the incredible ferocity of that violence in this instance that signals the impossibility of the fantasy, which is, finally, the fantasy that homosexuality cannot appear within heterosexuality, either within the community of heterosexual men or within the individual heterosexual male himself.

> "He [McKinney] said that a guy walked up to him, and said that he was gay and wanted to get with Aaron and Russ," Ms. Price [McKinney's girlfriend] recalled to 20-20. The two men beat him, she said, "to teach him a lesson not to come on to straight people."
>
> Two months before he was killed, Shepard was involved in another altercation, with a man who claims that he struck him because he had flirted with him.
>
> The kind of violence in this case fits national patterns in anti-gay crimes, several experts in the field say.
>
> "Once someone is labeled as homosexual, any glance or conversation by that person is perceived as sexual flirtation," Karen Frankin, a forensic psychologist, wrote in a recent paper. "Flirtation, in turn, is viewed as a legitimate reason to assault."
> —James Brooke, "Men Held in Beating Lived on the Fringes," New York Times, Oct. 16, 1998

If we are to believe the psychologist, "sexual flirtation"—the possibility of gay sex—is not really something that happens to the straight man: unwanted advances that come from someone else. If flirtation is a (heterosexual) projection, then its very trajectory as a projection—the movement outside—is intended to conceal the ontology that generates it: by definition, it is the externalization of the internal, of something within. This something need not necessarily be homosexual desire itself, of course. Yet, even if it is only the idea of homosexuality, the internalized other used to constitute the self, heterosexuality can thus never really demarcate an inside and an outside, can never establish a pure straight identity untainted by the homosexual.

A psychoanalytically inflected reading of a generalized heterosexual male "psyche" can thus at least begin to explain Henderson and McKinney's actions. It can even explain the media's own insistent re-marking of Matt, the fact that the news coverage, although sympathetic, nonetheless insists, relentlessly, on Matt as corporeally distinct from a straight man, if only by virtue of being presented as corporeal in the first place. Yet, such a reading, like the media coverage itself, actually functions, I would argue, to conceal something else: to distract attention from other operations. This can best be understood, perhaps, by asking a question.

Gay-bashing—and the murder of gay men—happens all the time. Why, then, did Matthew Shepard become so instantly and completely visible? In part the answer is the extreme brutality of the crime, which brings homophobic violence so sharply into focus that it is hard to ignore. But the brutality itself is highlighted in this instance because of its victim. Continually represented by the media as small, boyish, and immature, Matt Shepard is thus inscribed with a physicality that is not, finally, that of a gay man. Simply put, he is presented as being like a child. Hence, following the current hysterical insistence in American culture on both the asexual innocence and the extreme vulnerability of children, a hysteria that has recently been brilliantly anatomized by Lauren Berlant in *The Queen of America Goes to Washington City*, Matt can be assimilated to all the contemporary discourses about the mistreatment, abuse, and neglect of children ("Tied to a wooden fence along an old dirt road, the weight of his small body sagging against the cheap utility cord . . ."). In other words, the viciousness of Matt's murder is brought into visibility by the invocation of a complex of cultural ideologies that, at the same time and as a condition of this operation, virtually erase his homosexuality. Thus, while Matt can represent the idea of the victim of gay-bashing, he is a victim who has also been subtly but insistently cleansed of the threatening aspects of that sexuality. In fact, childlike, he has been cleansed of sexuality itself. Matthew Shepard may or may not have really flirted with Henderson and McKinney. Once he is displaced into media representations that stress his boyishness, however, the thought of "Matt" flirting becomes almost unthinkable; in the media construction of "Matt," such flirtation can only be seen as a homophobic fantasy.

Now, I do not mean to suggest that, even if Matt did flirt with Henderson and McKinney, there was anything wrong with this. The murder of Matthew Shepard was inexcusable. Rather, I am trying to emphasize the way in which, even beyond the basic homographic operations that it performs, media coverage of Matt begins a process of (complex, multiple) representation(s) of him, of which the portrait of him as a presexual innocent who is only looking for "friends" is merely one instance. As such, it seems crucial not only to analyze the homographic projections that caused this murder and that persist in the reporting of it but also to investigate how the (often) sentimentalized portraits of Matt that have emerged in public discourse perform a parallel, and at its core equally homophobic, process of projection. And this, I would argue, is where a Marxist paradigm becomes helpful, precisely because it shifts attention from the "content" of the incident to the very process of (media) representation itself: to the commodification of Matthew Shepard.

Although there will doubtless be, if there are not already, t-shirts that commemorate Matt, I am less concerned here with Matthew Shepard's metonymic reproduction in literal commodities than with his transformation into "Matthew Shepard," his (re)construction as a representation, which depends on (and demonstrates) the underlying logic of the commodity itself. As Slavoj Žižek (not to mention Marx) has made clear, the process of commodification is one of progressive abstraction away from the materiality of the object: the object's sensory properties are replaced by an idea of its "value"; more specifically, a perception of the commodity's use value is overwhelmed by an attention to its exchange value (*The Sublime Object of Ideology*, 17). Moreover, in the media-driven environment of late capitalism, as Baudrillard has pointed out, (monetary) exchange value eventually gives way to sign exchange value, to the image of the commodity (*Selected Writings*, 57–63). As such, once Matthew Shepard enters the circuits of representation, once he is transformed into the signifier "Matthew Shepard," he is submitted to an invisible ideological and representational labor that both creates a meaning for him and conceals its operations so that any meaning that is created seems to inhere in "Matt" himself. Like the literal commodity, "Matthew Shepard" is, thus, a fetish. Even more saliently, as Stuart Hall has made clear, because the labor in this instance is the production of signification, the meaning(s) created for "Matt" determine the use and exchange values of this image of him ("The Rediscovery of 'Ideology,'" in *Culture, Society, and the Media,* ed. Gurevitch, 56–90). As a product of signification, "Matt" thus becomes susceptible to ideological "use" and to circulation as part of media culture's discursive and semiotic "exchange" of signifiers.

> Let me also take a moment here to offer my prayers and my condolences to the family of Matthew Shepard, as well as to the community of Laramie, Wyoming and the university. . . . In our shock and grief one thing must remain clear, hate and prejudice are not American values. The public outrage in Laramie and all

across America today echoes what we heard at the White House Conference on
Hate Crimes last year—there is something we can do about this. Congress needs
to pass our tough Hate Crimes Legislation.
—*Bill Clinton, White House press release, Oct. 12, 1998*

In fact, I would argue that, as a signifier, "Matt" "himself" has undergone an
extremely rapid and multivalent process of semiotic and ideological transmutation. Identified as the exemplary victim of homophobic violence by both
President Clinton and gay activists, "Matt" becomes a premise, evidence for the
need to pass a bill that extends the definition of a hate crime under federal law
to include gay men and lesbians. Once positioned in this way, "Matt" comes to
mean something like "the gay man as victim" and thus becomes available as a
more generalized symbol of the effects not only of anti-gay violence but homophobia in general. Thus, a Web site like "Matthew Shepard Online Resources" (World Wide Web, Jan. 26, 1999, <http://www.wired strategies.com/
shepardx.html>) put together by Wired Strategies ("Political Internet Consulting—Washington, DC"), continually updates "Matt"-related material in such
a way that "his" meaning gradually expands outward to incorporate ever more
diverse aspects of the struggle for gay rights. Given the failure of Congress to
pass the Hate Crimes Prevention Act, the site, as of this writing (early in 1999),
has thus begun to report other incidents of anti-gay violence and homophobic death threats.

The fact that "Matt" need not intrinsically "mean" such things has been sig-
naled by both the direct and indirect repudiation of the notion that the original incident was a hate crime (rather than a simple robbery) by sources as diverse as the *New York Times*, McKinney's father, and the governor of Wyoming
(although the implication that Wyoming robberies are normally conducted in
this way can hardly be good for tourism). As this dispute over the representational significance of Matt's murder suggests, once "Matt" begins to circulate
as a sign, he quickly becomes abstracted into a synecdoche for all gay men that
intersects with a larger public dialogue of competing representations of homosexuality itself. This is evident, among other places, in "Matthew Shepard's
Memorial Website," put together by "Robby" (World Wide Web, Jan. 26, 1999,
<http://www.websine.com/shepard/matt.html>), which, like many of the
other sixty-one Web sites in the Matthew Shepard Memorial Web Ring, col-
lects and displays readers' comments and artistic tributes.

Precisely because it is an example of a sort of postmodern folk art, the ideological work of one such tribute, the homemade digital image Us.jpg is less self-
conscious than many of the more overtly political representations. As such,
its constitution of a certain idea of Matt as a metaphor for THE gay man is

naively and obviously encoded on the imagaic surface itself. Consisting of the familiar head and shoulders shot of Matt in a grey crewneck sweater reduplicated five times and overlapped along a roughly diagonal plane to form a sort of crowd of Matts, the image contains the caption "It could have been us!" and then, simply, "Matthew Shepard 1976–1998" printed in the lower righthand corner of the picture. This kitschy multiplication of "Matt" makes visible the operation by which the particular and the general are collapsed into each other. "Us" is a multiplicity, but that multiplicity is always "Matt." Intended to mean that any gay man could be the victim of a homophobic murder, the artwork distracts attention from the notion of the gay man that it constitutes: of the gay man as neither, finally, gay nor a man but, as I've already suggested, as an asexual, and hence innocent, child.

As I've also suggested, this child is important, finally, because of his victimization, because he has been abused by an irrational hatred. Yet, once positioned in this way, "Matt" enters the circuits of a bourgeois sentimentality that is so pure that it begins to float free of any relation to gay men at all, as another of the homemade images on "Matthew Shepard's Memorial Website" suggests. Like Us.jpg, Mattcollage.jpg is constructed through a process of superimposition of various images so that another familiar picture of Matt (in baggy sweats sitting with arms crossed on his knees) has been placed over an image of the sky so that Matt is now resting in the clouds looking up and to his right where a second, three-quarter profile shot of Matt has been placed, positioned over the light source of the original photograph and then airbrushed in a white oval to suggest, not entirely subtly, a halo. Below this is the caption, "A light to the world," and then, of course, "Matthew Shepard 1976–1998." This image may not have consciously intended to transvalue another of the recurrent images of "Matt" (being mistaken for a "scarecrow" by the cyclist who found him) into an image of sacrificial crucifixion, but the implicit analogy to Jesus suggests that, even if "Matt" is not exactly "the" light of the world, "he" is nonetheless a martyr. Yet the precise meaning or value of such a sacrifice is not made clear here, and I would argue that the use of Christian allusion in this image functions less as a means of recalling any particular aspect of Christian ideology than as the invocation of a certain formulaic sentimentality. In other words, the image's transmutation of the subhuman (Henderson and McKinney's view of Matt, or the cyclist's "scarecrow") into the superhuman (the divine: Matt as Jesus) does not finally work to reposition a "subhuman" group (gay men) as, at the very least, human. Instead, "Matt" simply becomes the latest in a recent series of icons of pathos, which includes, in slightly different ways, both Princess Diana and Baby Jessica, whose meaning is, ultimately, very little more than pathos itself. This series, that is to say, is a series of victims who, regardless of the ostensible cause of their victimization (homophobia, media attention, uncovered wells), and regardless of whether the "tragedy" can finally be averted by human effort (Baby Jessica) or not (Diana, Matt), derive their meaning only from their presentation as victims: innocent, helpless, prey to accident and misfortune. Thus, in "Matt's" case, once "he" reaches this level of semiotic and ideological abstraction as a victim of irrational hatred, any (political or interpretive) attention to the homophobia involved in gay-bashing is deflected into an emphasis on its irrationality, which becomes, as with Jessica and Diana, simply the irrationality of the universe, the apparent meaninglessness of (all) human "tragedy" itself.

At this level, of course, "Matt" does not simply cease to be political, but, having been inserted into a metonymic chain of cultural signifiers of pathos, he also ceases to be "gay" in any meaningful way. In fact, it could be said that he ceases to mean much of anything. Thus, the point is less that any resemblance between this "Matthew Shepard" and Matthew Shepard becomes purely a coincidence, but that one of the entirely incidental but nonetheless highly effective results of the process of commodification and representational circulation by which Matthew Shepard becomes an icon is to consume any use (political or otherwise) that that icon might have in the process of exchange itself. In other words, once the idea of "Matt" is commodified, put to various uses, and circulated and recirculated, it finally ceases to have any clear significance or effectiveness at all. In contrast, then, to a psychoanalytically inflected interpretation of Matt's murder, which seeks a (homophobic) Real within the incident, it might be more helpful to read it through a Marxist frame, which uncovers the equally homophobic but far more subtle process by which postindustrial consumer culture would seem to divest even the Symbolic of meaning.

"I'M LEBANESE"

For me this has been the most freeing experience because people can't hurt me anymore.
—Ellen DeGeneres

Like the iconized tragic figure of Matthew Shepard, the modern media role model Ellen DeGeneres seems best read through the psychoanalytic presumptions that ground understandings of identification. DeGeneres's success as a stand-up comedian and her accession to prime-time television stardom make her a spectacularly visible example of a woman who has achieved in a field generally dominated by men. Seeing a conspicuously eminent figure as in some ways the "same" as themselves, in the like-to-like logic of role modeling, others may be empowered to follow DeGeneres's trajectory to become, if not sit-com stars, then successful in their own endeavors.

But as the DeGeneres model complicates itself, becoming a figure not only of the successful woman but also of the successful lesbian, the stakes around identification become even more politicized. On the one hand, role modeling still holds sway, but for a slightly different group of modelers; lesbians can now find DeGeneres a role model, while straight women may be slightly decathected. On the other hand, DeGeneres also becomes a contested identity—gay—which not only outshines her prominence as comedian and female but becomes the pretext for more complex and vexed identificatory processes such as the displacements of homophobia and the anaclitic identifications of lesbian desire. Understood psychoanalytically, homophobia is the displacement onto another of one's fear of one's own homosexuality. Homophobia is indeed a kind of identification, which is why it so closely accompanies any discussion of a culturally taboo practice. Anaclitic identifications, or the desire to "have" someone, are, in the case of commodity culture, desires premised on the fantasy offered by the public image. Those who take such desires too literally become stalkers.

As an Identity, DeGeneres becomes an object of both hatred and love, spurring Web sites such as "Ellen DeGeneres or Ellen the Degenerate" that promote fundamentalist Christian intolerance or sites such as the "Ellen DeGeneres Internet Fan Club" "maintained by 15-year-old Alex LaVake of Pennsylvania, who idolizes Ellen—whatever her sexual orientation" or the "Ellen DeGeneres Shrine," an unfortunately defunct page whose title sums up the other nine Ellen-devoted sites' collection of Ellen photos, Ellen and Anne Heche photos, pithy sayings, bios, gossip, notes about future public appearances, musical recordings, stories about show tapings, quotes from her book, and the other electronically flashy flotsam of celebrity adulation.

But as in the apparently very different case of Matthew Shepard, the psychoanalytic assumptions of identification and even displacement don't seem adequate to account for what is, in DeGeneres's case, an identity made commodity. What DeGeneres exemplifies is more a complex psychology of the commodity identity. That DeGeneres is successful is not so much an indicator of public tolerance or the celebration of an identity category guaranteed through its tacit financing by advertisers and the support of fans, but is the symptom of a particular formulation of the identity category itself as an identity full of contradictions. Ellen DeGeneres's occupation of the totem site of public acceptance occurs not only because the time is right for commodity identities in general and a lesbian commodity identity in particular but also because of the particularly vexed and contradictory version of lesbian identity DeGeneres performs.

> We were like, "Whoa!"
> —*Dava Savel, executive producer,* Ellen

Like Matthew Shepard, Ellen DeGeneres becomes a gay icon because she mitigates whatever is threatening about being lesbian. The knowledge game that plays around her plays because she embodies both the contradictions between appearance and knowledge (she could easily pass as heterosexual) and compliance with a lesbian practice of encoded knowledge. Together these moor the knowledge game about identity that underlies a lesbian erotic and contemporary configurations of the lesbian as being itself a site of knowledge. In addition, the dynamic of DeGeneres's self-presentations where she poses as more inadvertent and indirect than deliberate or focused makes her seem less an evilly intentioned lesbian just waiting to venture triumphantly and in-your-face forth and more a victim of a nature that chooses some and not others. Even DeGeneres's comedy demonstrates this dynamic, simultaneously giving and taking away, asserting and deconstructing.

The character Ellen seems more aimless than deliberately funny, and her sexuality is more asexual than undiscovered. Even her lack of sexualness after her long-awaited coming out allayed any anxieties that a gay character would act true to "gay" form—that is, become a promiscuous, lascivious sexual predator. Ellen, in fact, becomes the opposite—a timid, shy, awkward, barely sexual being with an Identity. Although we might applaud the realism of DeGeneres's portrayal and the ways it fought against the unfair and unfounded stereotypes of the lesbian as man-hating, mannish, self-destructive, and single-mindedly sexual, it could survive as a portrayal only because it reduced Ellen to a kind of twilight zone adolescence, a pre–first kiss limbo of sexual immaturity. As Dava Savel, one of *Ellen*'s executive producers, points out, "Ellen Morgan is still in a very heterosexual situation. . . . Almost all her friends are heterosexuals. If one of the other characters has a guy that they're interested in, she's the first to say, 'Omigod, he's hot.' It's just not going to be an option for Ellen to date him" (Bruce Handy, "Roll Over, Ward Cleaver," *Time,* Apr. 14, 1997). As even *Time* points out, "This does smack a bit of the we're-doing-it-but-we're-not-doing-it attitude with which television often ends up approaching taboos" (Handy).

The character Ellen's sexuality was never separated from questions about DeGeneres's own sexual orientation just as the Ellen character was ambivalently both a character and DeGeneres herself. Curiosity about her sexuality was spurred not only by DeGeneres's unmistakable sub-code lesbian signals (those undefinable qualities that enable lesbians to identify other lesbians) but also by the sit-com's inability to find a sexual slot for an adult woman character (slots that are always spectacularly apparent from a character's first appearance). As *Time* relates it, "After the second season Ellen stopped dating—some writers say because DeGeneres was uncomfortable with overtly heterosexual story lines, although she says she simply wasn't interested in doing a show that focused on relationships" (Handy, "Roll Over, Ward Cleaver"). But the lesbian appears in the coming-out narrative by inadvertence as the unwilling but inevitable answer to a question that seemed to emerge organically from the show's difficulties. "Was Ellen Morgan really gay all along, before not only the character knew it but DeGeneres and the writers as well?" *Time* asks. Dava Savel comments on an episode with Janeane Garafalo: "There wasn't supposed to be a lesbian thing at all, but afterward we were watching the tape and we were like, 'Whoa!'"

> I'm Lebanese.
> —*Ellen DeGeneres*

Inadvertent, unwilling, but fated, Ellen Morgan's lesbian identity couldn't hide itself just as DeGeneres's lesbian identity eventually had to come out. "I always thought I could keep my personal life separate from my professional life," DeGeneres ruminated. "Everyone tried to trap me into saying I was gay. And I learned every way to dodge that" (Handy, "Roll Over, Ward Cleaver"). "I never wanted to be the lesbian actress. I never wanted to be the spokesperson for the gay community. Ever. I did it for my own truth," DeGeneres commented after Ellen came out ("Celebsite: Ellen DeGeneres," World Wide Web, Jan. 27, 1999, <http://www.celebsite.com/people/ellendegeneres/>). "Until recently I hated the word lesbian too. . . . I've said it enough now that it doesn't bother me. But lesbian sounded like somebody with some kind of disease. I didn't like that, so I used the word gay more often" (Handy). DeGeneres's ambivalence about identity politics is understandable as both a savvy anticipation of the tough loss of privacy demanded by commodity identity and as a vague sense of homophobia, a reluctance to see lesbian sexuality as anything but a personal and private predilection. Whether or not it should be so has already bowed to the pressures of a commodity dynamic that at certain points in history—here a point when homosexuality has become both an identifiable market group and a public scapegoat—emerges in figures whose presentation is the ultimate negotiation of multiple and contradictory fears and desires.

DeGeneres's reluctance to become this figure is not simply a level-headed reading of cultural cannibalism, however. Her reluctance is part of the commodity identity itself which has already determined that someone like DeGeneres would occupy that place. It is exactly DeGeneres's brand of hesitation, the strategies of withdrawal that define her humor, and the very indefiniteness of her self-presentation that make her the perfect commodity lesbian identity at this point in history. From the title of her best-selling book, *My Point—and I Do Have One,* to her comic routines, the method of her comedy is to first assert, then to withdraw into gradual uncertainty or to a point which undoes the original assertion. In an episode titled "Oh, Sweet Rapture" (where "Rapture" stands for Saturn), Ellen says to her annoying friend Audrey, "Audrey, it's nice to wanna belong to a group, I know, I felt that same way about the Girl Scouts . . . all right, that's not exactly true, I couldn't make a decent batch of S'mores and I was ridiculed and driven out in shame . . . but the point is . . . you don't need them." Or later in the episode: "If there's a company that has a philosophy of making their customers feel special, then more power to 'em . . . as a matter of fact, we should have more of that around here . . . Hello, how are you today? Okay . . . attention everybody, this lady has just bought a copy of *How to Please Your Partner* . . . Oh, you have change coming, please don't leave . . . well, well, we'll be callin' you in a couple of days to see if you're any better in bed! Alright then, come again!" (Moriah Nordahl, "Everything Ellen Sound Clips," World Wide Web, Jan. 27, 1999, <http://members.aol.com/ELLyNeSs/clips.html>).

While these snippets demonstrate the general pattern of DeGeneres's comedy of gradual degeneration, they are also and perhaps not uncoincidentally critiques of the commodity culture by which DeGeneres and Ellen become conflated and elevated to the position of commodity identity, that something to be consumed, either through the obsessive galleries of photographs provided on the Ellen Web sites, through the reruns that Lifetime has purchased at $600,000 per episode, through DeGeneres's continued stardom in the movie industry, and through DeGeneres's recent more publicly activist role in the Matthew Shepard vigil activities. The Australian Ellen DeGeneres Page reports that "entertainment figures Helen Hunt (Didn't turn up), Ellen DeGeneres, her mother Betty DeGeneres and Elton John (not yet confirmed at press time) will join on the steps of the U.S. Capitol in Washington D.C. They will remember Matthew Shepard and renew the call for the passage of the Hate Crimes Prevention Act by Congress, which President Clinton first called for over a year ago" (Linda Hillier, "The Australian Ellen DeGeneres Homepage," World Wide Web, Jan. 27, 1999, <http://www.geocities.com/Hollywood/1777/index.html>). The "Celebsite; Ellen DeGeneres" links to a slightly different version of the story: "*The Washington Post* reports that Helen Hunt and *3rd Rock from the Sun*'s Kristin Johnson will join super-couple Ellen DeGeneres and Anne Heche at a vigil at the U.S. Capitol tonight to honor the young man's life and politicize his death" (World Wide Web. Jan. 27, 1999. <http://www.celebsite.com/people/ellendegeneres/>). While never mentioned first, DeGeneres's is the only name that turns up consistently both in reports of the vigil and apparently at the vigil. After the vigil DeGeneres was also reported to have been a guest of ABC's *The View* (Oct. 15, 1998), "talking about hate crimes following the brutal murder of Matthew Shepard" (Hillier).

DeGeneres's leap from the uncertain and private to the public and political occurs around the question of identity, an identity that as embodied by her is both indefinite and unthreatening. Although she becomes a vague political figure who, in the instance of the Matthew Shepard vigil, stands in for the lesbian identity commodity, DeGeneres's lesbian is a perpetual palimpsest, a constantly disappearing shadow of an identity that in her case can only be pinned down when she is in the apparent act of being a lesbian. DeGeneres's lesbian presence is so precarious that to solidify and guarantee it, DeGeneres must constantly be imaged with Anne Heche as part of a lesbian "super-couple." In all of the Ellen Web sites (except the Ellen Internet Fan Club, which states explicitly on its opening page that "The EDIFC would like to note that this page is a dedication to Ellen's comedy and her show, NOT because she is gay, that has nothing to do with this site") (LaVake, "The Ellen DeGeneres Internet Fan Club," World Wide Web, Jan. 27, 1999, <http://www.geocities.com/Hollywood/4566/index.html>), Ellen is pictured as often (or more often) with Heche as without her. The Identity that is Commodity functions best when it is constantly reperformed, but this reperformance also closes the figure of DeGeneres off from all but the most vicarious fantasies of her lesbian viewers who, if they lust for Ellen, do so within the spectacle of her coupledom. DeGeneres's couple status, in fact, makes DeGeneres a very safe lesbian figure indeed; whatever figments of untrammeled sexuality might circulate around the lesbian, those fantasies are contained by Heche. In fact, this is exactly the case; in November, 1998, Jay Leno told a series of jokes centered around DeGeneres's and Heche's first date where they reportedly made love for seventeen hours. Lesbians can be sexual as long as such sexuality is safely contained by another lesbian and by the absence of any overt signs of sexual desire or homographesis.

However safe, disavowed, desexualized, or comically hypersexualized DeGeneres's commodity identity may be, it raises the question of why such an identity is necessary and what functions it serves other than to allay anxieties and represent and negotiate complications around the category itself. Both DeGeneres and Shepard are fetishes in the ways they negotiate ambivalences around contested sites of sexuality and death, DeGeneres by figuring the constant disappearance of the desexualized lesbian and Shepard by perpetually playing out the sacrifice of the desexualized gay male. In both cases, the figures can both function as emblems of gay and lesbian communities and perform the detoxification and ritual containment of the categories. This fetish, as read psychoanalytically, links to the Marxist idea of the commodity fetish, since these figures are essentially traded as figures for the fantasies, negotiations, and disavowals they can provide rather than for any use value they might have.

Arriving at the all-purpose or hybrid fetish in this discussion may not be that much of a surprise; what is instructive is the way this commodity fetish Identity also exists in the academic practice of lesbian and gay studies as the guarantor of authority, continued presence and visibility, and ritualized tribute. While almost every prominent gay, lesbian, or queer critic uses some combination of psychoanalytic and materialist thought in their writing, their work is often taken as a shorthand totem of particular, sloganized propositions that are very close in operation to the commodity identities represented by Shepard and DeGeneres. These propositions are never separated from the figures to whom they are attributed; the names (and we know what they are) work like commodity identities to negotiate ambivalence around the dual and difficult project of sorting the multiple and sometimes conflicting interests of gays, lesbians, queers, and others. And like DeGeneres and Shepard, that the complexity of knowledges and desires is concentrated in persons instead in ideas makes these professional totems function paradoxically to contain and delimit the circulation of ideas even as their visibility seems to disseminate them.

As in other segments of the academy, the reliance on the commodity identity of certain scholars (some of whom actually try to position themselves this way by making their own lives the object of "critical scrutiny" or by preening themselves as if they were "stars") is a signal of an ambivalence and difficulty around the intellectual project in general where identity and personae are substituted for interchange and process. While we might attribute the rise of the academic "star" to commodity culture's inroads into academe, the very special case of the complexly totemized figures of gay and lesbian studies shows the extent to which this stardom is not the innocent effect of market forces, but is rather, as DeGeneres's and Shepard's examples demonstrate, a suspicious fetish operation around the threats and uncertainties posed by gay and lesbian studies in the first place.

"I WANNA BE ADORED"

I wanna be adored.
—*The Stone Roses*

If the academic star system in lesbian and gay studies serves to contain the anxieties and uncertainties created by the very existence of the discipline in the first place, then a closer look at exactly how that process of containment works seems to be both intellectually and politically necessary. The convergence of the psychoanalytic and Marxist notions of the fetish in the figure of the star provides a clue about how to proceed with such an analysis. As Žižek notes in relation to the homology of Freud's and Marx's interpretive procedures, "the 'secret' to be unveiled through analysis is not the content hidden by the form. . . . but, on the contrary, *the 'secret' of this form itself*" (*Sublime Object of Ideology*, 11, emphasis in the original). Žižek is speaking here of the hermeneutic goals of Freudian and Marxist analysis themselves, but the principle also seems helpful in analyzing the very idea of the fetish produced by those procedures. At least insofar as the objects we've been analyzing (Shepard, DeGeneres, academic stars) are concerned, I would argue that the prevalent understandings of the idea of the fetish are catachrestic. Generally, the form of the fetish is understood to be a metonymic process: the commodity stands in for and replaces the labor that produced it; other objects or body parts (both do and do not) take the place of the phallus. Yet, if we look back at the examples discussed so far, it becomes clear that in media culture or the academic star system, the process of fetishization is NOT metonymic but synecdochic, with an individual standing in for an "identity category," the one standing in for the many. Thus Matthew Shepard becomes all gay men ("us"), Ellen DeGeneres all lesbians, certain prominent scholars the emblematic practitioners of a particular academic discipline. Analyzed from both the psychoanalytic and Marxist perspectives, this synecdochic operation can, then, help to explain not only how the star system contains the political and intellectual energies of lesbian and gay studies but it can also clarify the implications of the use of representational figures for gayness and lesbianism in a media culture in general.

Read psychoanalytically, the "form" of this synecdochic fetish is already a complex configuration of several different identificatory dynamics that Freud bases on "the analysis of being in love," operating at the conjunction of individual and group. On the one hand, individuals' identification with star figures occurs as a narcissistic project, "as loving oneself in the other," as Jacques-Alain Miller describes it ("Duty and the Drives," *Newsletter of the Freudian Field* 6 [Spring/Fall 1992]: 5–15, esp. 9). On this imaginary level, the star object is deployed for the individual's own ego because that object, in being the same as self (or ego), makes the ego feel better. This is the underlying logic of the role model. On the other hand, individuals with very disparate fundamental fantasies nonetheless invest in the same object, a "master signifier," that impoverishes the ego but sustains a group of egos that have all introjected the same ideal, "so that the whole series of these egos can feel equal and the same." This ideal "master signifier," or "Other" is idealized; it is not subject to castration like all of those who idealize it. This is the overt logic of the star's power as the ideal one not subject to the weaknesses of the many; the idealized star, thus, becomes the source of the "law," in the case of academe, the sets of oft-quoted principles generally accepted as foundational in a field or discipline. The relation of the many to this exemplary "one," a relation of desire and identification, would thus be played out in the profession in forms as diverse as envy, citation, mentoring (or the desire for it), and the validation of the discipline of lesbian and gay studies itself.

In the United States, there is a certain tension between these two modes of identification; because the dynamic of "equal and same" is privileged over the hierarchical dynamic of the ideal (as in monarchies), ideal figures are either themselves ambivalent or the objects of ambivalence. While Shepard and DeGeneres can function as idealized figures precisely because they are ambivalent, academic stars are treated ambivalently. Subject to both adulation and attack, idealized academic stars are venerated for their talent and insight and blamed for not being a part of the egalitarian mass. Insofar as stars have indeed gained their status as ideal as a by-product of accomplishment, blame is an effect of the group egalitarian fantasy that seeks to level the ideal. Such blame takes the form either of an attack on the work that produced the idealization or an ad hominem critique of often irrelevant behaviors, infidelities, or inconsistencies that prove the star's unworthiness as an ideal.

Insofar as some academics deliberately seek idealization by simulating stardom rather than through spectacular accomplishment, the function of the ideal is a part of the individual's own fundamental fantasy, a narcissistic guarantor of personal significance. The notion of the ideal, thus, itself becomes introjected as a site of narcissistic identification, encouraging the envaluation of appearance (idealization) over substance (accomplishment). This ultimately pushes the notion of the ideal into simulation where it conveniently allies with commodity fetishism to produce the idealization that far exceeds either the scholarly persona or the reasonable status that might be accorded respected colleagues. General disdain for star wannabes is not catalyzed by group egalitarianism, but rather by the embarrassment produced by the overt performance of lack such posturing signifies, so that the wannabe star often accomplishes the opposite of his/her desire; one might become spectacular and a commodity without being idealized. Commodity culture is all too willing, in fact, to reward the spectacle for being substanceless, for being in fact the same kind of ambivalent, detoxified figure as Shepard or DeGeneres (though few of those so rewarded think that is the case with them and hence the fantasy can continue).

Synecdoche and representativeness are, thus, already fraught with an ambivalence that turns idealized figures into sites, not for the contest of ideas or political positions but rather for the fantasmatic playing out of individual anxieties around meaning and self-worth. And when these figures are the totem figures of identity categories, the anxiety is multiplied as the ideal comes to represent the law of inclusion and exclusion, membership in the group itself. Either one belongs to a group as a partial effect of having introjected the same idealized figure or one is not in the group because of a failure to accept the ideal as such because of a stronger attachment to the egalitarian model. The effect of this is to fracture any community centered around an identity, since the community's existence depends upon ambivalence, upon sustaining both narcissistic and idealized identifications at the same time. When individuals refuse such ambivalence, as is often the case around identity categories which in themselves promise (perhaps fraudulently) an unambivalent identity, they must relinquish either the ideal (and gain identity as a rebel or "other" to the orthodox) or their sense of egalitarianism (their sense that they are as good as other scholars). The only other way around the paradox of ambivalence is the production of the down-home folksy star who in fact idealizes egalitarianism.

> We are all in the gutter, but some of us are looking at the stars.
> —*Oscar Wilde*

The synecdochic nature of the star system implies slightly different readings when viewed from the perspective of a neo-Marxist point of view that stresses the ideological work performed by signification and representation. If we return to the "form" itself, as Žižek suggests, we might see that synecdoche, unlike metonymy, which invokes the endless *glissement* of the signifying chain, performs a delimitation, a reduction of semiotic possibility. To put it another way, if a part is taken to represent the whole, then the whole is only ever partially represented. "All hands on deck," to take the classic textbook example of synecdoche, implicitly restricts the potential significations of the seamen synecdochized by "hands" to the corporeal, first of all, and, even more narrowly, to the association with labor power implied by "hand." This delimitation of potential meaning becomes apparent when one realizes that alternate synecdoches are possible: "All minds on deck," say. As a result, when the whole being represented by the part is an identity category, the very form of the fetish, the selection of the exemplary individual, performs a process of ideological containment, restricting the possible meanings of the identity label. Thus, as we've seen, both gay activists and the (straight) media cooperate to produce, for different reasons, such nonthreatening representations of queer identity as Matthew Shepard and Ellen DeGeneres.

This process works slightly differently in relation to the academic star system, of course. Usually scholars are idealized because they are talented individuals who have been instrumental in creating the concept repertoire of lesbian and gay studies. And, in this respect, "queer theory" is no different from other disciplinary specializations such as American literature or early modern studies in which the creation of stars is implicitly understood to follow a vaguely entrepreneurial model: the production of a product (a corpus of work) leads to the accumulation of a certain intellectual "capital" (which can often be exchanged for literal capital, of course, in the form of higher salaries). As such, the analogy to the Hollywood star system is particularly apt. Unlike the literal capitalist, whose capital is owned by the self but is not literally the self, both the Hollywood star's "product" (his/her film roles) and his/her cultural capital (his/her "image," his/her stardom) are quite literally produced through and embodied in the star him- or herself. Similarly, the academic star is personally indistinguishable from the "intellectual capital" he or she can less be said to possess than to be.

Now, as has already been suggested, the synecdochic creation of the academic star is particularly problematic when the stars in question come to represent the study of a minority identity. While, on the one hand, they differ from media icons such as Shepard or DeGeneres in that their exemplary status does not derive from the projection of a relatively unthreatening image of the queer but rather from talent and intellectual ability, yet, on the other hand, one might argue that the implicit function of ideological containment enacted through them is thus even more subtle. This is precisely because such containment works through the form of the star system and not through its content. Regardless of who the stars are or of the actual intellectual paradigms established in their work, the very existence of a star system presents synecdochic figures who stand for the discipline as a whole. The effect of this is to organize and delimit the field, to establish valued and devalued lines of inquiry, modes of reading, and even of (queer) identities themselves. In the case of lesbian and gay studies in particular, the resulting irony is that, while the content of much of this work involves a radical questioning of the notions of "identity" or "gender" or "sexual orientation" in an attempt to evade culturally restrictive processes of labeling the self (and even to explode the very conceptual categories of western culture), the form of the star system serves precisely the opposite function: its synecdochic logic of exemplarity contains the potentially disruptive energies of this area of study and their impact on the academy, if only by delimiting the dominant intellectual paradigm(s) of the field. Moreover, the implicit structure of the star system—the positing of an exemplary individual identity—also serves to frame queer theory's theoretical questioning of "identity" within the larger and often unrecognized ideal of the (entrepreneurial) bourgeois individual. As such, it works to contain the anti-identity content of the field itself. In fact, in a final twist, even most critiques of the star system distract attention from an additional mystification: the cynical criticism of the star conceals, through its very focus on that individualized figure, the synecdochic operation of exemplarity, the representationality, that is the underlying logic of the system itself.

What is omitted, then, is the group. Politically, this also becomes a problem, since the whole for which the part stands is made to disappear through the agency of the idealized part, a disappearance welcomed by many. Even if the very presence of a media lesbian is irksome to some and an indication of some degree of social progress, that Ellen DeGeneres becomes the lesbian renders the mass of gays and lesbians fairly invisible (well, there is k d lang and Chastity Bono and Melissa Etheridge and George Michael and Elton John and Rock Hudson, but these, too, are all special cases). If there is no perceivable group in American politics, there is no vector of pressure, no sense of an interest that must be attended to. In fact, the appearance of the commodity identity icon is enough in itself; it substitutes for political action and social change. Even if the idea of a minority voice is itself a fiction in these postnationalist days, the mechanism by which the minority is made to disappear by being made visible indeed does serve the ends of a democracy that counts the appearance of being represented as the same thing as having representation.

This mechanism does have material effects. It accounts for how it is that women and gays can be quite visible in academe and still not have much of a voice. It accounts for how certain fields of study can be cordoned off from the mainstream even as their precepts seem to be adopted (feminism is the prime example of this, though gay and lesbian studies is a close second). It accounts for the divide-and-conquer strategies by which minority groups have chronically been prevented from organizing themselves effectively. But it is not the answer to everything. What we need to understand is how to operate the image system we are so deft at analyzing, either as psychoanalytic or Marxist critics or both.

"... A LITTLE BIT COUNTRY"

I'm a little bit country.
I'm a little bit rock and roll.
—*Donny and Marie*

. . . as psychoanalytic or Marxist critics or both. As our own exemplary readings would seem to demonstrate, the issue of an appropriate methodology for lesbian and gay studies, the question of the relative merits of a psychoanalytic or a Marxist approach, can most easily be resolved by the now familiar substitution of "both/and" for "either/or." As even a quick glance back at the preceding analyses makes clear, not only do the "psychoanalytic" and "Marxist" halves of the dialogue complement each other but both "sides" of this debate are themselves amalgams of both methodologies, with ideas from one approach informing and blending with ideas from the other approach within each half of the dialogue. Now, in an era of methodological eclecticism, such syncretism is hardly surprising, making "both/and" the obvious response to the question with which we began. Yet this "both/and" can also be read less as a dialectic synthesis of two theories than as an inherent interpretive ambivalence at the heart of gay and lesbian studies, itself the signal of a certain hesitation about how we understand the identities that are taken as the basis of the discipline.

On the one hand, gay and lesbian identities, roughly in line with the psychoanalytic model, are implicitly understood both academically and in popular culture to be internal to the individual and inherent. Whether such an identity is defined in terms of (same sex) desire or as a certain configuration of the self (as campy or butch or femme or . . .), gayness or lesbianism is conceived not only as innate but also as prior to whatever social interactions or cultural stereotypes or prejudices or, indeed, social organization the (gay or lesbian) self encounters. This notion, which is really the idea that gayness or lesbianism are identities in the first place, that they have a certain transcendental "reality," is suggested by our implicit assumption of the literal priority of Matthew Shepard's and Ellen DeGeneres's sexual identities in the preceding analysis. Matthew Shepard was gay and then was murdered because of this fact. Ellen DeGeneres was a closeted lesbian but then both she and Ellen Morgan came out. Such narratives assume the sexual identity categories of their characters, assume the idea of sexual identity categories itself, as a precondition of the stories they tell.

On the other hand, roughly in line with a (neo-)Marxist model (as well as with performative notions of identity and the general tendency to historicize sexual identity categories in lesbian and gay studies), queer theory (although not necessarily the queer on the street) tends to understand gayness or lesbianism as external to the individual: as culturally constructed categories of identity or as commodified images of such categories. While this perspective is not completely incompatible with the notion of an innate same sex desire and often works in concert with it, such desire is usually understood, in this view, as something that cannot be known apart from or prior to its symbolization. Thus, in a sense, the focus here is not on the prior (existence of the identity) but on the present, on the individual's performance of the identity in the moment or the organization of the sexual field at the time, and an attention to etiology is replaced by an emphasis on effects, on the significations applied to the identity categories. The narrative in this instance thus becomes the story of how representation and commodification shape and inflect "Matthew Shepard" or "Ellen DeGeneres" and of how such representations work to produce a particular political end. Specifically, in the case of the preceding dialogue, the narrative becomes the story of the ideological containment of the idea of the gay man or of the lesbian or, as with the academic star system, of lesbian and gay studies itself.

As this dialogue has itself demonstrated, these conflicting assumptions about the nature of "identity" can be reconciled. But to stress the compatibility of the two methodologies, to focus on the "both/and," is also to gloss over the inherent ambivalence about what we understand "identity" to mean in the first place, an ambivalence that it seems necessary for lesbian and gay studies itself to explore in more detail. Moreover, this ambivalence predicts other discords: over whether identity is a basis for "queer theory" in the first place; over what political goals ought to be sought—gay marriage, the repeal of anti-sodomy laws, rights for gay parents, or larger more systemic shifts in our notions of gender and gendered identities. And do gay and lesbian studies focus only on gay and lesbian subjects, retrieving lost histories, collecting gay and lesbian texts, explaining gay and lesbian

*existence, or do they employ the insights of "queer theory" in other venues? Like
assumptions around identity, the ambivalences between and within the political
and the scholarly can be reconciled, at least provisionally, with the buffering "both/
and," while what is probably necessary, as in the case of identity, is a rethinking
of what "political action" might mean.*

*Yet to end with either a call to investigate further or happy reconciliation would
be to miss a deeper issue that this dialogue has been gradually approaching: what
presuppositions are contained in the very notion of (the necessity of having a)
methodology in the first place? In answer to this question, one could argue that
any methodology, even an unstated or untheorized one such as the New Criticism, functions very much in the way that we have argued that the star system
does: as a form of synecdoche that limits and contains the conceptual play of a/
the discipline. As the (pre)selection of a concept repertoire or set of assumptions,
a methodology, standing in synecdochically for something like "analysis" or "interpretation" or "thought" in general, thus restricts the discipline's conceptual
potential. Again, this conclusion is a fairly obvious extension of our previous discussion, however, and it seems possible to take this analysis even further. Thus,
one could argue that, seen from another angle, methodology works less as a synecdoche than as a sort of reverse synecdoche, that methodology tends less to substitute a part for the whole than to substitute a whole for the part. Or, more accurately, that methodology functions through the inevitable interpretation of the
part in light of (or "through") the whole. Thus, for example, someone like Matthew Shepard or Ellen DeGeneres is read not as an individual but as an illustration of larger interpretive paradigms: as evidence of homographesis, say, or of the
ambivalence inherent in any assertion of the possibility of a lesbian sexuality.*

*In this context, Mikkel Borch-Jacobsen's recent reevaluation of psychoanalysis
is entirely apposite ("Is Psychoanalysis a Scientific Fairy Tale?" Narrative 7 [1999]:
56–70). Although Freud claimed that the larger theoretical principles of psychoanalysis were derived from the details of the case histories, Borch-Jacobsen argues
that, in fact, the opposite is true, that the case histories are "artifacts" of the theory,
that they are not finally based on observation but rather derive their coherence
and meaning from the imposition of psychoanalytic theory onto the material to
be interpreted. Borch-Jacobsen goes on to demonstrate how, in Freud's case, this
led to the suppression or revision of the facts, including the clinical outcomes of
many of the cases. Even if such an overt manipulation of the "evidence" had not
taken place, however, Borch-Jacobsen argues that psychoanalysis would still need
to be considered a "theoretical novel": "This theory is a novel because it creates
its own evidence. . . . And this novel is theoretical, for the narrative coherence of
its plots is nothing other than a coherence with the theory" (65). Now, we would*

argue that it is not only psychoanalysis that is a theoretical novel in this sense. All methodologies, including Marxism, work in the same way. Thus, an incident like the murder of Matthew Shepard can be read as either the result of a certain projective homophobia or as an example of how media representations create the meanings of events or as evidence of both. Yet, any or all of these interpretations work, finally, by imposing a fictional coherence—the coherence of the theory (or even the syncretic combination of theories) applied to them—onto the raw material of the incident itself. And, once interpreted in this way, the incident then becomes further evidence for the theory, confirmation of its interpretive value. Rather than simply assuming that the methodologies employed in lesbian and gay studies are objective interpretive tools, then, we need to look more closely at the ways in which they actually create the meanings that they purport to discover.

One way interpretation is conceived of is through metaphors of transformation at the heart of almost all interpretive paradigms. The model we typically use—a model that is used, in fact, in the previous paragraph—is one in which the events of life, a text, or a cultural representation are taken as "raw" material that both (a) is given meaning through one or more methodologies' interpretive gloss and (b) gives meaning to interpretive methodologies by seeming to provide, as if from a pure, untouched landscape, material that proves the methodology's hypotheses correct. This two-way function is yet another instance of an ambivalence, this time located not in the object of study or its functions but in the very ways we interpret, which in setting up or at least depending on surface/depth, raw/cooked, "natural"/interpreted dichotomies, actually define the structures through which they will always prove themselves valuable. But just as Michel Foucault observes in The Archaeology of Knowledge and the Discourse on Language *that structuralism cannot escape its own assumptions and will inevitably reiterate a structuralist paradigm, so any methodology that proceeds within the part/whole schema of example/paradigm will inevitably reconfirm its own model in an interpretive tautology that lets us feel that our methodologies themselves are whole and effective. In this light the purpose of interpretation and its design is ultimately self-confirmation, not unlike the identification functions of star personae which seem to provide objective evidence of the viable nonpathology of nonmainstream identity categories.*

We might also, however, view this ambivalence as potentially productive, especially if we conceive of interpretation less as a paradigmatic production and more as a cybernetic process. Cybernetics is based on a "'bootstrapping' principle: the expression of a theory affects its content and meaning, and vice versa" (C. Joslyn et al., "Metasystem Transition Theory," World Wide Web, Feb. 2, 1999, <http://pespmc1.vub.ac.be/MSTT.html>). In other words even in the selection *of an apt example, a methodology changes in relation to the act of choosing that example. The example itself is altered by having become an example and is further transformed through the interpretive processes that also bootstrap on their own preliminary observations and conclusions. The interpreted example provides feedback to the evolving hypotheses as long as interpretation takes into account those things in the example that clash with the paradigm rather than merely seeking proof of the paradigm's "truth" in the example. Instead of producing a rounded metaphor where the example serves as a displaced expression of a paradigm (which is itself already an elaborated metaphor), a cybernetic method pushes hypotheses along a series of contiguous evolving stages in a more metonymically inclined process that drives past self-reification and reaffirmation into the perpetual movement, complication, and elaboration of questions and hypotheses which become dynamic, responsive, and constantly shifting.*

Where might this more cybernetic or metonymical method go in our Marxist-psychoanalytic critique of the commodity identities of Matthew Shepard and Ellen DeGeneres? Shepard and DeGeneres are excellent examples of commodity identity because they confirm the ability of both psychoanalytic and Marxist methodologies to ferret out a truth of sorts, the presence of ambivalence at the core of identity politics, gay and lesbian studies, and methodology itself. But what in their examples doesn't fit into our tidy mapping? Perhaps many things, including the materiality of death, the implied nonpublic persona of DeGeneres, the possibility of nonidentification with the sometimes irritating quality of Ellen Morgan, and the punishment of the perpetrators of antigay violence. What both examples push back with, however, is their own association with another figure—Elton John—who appears in the Web sites of both DeGeneres and Shepard, but who seems to have a very different kind of fame. While it might appear that Elton John is merely another example of a gay commodity identity, his celebrity comes instead from a long career of successful songwriting and performance. His image, thus, already works slightly differently than both DeGeneres's and Shepard's. John's presence in the Shepard and DeGeneres Web sites is linked to the more overtly political function of a promised appearance at an anti–hate crimes rally in Washington, D.C., in memory of Matthew Shepard and in the company of Ellen DeGeneres. But Elton John is a phantom, since we never know from any of the Web sites whether or not he ever actually appeared at the rally; and if we examine his many Web sites (as we did thoroughly, of course), there are no references to this possible appearance, nor do the sites devote much space to the singer's sexuality. Against expectations, John's connections to gayness are almost as phantom as his appearance at the rally, made mostly through the indirect vector of his AIDS Foundation (which itself never mentions any word meaning "homosexual"), with the exception of one linked Web site devoted to David Furnish, "The love of Elton's life," and one very odd statement about Elton John's coming out in an interview with Rolling Stone which ends up discussing his drug addictions and his futile marriage to Renate Blauel (because "he realized he was homosexual before his marriage").

What Elton John's Web sites lead us to is not more confirmation of our theories about commodity identity but rather the vanishing point of this identity as a positive political statement and its transformation into something else—in the case of Elton John, into loss and mourning. Elton John's Web sites do not link back either to Ellen DeGeneres or to Matthew Shepard, but to Gianni Versace and Princess Diana. The ambivalence of both Shepard's and DeGeneres's figurations transmogrifies into a spiritual melancholia as the Elton John fan pages mostly focus on how important the man and his music are to various Web masters' lives. While the sites have the same photo albums, lists of achievements, and concert dates as most fanzine pages, their tone shifts from the excited adulation of the Ellen DeGeneres pages or the shocked monumentalism of the various Matthew Shepard sites to a greater focus on the music and a more reserved and serious admiration. The Elton John pages pick up the mourning of the Matthew Shepard pages, but distanced completely from any fixation on gay identity. Elton John's contiguity to mourning comes through losses made personal by John's much-publicized association with both Versace and Diana. This loss itself became a synecdoche for the mourning around Princess Diana in the "English Rose" remake of "Candle in the Wind." Elton John's connection to the tragedies of Versace and Diana re-animated his career, propelling him to the top concert gross for 1998.

So if we follow Elton John, we go from phantom political action to loss to mourning to career success, a success that comes not from gayness as a commodity identity but from a figure's contiguity to supreme death. The connections among death, mourning, sentimentality, and market cash would be a way this more metonymical trajectory pushes back on the commodity identity paradigm of ambivalence we previously mapped, suggesting a very different set of motivations behind the commodification of sexual identity and academic stardom. Culling out these motivations would again be both a psychoanalytic and a Marxist task, as would an analysis of the connections between the market and processes of public mourning and a scrutiny of mourning itself as a commodity. And this, too, would lead to something else, ad infinitum. While the figure of Matthew Shepard suggests loss and mourning as an obvious motivation for his figuration from the very start, the complex meanings of that mourning may not be available except through the detours, Deleuzian rhizomes, and complex displacements of a process of traveling interpretation, whose end may well be in its beginning, but whose efforts nonetheless continue.

PART THREE

A Changing Profession

7

The New Challenges of Academic Publishing

*Niko Pfund, Gordon Hutner, and Martha Banta
(Interviewed by Donald E. Hall)*

Niko Pfund: In his short story, "Funes the Memorious," the Argentinean writer Jorge Luis Borges tells of a man who boasts a truly encyclopedic memory. In fact, the protagonist of the title never forgets anything. Funes is able to remember every moment of his life in such detail, and so distinctly, that it seems absurd to him that a dog running across a field at midday should have the same name—"Dog"—as that same dog running across the same field at dusk. To Funes, the same moniker for two things so different is incomprehensible.

Were Funes reincarnated today in the guise of a university press publisher or a research librarian, surveying university press publishing and, relatedly, the brave new world of electronic publishing and its consequences for the book, he would surely argue along similar lines, that (with apologies to Gertrude Stein) a book is not a book is not a book. Just as the word "drugs" in our cultural lexicon is applied as a blanket term to refer to everything from marijuana to heroin (and bear in mind that "drugs" heal many more people than they kill), the term "books"—as in "Is this the end of books?"—has been bandied about in a similarly loose fashion. At the risk of stating the obvious, books are enormously disparate in content, purpose, and utility. Jay Leno's biography or John Grisham's latest formula thriller has so little in common with a research monograph on nineteenth-century Lapp society that to describe them with the same word is deceptive in all but a strictly physical sense.

So let's narrow down our definition. In the context of this discussion, "book" will refer to a volume the primary constituency for which is students and professors in American higher education. Further, let us establish certain developments as baseline facts:

1. It has become increasingly difficult for academics to find publishers for

high-level academic research monographs. Whereas getting published as a first-time academic was once a relatively straightforward process—send out a prospectus, ask your mentors to call a few friends who edit appropriate series, et cetera—today many scholars are finding it virtually impossible to place their revised dissertations, especially those working in such fields as literary criticism and Latin American politics and history, to name two.

2. The reasons for this squeeze are numerous and of course interconnected, but none has had a more profound effect on the evolution of academic publishing than the skyrocketing costs of journals, particularly those published by European commercial conglomerates, which has put an enormous strain on research library budgets and has had a profound effect on libraries' ability to purchase books.

3. The primary obstacle to the extinction of the monograph is its continual role as a credentialization vehicle for (young) faculty. However, this system of credentialization has become greatly skewed in recent years as university presses, squeezed by the double whammy of shrinking markets and declining subsidies, increasingly weigh the size of a book's prospective audience when deciding whether to publish. To acknowledge the changing economic equations, is, to be clear, in no way to dismiss or underestimate the value-added contribution of university presses—which, despite economic hardship, continue to serve as a filter for academic work. However, unless we are willing to embrace an academic environment increasingly governed by the market economy, where the "publishability" of one's work and thus tenure or, more generally, success is gauged ever more by economic rather than intellectual relevance, this system requires overhaul.

4. But overhaul makes people nervous. Every new endeavor which seeks to involve many players, all with different interests, in a paradigm shift must ensure that each player—author, university press, research library, commercial publisher—has a compelling interest to engage energetically in this new endeavor. (One venture, the International Scholars Academic Network [ISCAN], proposed a few years back by the Association of Research Libraries as a "not-for-profit consortium" which would serve as "both a publisher and coordinator of the publishing activities of its members," foundered precisely on these grounds.) This interest must be compelling enough to override the natural human resistance to any change in the status quo.

By now, many will have heard the lament, whether from authors, agents, graduate students, or book editors: Publishing houses are setting the bar higher and higher for new books. Midlist authors with a half-dozen books under their belt are having a hard time placing their new projects and freshly minted

Ph.D.s, casting around for a hospitable university press, are finding fewer and fewer takers.

But at a time when commercial publishing is increasingly going the route of Hollywood, opting more and more for the seemingly safe, formulaic book by an established author—university presses have also been quick to take advantage of the opportunities this development presents. Rather than pine away for some long-lost and increasingly nostalgized golden era of academic publishing, many presses have simply moved their programs up a notch, or several, leaving behind much specialized work as unpublishable, and increasingly directing their energies to trade books and college texts.

Understandable as this strategy is, some university presses are now reconsidering their aggressive inroads to the bookstores, more specifically to the chains. The higher discounts and, as importantly, higher returns associated with the chains have wreaked havoc with budgets, projections, print runs, and inventory, often with less than stellar final results. The professed desire to appeal to the spectral "general reader" or "lay public," by now offered almost reflexively by editor and author alike, overlooks two fundamental truths: (1) the core audience for university presses remains academic (whether institutional, individual, or pedagogic), and (2) the core outlet for most academic work in the social sciences and humanities remains the 100-plus university presses.

5. Simply because university presses once consistently sold one thousand copies of their titles to research libraries and now sell half that number of similar titles doesn't mean that these books are of less utility now than they were then. There are simply fewer dollars available for libraries to purchase them (thus the rise of the interlibrary loan). A quarter-century ago, the actual readership for the average monograph was arguably no larger than it is today.

Gordon Hutner: Niko describes the problems besetting the publishing of academic books very cogently. In the following, I hope to explore a few of the implications of his positions, though in general, his description seems to me apt and smart. On the other hand, as central as the question of publishing literary criticism manuscripts is, it's the word "publishing" at least as much as "book" that warrants our attention. The crisis facing critical monographs is the subject that most notoriously opens up the question of the relation between publishers and scholars, but there are a variety of ways that publishers are changing the way we do business. These include the current state of coursepacks, the proliferation of literary anthologies and critical collections by diverse hands, as well as the constraints placed on journal publication (at least in the humanities). Publishing, in so many ways, is the lifeblood of the profession: writing introductions to new editions, editing collections, contributing to anthologies, publishing articles in journals, reviewing books—all of these things matter to members of the professoriate as much as, if not more than, writing thesis-length books.

Of course, in a limited, if troublesome, sense, the crisis is of our own making: Literature professors do not consume what they produce. If we don't buy our books, who will? Not, we have learned, the much-fantasized but increasingly remote "general reader." And we don't buy them because we don't have to! We don't ask our initiates to be responsible for an agreed upon canon of writers, much less critics or theorists. There's very little sense of an obdurate orthodoxy, despite the posturing of academics for general circulation periodicals. So problematized is our conception of authority, and certainly our value for the definitive, that we float in a universe of the provocative, at worst, and the influential, at best. As an editor of a journal I know the shared sense of reigning authorities that students and scholars feel obliged to invoke. A quick look at our own bookshelves tells us that nothing ages faster than the authorities of the moment. And these are the books we are likely to buy. What does it say that we do not think enough of our colleagues' work to spend money on their books? Or they ours? It's regrettable but inevitable that we generally don't feel obliged to invest much disposable income in our personal libraries—and, given hardcover costs, how could we afford to, we wonder. So we hunt for remainders and crowd the stalls on the last day of the MLA conference.

But publishers set the bar in ways that many professors don't consider higher but lower—lower because they see publishers living out professors' nightmares of mediation, pursuing as they do so foolishly bad, superficial, or trivial books in the name of being au courant. There is never enough good scholarship to go around, in the first place. Now that scholarship seems to be the kind ratified by stories in *Lingua Franca* or the *Chronicle* as the ideas worth talking about, presses try to secure manuscripts on hot topics. Inevitable is the anxiety that publishers will lower their standards to tap into the market they see as their best bet to show a profit. Of course, the acquisition editors of academic presses might reap the riches in excellent manuscripts that are going wholly unread by the prestigious ones. Apparently, they think that it is more prudent for them to continue to ignore those and simply bring out weak manuscripts on hot topics that more renowned university presses have rejected. I suppose there's a logic, perhaps even a justification, in doing so, but is it healthy—for all of us?

Professors who have been heedless of trends find themselves having difficulty finding venues for their new work. Sometimes, someone who hasn't published a book in years is astounded at what he or she finds upon sending out letters of inquiry, so dramatically has the situation changed. What they find is not a pretty sight, if you were raised in the tradition of the profession as a meritocracy. Publishers who have had their eyes fixed only on what sells find themselves less and less concerned about quality, more and more willing to forego readers' reports from the field, hastier and hastier in bringing out the work of younger scholars. The bar isn't higher, in this sense either, but much lower. Too many books go from doctoral thesis to publisher's catalogue without sufficient revision, meditation, or criticism. A couple of good dissertations turned books may be as short as 135 pages, but most of the short ones can be superficial and predictable. One hears so many war stories about the longish book that has to be cut. Of course, it goes without saying that long books, like long articles, can always be shorter, but publishers just don't want to lose money anymore on 500-page books. OK, we live in that kind of world, but it changes the way we project our research, changes how we think about history or categories.

Niko is quite right to say that upheaval is inevitable, and it will come as a result of our own incapacity to police ourselves, that is, to govern our press boards sensibly, run our departments honestly, judge our junior colleagues fairly. In a sense, we have surrendered ourselves to the publishers and their commercial discontents. Part of the problem is the change in the object of literary inquiry and the revolution in subject matter to which this has given rise. Once upon a time, professors could write books, drawn largely from the four or five poets or eight or nine novelists that they grouped together in their courses. These books were a great deal easier to evaluate according to the critical contours of the profession. Readers' reports may still have been based on what one judge or another imagined he or she would do with the topic, but the community of scholars could rely on these assessments of the way books were analyzed since very often they were books that any member of the community (or its subgroup) could be counted upon to know intimately. The courses we teach now, however, don't usually yield such conceptualizations; the ways we think about literary and cultural history certainly don't allow such a ready faith in our professional readers.

Niko suggests that publishers moved up a notch, in their newly aggressive pursuit of sales, as a tactic made in the name of keeping the presses afloat. But I don't think so. I am delighted by the publishers' efforts to publish more fiction and poetry, just as I'm glad to see them try to be of more service to a community, as in the case of state university presses, where they can do some positive good by circulating works of regional interest. (The best-selling book of the University of Wisconsin Press, I'm told, is focused on the work of the painter

Owen Groome and his scenes of nature.) But when publishers do so, the move is not meant to bring better critical books aboard the list. Hollywood rationalizes its blockbuster mentality by saying that the profits, in turn, make more little films. We know that this is simply more bad faith; not one little film gets made because of *Titanic's* success.

We clearly need help—help in the form of increased budgets for libraries, especially. Niko's right: for all the distribution of blame, a basic problem is the decline in buying power of college and university libraries as a result of ridiculously expensive journals. Why can't those journals be available on loan, instead of books, anyway?

Niko Pfund: The idea that some presses are simply bringing out manuscripts their betters have rejected is just too facile. Of course, anyone who's worked in the university press world for a while will have published books that other presses have rejected or will have rejected books others have published, but there simply is no easy, trickle-down theory here. For example, in my first year at NYU, when the press was still being distributed by Columbia University Press and had a fairly low profile, we turned down a baseball book which would have fit in marvelously with our regional list but which we ultimately felt was not sufficiently well written to take on. It was almost immediately picked up by one of the juggernaut presses, where it was published, essentially unrevised (to unflattering reviews). Who turns down what, and who publishes what, generally has less to do with presses than with editors. Books in one particular discipline that I turned down kept showing up on one press's list for several years, until the editor there left for another house. Lest you think I say all this for reasons of self-aggrandizement, let me be clear: the reasons one editor will turn down one book while another will publish don't always have to do with good judgment versus bad judgment. More often an editor is trying to expand (or cut back on) a list in a certain area and doing that (expanding, that is) requires that one generate a corpus of titles on which to build. So, it simply isn't the case that the larger presses associated with the Ivys are somehow retaining their standards while other presses are snapping up the scraps. (I realize that's not entirely what you said, Gordon, and that I'm being a bit dramatic here.)

Relatedly, some presses (more and more) will make the decision to publish a "current events" book that will get lots of reviews, sell quickly, and then die within twenty-four months, a decision based admittedly more on making a name for a press and on a "quick strike" than on building the backlist. There's no better example of this than an anthology published several years ago, called

Women on Ice, consisting of feminist readings of the Tonya Harding–Nancy Kerrigan business. The book received formidable review attention, sold three thousand copies in eighteen months, and died. It's precisely because a book like that gets a lot of reviews that folks think it's all a press is doing (this was Routledge). Well, any cursory survey of the Routledge catalog reveals at least as many "traditional" philosophy, literature, history, politics, psychology, sociology, religion, et cetera, titles as any catalog published by the above-named presses; it's just that those titles don't get the press and attention that something more sensationalist does.

During the past decade I've read hundreds, if not thousands, of readers' reports and this process has convinced me that while there is of course Good Work and Bad Work (smart versus unimaginative, original versus derivative, well-written versus obfuscating), quality can, in the academic world, be very much in the eye of the beholder, especially once you migrate out of the little microcosms in which scholars exist and get projects reviewed by people outside the subfield. Historians aren't particularly sympathetic to sociologists whom they often perceive, as someone once said to me, as empiricizing the intuitive; some political scientists I know similarly perceive some anthropologists as heroicizing the mundane; data-driven sociologists don't have much truck with cultural studies; cultural studies people find much social science work woefully undertheorized; humanities and social scientists deplore the overfootnoting in law reviews, while legal academics abhor the bracketed textual notes in social science, and so on. For extra-academic support of this point, one need look no further than the Modern Library 100 Best Books List, and the demographics of the judges and their critics.

This then brings me back to one of your first points, where you, rightly, say that "we" aren't buying our own books anymore. True enough in a way. But who's we? When North Carolina sells a dozen copies of its latest OAH-award-winning title at a history conference, when Duke's traveling bookstore runs dry by exhibit's end, when the academic hordes descend on the exhibit hall on the last day, "we," meaning you, are in fact buying books. If "we" are the lively minds who beat a path to the NYU book display to request two dozen exam copies of a book such as *Women Transforming Politics, World History in Documents,* or *The Children's Culture Reader,* then I'm here to tell you that you are buying certain books, and buying and assigning them in large, enthusiastic numbers.

Too often this debate is dichotomized into "them" and "us": one lobby groans that all the high-quality works are left at the altar while books on lesbian erotics flood the market. In the other lobby, junior faculty moan about deadwood faculty and resent the criticism of people who have made little attempt, as they see it, to engage their work on its own terms. To a publisher, it's not that easy. Sure, some folks who are seeking to establish the legitimacy of certain fields of inquiry or certain approaches to literature, history, et cetera, are overly tolerant of fringe work; that comes with the terrain and should be actively discouraged. And some reviewers genuinely do try to engage this new work and find they just hate it, and righteously, while some are simply disgruntled and feel left out or behind. My overall point is that university presses should not shy from publishing provocative, new work, if for no other reason than to let folks judge for themselves whether it's valid, useful, substantive, or not.

The baseline issue here is that university presses want to survive and that, as university support erodes and expectations change about what we should be accomplishing, we scramble to make ends meet. And this means publishing books that people WILL read. If that takes the form of a teachable anthology, over a single-authored book of literary criticism, that's the way it is. Mind you, I'm not endorsing the current status quo but, having been the director of a publishing house with a very specific financial mandate, I must exist within it. Unless supported by outside funding (witness, for instance the recent donation of $1 million to Yale University Press for their magnificent 75-volume series on China), some work simply won't get published under the current structure. University presses are the reflectors of a quantum change in higher education, not the agents. I think we can certainly agree that this is a matter of effect, not cause, and that if, as James Shapiro has suggested in the *Chronicle*, universities would better fund their libraries, the system would continue to work.

Gordon Hutner: It's just too facile to characterize as facile my view that presses often look for mediocre manuscripts on ostensibly saleable topics while neglecting good manuscripts of literary criticism that are wanting a worthy publisher. Anyone who's spent any time hassling tenure or meditating promotion knows that professors have lists—a shopping list, if you like; a wish list to be sure—of where they'd like to send their books. Guess what? Venerated or extremely hot presses are on top and second or third choices follow. These lists, drawn up on paper or in the imagination, seldom reflect a great deal of thought but fairly well reflect one professor's sense of the prestige that his or her book is able to command (or his or her sense of a department's view of status or his or her sense of the academic world's vision of success). Silly? Sure, but, simply put, the way things are done. So I don't understand why you think some presses are not seeing numerous passed-over manuscripts in some subjects, while excellent studies on other subjects can't even get a reading.

Of course, publishers turn down what others accept. Journals too. It makes for a much more vitalized publishing world, since, among other things, it means that no one exercises absolute authority. And no one said otherwise. I've published a dozen articles that other editors either did not know how to or did not care to edit, essays I'm just as gratified to publish as many of the excellent ones that barely needed any work. Similarly, I'm delighted to see other journals publish pieces we've had to decline, if only because *ALH* cannot publish all the wonderful submissions we get, essays that I know deserve circulation. What I was saying was that presses could make an impressive show of quality by seeking books on subjects that may not be popular (I believe the University Press of Virginia is doing this in eighteenth-century studies; SUNY in Romantics.) And this seems to me much more sensible and admirable than the prevailing practice of publishing manuscripts not even as good as the Harding-Kerrigan one in the hope of seeing three thousand copies sold in eighteen months.

I have no trouble with the scholar-critics devoting their time and intellects to the Harding-Kerrigan affair, nor do I object to Routledge publishing the book. Nor do I think that in itself it represents some decline in the intellectual life of our time. But the example is not so compelling as you think. Of course, from a publisher's point of view, it was a good book; it showed a nice profit and brought some attention to the press. But the proof of a book's worth is not only in the selling. Maybe the essays are of uniformly high quality; certainly there are several contributors whose work on other subjects I've found instructive. But you don't say that its success derived from that as much as from its topicality, its newsworthiness.

What's wrong with *Women on Ice*—as an example—is precisely that it disappears so quickly. If these professors think they're acting as public intellectuals, instructing the citizenry in the whys and wherefores of our culture, they are deluded. What does the public care if a dozen professors lend their voice to the latest instance of media frenzy? Three thousand sales is five or six times better than many critical books are likely to generate, but it is not thirty thousand or three hundred thousand. Surely you're not suggesting that these professors were able to reach the minds and hearts of the populace, hungering for academic explanations of that grim scandal? I wonder who the audience for this book is: like-minded professionals? Students in pop culture courses? As much as I respect the authors and applaud the editor for her industry, I also don't see this kind of book as the answer to our woes, or even as part of a

significant model for a new, multivalent paradigm—which we sorely need. If
it is, all it seems to mean is that we should study popular culture from unpopular perspectives. You suggest that, if these are the books that are to succeed, then
this is just the way it is and that we should accept this as our lot.

I hope you're wrong, because I believe that humanities scholar-critics have
more interesting and important things to say, if only to each other, than op-
ed pieces in the *New York Times,* though most of us would be tickled pink to
publish our views there. We worry, even a little insanely, about reaching a wider
audience, as if the discussion among academics is, by definition, a degraded
or trivial conversation. I don't believe it is, in the first place. In the second,
academics seldom command this kind of attention. A few professors, in each
generation, have been good at it, but most of us should realize that there's a
very limited market for such address, and that we should be satisfied to address the public that enters our classroom, semester in and semester out. Or
we can address other professors, in papers and essays, and books, who in turn
will address their students, that is, their larger public. What's wrong with this
anyway? And this is what so many of us do, however begrudgingly or enthu-
siastically, though for some there's the gnawing disillusionment that neither
the general public nor our students want what we have to offer. In fact, those
students often dislike intensely our takes on Harding-Kerrigan since for them
we're "overanalyzing" something that everyone is supposed to understand or
can take for granted as meaning nothing but the interest that someone wants
to draw from it.

Still, professors want an audience, but where to find it? One of the hardest
things about being a professor is that you can work years on a book, really drive
yourself—over winter holidays and summer, in between classes during the
term. Polish and revise. And then revise again according to helpful readers'
reports. Then, you see the book through publication. And await its release,
perhaps with the expectation that you'll be lighting celebratory cigars with
rolled-up twenties. The reality is the book turns out to be just another title at
the convention book stall. It takes forever for the journals to review it (and then
you're lucky if the review is by a sensible peer). In the meantime, publishing
seasons come and go; whatever chance your book has had of being noticed and
valued seems to have passed. Now and again you get a modest royalty check.
A couple of years later, you might get a friendly word of recognition here or
there, but basically, you're left wondering why you spent so long on the project.
Shouldn't you really have been playing with your kids?

Why work so hard for such an unappreciative audience? To be sure, many
professors, including younger ones, have abjured this traditional publishing

model in favor of a quicker take. Saner perhaps, but what do their books look like? Provocative readings? Reinvented wheels? Insufficiently researched monographs, haphazardly argued but very stimulating? Important interventions in an ongoing critical dialogue? As a group, we've taken up the collection of essays with a renewed vigor—sometimes with troubling results. Occasionally, these books make some sort of impact, but I suggest that most of them are forgotten within the same publishing season that they're produced. The topic might be a good one, and so they may attract a couple of excellent pieces. But the chances of the collection being uniformly excellent are quite slender. (I'm saying that it would be preferable to have fewer collections of higher quality than to have as many negligible ones as we have. I'm not saying I expect this to happen, but I don't think I'm alone in thinking it would make for a healthier state of affairs. I don't think excellence is in the eye of whoever happens to be writing a report. I've read nearly as many thousands of reports as you have, and I think I've done my job as an editor when I'm able to secure assessments that speak honestly and responsively to an argument, even when the judges cannot come to as a consensus.) Mostly, these collections are as a good as a the best two essays and as a weak as a the worst ones. Most of the pieces are still in need of meditation, revision, and editing, as a they might have received had they been vetted by a journal. Indeed, the journals are being bypassed in this respect, perhaps because they take so damned long to get their essays in print. But many professors who have opted to publish an essay in someone else's collection have had the dismaying experience of seeing their essays held up there also, first by uncooperative fellow contributors, then by the book editor, and then by the press, for all the usual publishing delays. So instead of making a quick strike, we're left with collections, like the present one perhaps, that have no core audience.

I think we've turned to this model, which can be very exciting when it's effective but which can be quite depressing when it isn't, because somehow or other we now think it is better to move through our ideas quickly. If we could be sure that we even constituted an audience for ourselves, it would be one thing, but we're not.

Niko Pfund: How dare you accuse me of being facile in accusing you of being facile? That is so facile of you.

Seriously, my point there was simply to complicate a little the idea that there's a predictable hierarchy of presses. That hierarchy exists, to be sure, but it varies enormously from discipline to discipline. I agree wholeheartedly that presses should make an attempt to publish high quality work regardless of market or popularity, but that's a luxury that some presses (those with enormously profitable backlists, big endowments, large annual subsidies, etc.) can afford, while others can't. It depends on the finances of the particular press.

As for the *Women on Ice* example, touché on most points you make. While I agree with you that that book is highly unlikely to have reached the minds and hearts of a populace hungering for academic explanations of that mess, and while it would be difficult—and senseless—to argue otherwise, bear in mind that that volume received a great deal of review attention. There's a school of thought that believes that the value of certain books, as cultural capital if you will, lies not in their actual value as books per se, but in that they foster discussion when they are widely reviewed. Again, I don't want to overstate the case for *Women on Ice* as this is not necessarily the best example of what I'm talking about, but I do think that the nonacademic reviews of that book did serve the purpose of making at least some people think a little more deeply about why folks reacted to the various players in the way they did. But you're right, such projects are certainly not solutions to the problem; they can, however, be a useful component of a publisher's overall list, when combined with books that speak to less fleeting subjects and will enjoy a slow, steady, consistent readership for years to come (which is, of course, the model for 90 percent of university press books).

As for your observation that many professors should realize the inherently limited audience for their intellectual output, well, yes, I couldn't agree more. However, university press publishing is an increasingly competitive industry and you don't necessarily win important authors/projects to your fold by candidly stressing the intrinsically limited nature of their readership.

And finally, I have no answer for your "why bother?" complaint about the dissatisfaction of working hard on a book for years, with very modest emotional/psychological return. You're right. It must be the most disheartening thing in the world.

I don't know whether you've followed this but I've been fascinated by the response to Jodi Dean's book *Aliens in America,* published by Cornell. Cornell pushed the book hard, hired a publicist, and received an enormous amount of press for it, with cover pieces in the *New York Review of Books* and the *New York Times Book Review.* And yet, despite the fact that the book is on a "sexy" topic, it's a work of cultural studies–informed political theory and has thus been slammed aggressively in both places. My argument as regards this particular book is that we publishers aren't necessarily doing our authors any favors—and many academic presses have been guilty of this—by pushing books to a certain mainstream audience when we can easily predict that those audiences are going to have little sympathy with the particular approach a given title takes. But, again, that's a very difficult thing to convey to an author whose head is being filled with promises of lead reviews and book tours (however modest) by other university press editors.

To clarify my point about anthologies, I'm speaking of very particular types of anthologies: proactive, platform anthologies that seek to anticipate a development in a field or influence pedagogy in a certain way. It makes me a little crazy when I hear some young editors sniff, "Oh, we don't publish anthologies." Again, an anthology is not an anthology is not an anthology (Gertrude Stein is now spinning in her grave). A collection of conference papers, with all its weaknesses, is a very different creature from a carefully developed, painstakingly edited anthology on the development of mental retardation in America, or on the history of miscegenation, or on the role of culture in causing and mediating conflict. Likewise, for me, affirmation comes twice a year when certain anthologies we've labored over, from conception, are adopted by the hundreds. That to me is evidence that professors and students like the books and find them useful.

Having said all that, yes, you're absolutely right: there are too many books out there, and too many books that are published too soon or shouldn't be published at all. Even university press publishers (maybe especially university press publishers) acknowledge that. And in fact some presses, NYU among them, have cut back on the number of books they're publishing, devoting greater energy to fewer titles. (NYU's Fall/Winter 1996 catalog featured ninety-nine books; more recently that figure is closer to sixty.) But too often the "fewer, better books" model can work out simply to "fewer books" and that's when the trouble begins for publishers and authors.

So, what now? What are the answers for young scholars hoping to get published in fields that can no longer sustain the number of books they once could?

Editor's note: Given the "realities" of the current state of academic book publishing, as discussed above, I asked Niko Pfund to speak directly to aspiring authors on how best to approach a press and work toward the placement of a manuscript. I then asked Gordon Hutner to respond to Niko's advice.

Niko Pfund:

Dos:

—Identify those presses most likely to publish your work, given their past publications, by consulting the American Association of University Presses directory, available from the AAUP or in every academic library. Send letters to an editor by name (editors are listed by name in the directory), not to "Editor." Indicate a basic familiarity with the list and indicate, briefly, why you are sending it to this particular publisher.

—Provide editors with a concise summary of your work that will give them some sense of the subject and scope of your project. I would suggest a 1–2 page cover letter, a proposal or annotated table of contents or abstract, perhaps a representative chapter, and an up-to-date CV.

—Credentialize yourself. This is no time to be modest. Include letters of support for your work by prominent scholars, emphasize your committee members (especially if well-known), et cetera. Basically, sell yourself.

—Tell the editor about audiences and readership about which s/he might not know. If, for instance, your work is one about, say, the rise of objectivity as the holy grail of modern journalism, and you are a member of the American Society of Journalism Historians, let the editor know that. Even if the society only numbers 328 folks, if the mailing list is attainable and inexpensive, that's a hard-target audience of the kind university presses very much like.

—Realize that the editor will ultimately have to make a decision about whether or not s/he wants to works with you, on a fairly intensive and intimate basis, for the next several years. This is a major commitment and some editors approach prospective authors like patients do doctors. (Relatedly, I would argue that more authors should approach a potential collaboration with an editor in a similar vein.) If an editor gets the sense from you that you are obsessive or unrealistic or unpleasant or in need of an inordinate amount of handholding, s/he might bail.

Don'ts

—Blanket every university press with an obviously cold canvas submission.

—Email submissions. Editors are overwhelmed with paper and don't want to take on the additional step of printing out your submission. Few acquisitions editors actually edit manuscripts, or review submissions in detail, in their office; rather, they take them home and work on them there, in the evenings or on weekends. Make this easy for them by sending them a neat package, rather than forcing them to print something out themselves.

—Go overboard with flattery. It's one thing to show a familiarity with a press's list, quite another to fawn over it for obviously self-interested reasons. This is not of huge importance, mind you, but it's better to err on the side of caution here, simply alluding to other works that you respect, rather than gushing.

—Try to persuade the editor that your work has a large audience among "general readers." The business about "appealing to the general reader" has become so clichéd that it's a virtual throwaway line these days, right up there with touting prose as "eminently readable." The "general reader," especially of scholarly nonfiction, is an elusive demographic and literally four of five unsolicited submissions presses receive that tout their likely interest to the general reader don't, honestly, stand a chance in that respect. So be realistic. Realize that there is a big difference between a general reader and an academic reader who may not be in your particular (sub)discipline.

—Be too compliant or, alternately, distrustful. Editors want a constructive, cooperative, dialectical relationship, a genuine give-and-take. The author-editor relationship is an unusual one in that no one is working *for* anyone else, per se. While some editors like malleable authors, and few like pushy authors, the best editors prefer a relationship in which they themselves are challenged and the author her/himself enjoys the same. Relatedly, if you've had a bad experience with editors, don't go overboard in projecting that. It's one thing to state that you feel strongly that you'd like to have some input on the jacket, it's another to say that you've heard so many horror stories about bad jackets that you are going to insist that you see the very final proof before the book goes to print. It's important that you engage the editors, but equally important that you let them do their jobs.

Gordon Hutner: Dos and Don'ts

1. Do: Follow Niko Pfund's advice. The first thing to observe is that quality tells, but there are a few things you can do about marketability. Although the dissertation topic better be something that you want to think about for several years, it also needs to be something that others are willing to think about too—not just you and your director. Why not examine the contents of several publishers' catalogs? If your dissertation sounds like some of these books, you're probably a little late, since it will take you years to write a thesis and revise it into a book. Of course, you can always take the worthy chance that your work is smarter, more thorough, and more refined.

2. Don't get hung up on any one press. There are plenty of good ones. And of course the best one, in this market, is the one that is wise enough to offer you a contract! Some people get hung up over prestige, even fixated on one or two presses, but publishing a book can be such a crapshoot that this seems foolish to me. Consider whether a press markets its books aggressively. Some people insist on simultaneous paperback and hardcover distribution, but only a few presses seem willing to go that route.

Again, look over a couple of their recent catalogs. (It's easy enough to get put on their mailing list.) What are they committing themselves to lately? If your manuscript has some regional appeal—southern writing, for example—you might want to look at those presses that might actually sell the book, first to their board of faculty overseers, then to academics, then to a constituency of special interest.

There's nothing wrong with asking your professors and colleagues to recommend your work to editors they may know, but there's no sense in reposing a great deal of confidence in that avenue either. Such word-of-mouth can help get you a reading, but no press is going to accept a manuscript for fear of alienating your dissertation director. If you're an assistant professor, it may pay to look where your immediate predecessors published their books; that's an informal guide to a department's expectations.

3. When going up for tenure, make sure your colleagues know a little about the press you've chosen: is it strong in your area of expertise, for example? What books has it recently published that they may have heard of? Do not let them rely solely on their general impressions, since you don't want to risk any misconceptions, not to mention their failing memories.

4. Take readers' reports seriously. If they are negative, do not contest their legitimacy. Address instead the needs of the readers that your unfair critic represents. To an editor, they represent predictions about a book's reception, which a press is bound to consider, even if you're not. The editor may have chosen badly, but there's nothing to be done about it, so don't get into arguments about the authority of the report or a judge's motives. You're the only one who really cares; the editor has a deskful of manuscripts to worry about.

A true consensus doesn't really begin to form until the fourth report, but no editor will sink that much money into your manuscript. Two reports are standard. If you've been rejected by more than one press, and all the reports are consistent, then you may want to revise to meet the shared sense of the book's limitations. Try not to revise simply on the basis of one report—or two—unless a contract is forthcoming.

5. Dealing with presses is a bit like the job market; how you're treated in the initial stages is a good indication of how you can expect the negotiation to go. If an editor loses a report, or sits on a manuscript, and you have another opportunity elsewhere, pursue it. Your editor may renew attention momentarily, but more lapses are probably coming.

6. Count on a press taking 9–10 months at the very least. Press editors, like journal editors, often resist the obligation a job candidate or tenure hopeful may put before them to respond by a certain date. Leave plenty of time in your

calculations and indicate to the editor the time framework. If you need a decision in the early fall, don't expect that sending the manuscript out in the late spring is enough time. It's likely to sit in-house for a while; the judges will consider your manuscript as summer reading. Then the reports; then, maybe, the directors' meeting. Too many variables for such a tight deadline, especially if you are also asked to respond to a critic's assessment. That letter, by the way, could prove to be the single most important document of your early career, so it's not the time to get bratty, no matter how unjust the critique. Remember, your editor will be presenting the case to the board on the basis of the reports and your reply. Make a good impression.

7. Multiple submissions: the new etiquette seems to be that it's okay, if all the parties know about it. As a journal editor, I generally forego the chance to compete with other publications for material, if only because our judges—who don't get paid—ought not to be called upon to sacrifice their time and trouble and expertise for submissions for which we do not have exclusive rights. Press editors, on the other hand, may take a longer view, so that they do not miss out on a really hot prospect of a manuscript. The only honest thing to do is to ask whether they accept multiple submissions.

8. When to pull your manuscript? No later than nine months before you need a decisive word, and then only if you have another press lined up and if your editor has a record of not fulfilling promises or meeting expectations. I don't know why some editors give authors the runaround, but it happens and, after a very long stall, you may lose confidence in an editor's interest in your book. In which case, write a humble letter to one of the presses that earlier did avow an interest.

9. Use wisely MLA and other professional conferences where you are likely to meet press representatives. It might be useful to have a (very) short paragraph ready, but you can expect editors whom you have engaged to ask you to send an abstract. (Remember, they're usually on overload at these conference.) Brush-off or not, send the abstract if you have one ready. In all ways, be professional, and make them think you might be the kind of person they might like to work with.

10. And finally, try not to fetishize your manuscript in the various stages. Answer the copyeditor's questions politely and promptly. And answer the marketing questionnaire. Help yourself by helping the press to sell your book.

Editor's Note: On similar and other topics, I spoke with Martha Banta, who assumed the editorship of PMLA in the summer of 1997, for a three-year term. Professor Banta has a long and successful history as a published scholar from which

she draws as she offers her own insights into the state of academic publishing to-
day. She echoes some of the thoughts of the two essayists above, but also offers some
significantly different perspectives that are well worth considering, by new and
seasoned writers alike.

Donald Hall: While I would like this interview to focus largely on your opinion of the current state of academic publishing, I want to start our conversation by asking more generally about your perspective on the profession; in
particular, what do you see as the most serious challenge we are facing today?

Martha Banta: I find most troubling, as do many of my colleagues, a growing domination of what I will call a "business ethos." We all know what
"downsizing" means now, and that it doesn't just apply to IBM or hospitals,
but also to colleges and universities. Certainly one of the clearest results of
this business ethos is restrictions on hiring tenure-track faculty and, most
devastatingly, an excessive reliance upon part-time lecturers. You and I both
know the terrible tale in the Los Angeles area where people dash around from
community college to community college on the freeways for hours trying
to pick up jobs, because the budgeteers are simply deciding "why go for expensive help?"

At the same time, administrators are attempting to convert our entire humanities curriculum into service courses. This too comes out of an overall
business ethos, which emphasizes going to college to get a piece of paper that
will get you a salary: a contractual relationship. I was reading recently of a
commentator who said that if a teacher cannot prove to a student, when as-
sailed by that student, "how is what you are saying in the classroom today going
to help me get a job and 'x' number of dollars a year," then that teacher's course
has no reason to be taught. Today, even the humanities curriculum has to translate simply into money.

In fact, we are even faced with an emerging possibility of the complete elimination of personal faculty contact through computer-based courses. Now please
let it go on record that I am not an "old fogey"—I'm not living in the past—
I'm still eager and excited about the future—but I do see some very troublesome trends. Someone at home turns on the computer and gets x number of
facts and takes some kind of exam and gets a piece of paper to go forth into
the world to make money. That doesn't help one's intellectual quality or one's
soul. One of the more troubling recent developments along these lines at UCLA
is the request (requirement) to put all of our courses in advance on the Web.
Of course, the people who are asking us to do so generally have no idea what

goes on in the classroom. Yes, you have to have a syllabus and a well-planned course, but at least for me and most of my colleagues, a course is also about comments raised during class, in office hours, in encounters in the corridors; you are revising things constantly because you are responding to students' points of interest. If you have a fixed, contracted program already on line, it will kill any sense of spontaneous give-and-take and intellectual engagement. Certainly it is the best way of killing excitement I know; what you get is quite simply boring. But after all true service courses are meant to be boring. They are contracted in a certain way so you can take a test and then get your salary.

And the commitment to this larger business ethos—of quantity over quality—directly affects the question of publishing, and has a very insidious effect upon scholarship. We know that in the trade publishing business, what gets published is what sells, what has a quick turnover, what won't be remaindered, what is trendy, especially what has (by marketing surveys) a wide potential for "quick" sales. That ethos has not only hurt the trade press, it is also now hurting the academic world, which is not supposed to be thinking about marketing strategies and quick sales and so on. Serious intellectual work does not always mean quick sales; in many ways, you have diametrically opposed projects. But then Niko Pfund and Gordon Hutner have already spoken to this problem, far more elegantly and eloquently.

Donald Hall: Please, speak a little more about that "insidious effect" that you refer to. What concerns you most, as a mentor of writers, about the current state of book publishing?

Martha Banta: First I want to mention some early, necessary struggles: to find the right voice, a distinctive, unique scholar's voice, a critic's voice, and through that voice the best way to put forth a convincing argument. Now in my case (because of my own experience in graduate school in the long ago and far away years of the sixties), my problem was *not* that I brought to my early work the signs of an inadequate training in research and scholarship techniques. However these inadequacies are too frequently the case with the essays and book manuscripts that pass through my hands today. Not only have too many academics a problem with finding a unique scholar/critic's voice and a smart, exciting way of putting forth the argument, in many ways they just haven't been sufficiently trained in how to do the kinds of research that holds up. It is hard enough to discover a scholar's voice, to discover your own way of making a powerful argument, don't make it harder yet by not knowing how to substantiate your argument with first-rate archival work.

But there was another struggle as well, for as I worked to discover that voice, I also had to find the appropriate journal or book publisher for my particular subject and topics, particularly when, about ten years into my career, I was becoming increasingly interdisciplinary. Moving around between different disciplines was not as accepted then as it is now; book publishers had yet to wake up to the fact that this was an important scholarly enterprise. But even today, the more interesting and innovative you might be, the more trouble you may have finding a nest for your material.

Later on, I began to see the difficulties from both sides. I have served as a reader for lots of book publishers and on the advisory board of a number of journals. I started asking, does that book publisher or does that journal have sensible editorial procedures and policies in the way they organize the review process, their overall turn-around time, the letters they send back, and how they handle their readers' reports? Of course you can be an excellent journal or an excellent book publisher and wait endlessly for the best material to come to your desk, but I'm saying it must work the other way too. I don't mean the publishers or readers are hostile, but rather that some of them don't know their business. They are too hasty or just not up to their task. Of course, they may soon be out looking for another job.

Since it can be a jungle out there, as well as paradise island, I want to speak in specific ways to graduate students and to young faculty concerning publishing. Today there is severe pressure to publish very quickly and in great quantity, even before one is an accredited professional. My graduate students come to me, ready to go on the market; they are very nervous if they don't have a couple of essays accepted, if not already published in the "big" journals. They have a right to be nervous, because now the stakes are very high. I had a couple of pieces published before I got out of graduate school, but it certainly wasn't needed or expected of my generation; it was nice, but it wasn't as if my professional life were in danger if I hadn't done so. But now students, who have already gone on the market one year and must go back out the next because they didn't get a job the first time, know they had better have a book manuscript in hand. *And they are still just emerging from graduate school.* Pressures like these simply don't give your mind, your intellect, enough time to think clearly about your book project; it leads to very hasty scholarship. My point is meant to be a paradox: we lament the fact that good first-time manuscripts don't get accepted by the presses; we should also regret the unwise publication of material that is not good enough.

We must resist the temptation to rush half-baked and raw-edged dissertations into print. It is a difficult temptation to resist, especially when the academic novice is lured by the offer of an advance contract, offered by less responsible publishers. Frankly, I'm putting a lot of the blame on those academic houses who respond to nervous sales representatives and nervous editors who feel they have to grab some of this "stuff" while it is hot. They'll sign people up for an advance contract when the dissertation isn't even finished, perhaps after having heard only a snippet of it presented as a paper at a conference. They take the graduate student to coffee, and she or he says "I hope to finish my dissertation next summer," and the publisher says "fine, here is an advance contract." Well, psychologically and intellectually that is very bad news. If Niko and Gordon declare this does not happen all that often, then I say, thank goodness!

When I listen to conference papers, when I read essays sent my way, read dissertations struggling to be transformed into book manuscripts, I find they often fail because the person has not yet arrived at an appropriate level of intellectual independence. If you are just coming out of graduate school or you are a new assistant professor, you are still very close to the world of the seminar room, where you have been reading up on all the most current theory and criticism; certainly you are very bright, and are starting what may be a great career, but what your brain has been absorbing usually hasn't had time to meld and come together. What I often "hear" as I read raw manuscripts is that they sound like everybody else talking in that seminar or at that conference. By the way, understand, I'm not saying I'm against the newest theories or critical positions. Let's hope you're getting a lot out of reading Lacan, Derrida, or Kristeva. But you need to test where their weaknesses are, as well as the strengths. When you do that you are not throwing away the theory, you are making a stronger case for your own argument. You can't become your own scholar and critic if you don't do that testing. In fact, the consequence of any "hurry up and do it" mentality is that you can't even break free from the language which is being exacted by, expected by, and is inherent to one established position or the other. It is not a matter of rejecting the position you are learning to love; it is being able to come up with fresh language or modes of discourse that demonstrate that you have been doing your own thinking.

And so our new "business ethos" contributes to this undue and harmful pressure to publish. Certainly there has always been concern over "publish or perish" in the groves of academe. Frankly, in the past, I was pretty sick of hearing about this all the time. After all, if you go into the academic world, you should want to be a wonderful teacher, and to me being a wonderful teacher means you want to do wonderful research and writing. It's a reciprocal action: the books and essays you write come directly out of student contact; then, what you write goes back into your courses. People used to say it was either black or white: you either published or you were a good teacher, and if you were a good teacher you were going to perish. Well, it has never been that simple. But now we are getting to an impossible situation: if you don't publish fast, which usually means publishing very raw material, you *are* going to perish. Without the proper time, you are not able to become a very good teacher and scholar, and to do it in your own wonderful way. Then (and I dread having to bring up this awful truth once more), how are you to manage any of the above if "bottom-line" demands mean you're a part-time instructor, unable to do anything well that brought you to this profession in the first place?

Donald Hall: But how do we effectively counter those forces? Do we do it in our role as members of tenure and promotion committees; does it lie with the individual graduate student who has to make almost impossible choices; or does the responsibility lie at some larger administrative level?

Martha Banta: There are things all of us can do, or try very hard to do. The faculty who sit in judgment for hiring and tenure, and of course merit and promotion, should have the awareness and wit to take these contending issues into consideration when they are evaluating someone. They must take care not to promote mindlessly someone who has a long bibliography that seems to hit all of the buzz buttons, or wrongly hire or tenure someone who really isn't going to be much of an asset to a department. The reverse is also true: the department should be aware and witty enough not to penalize or to react negatively to someone who has a smaller bibliography though of wonderful quality, or to fail to recognize the merit of scholarly approaches that don't duplicate their own interests. Faculty, in its actions, votes, and decisions, can either reinforce a bad situation or they can act to work to change it. After all, if enough people on the faculty did that at enough schools, we might see major changes in this business ethos. There still would be the occasional dean saying, "why haven't you hired this hot shot?" but then the faculty should reply that that person really isn't the kind of scholar/teacher we want because what's offered here is just a lot of flash rather than something solid. This argument chairs must make when they go to the dean, to try to either put forward a certain person who doesn't fit the superstar profile, or to try to explain why they wisely choose not to go after a superstar.

On the individual faculty level, it means an awful lot of time spent talking with graduate students, and I mean *hours* of discussing the pros and cons of publishing, of going to conferences, of accepting offers to write book reviews or encyclopedia entries while still at work on a dissertation. On those latter two issues, I generally tell students, given the situation today, to hold back on writing in dribs and drabs. Encyclopedia entries can take months of research, and even a book review will take up a couple of weeks. I give the same advice to junior, pre-tenure faculty too: wait until you get tenure, and then you can take the time to review books and do short entries, which can be fascinating and intellectually rewarding work. Focus first on essays and book manuscripts. But most importantly, I say: *avoid the blandishments of the Satan who holds out the apple of an advance contract.* Be sure you are ready to turn over a piece of writing to an editor that you are really proud of, don't be lured by the first publisher who knows your name and asks you out for coffee at a conference. And when it comes time to try to peddle your work (and "peddle" is what you're doing) be smart about the publisher you go with. Some of the biggest name publishers have bad reputations for signing on far too many new books a season, which then get a tiny space in a *PMLA* ad (and for one issue only) and then disappear. Be alert to the fact that when a publisher accepts too many books and rushes them quickly into press, the copyediting and the overall editing work can doubtlessly be very slovenly. So if you can, hold out for a publisher who is going to pay attention to your book and carry through on it, and give you attention in their catalog and more than five minutes' worth of academic fame.

Giving advice along these lines is the responsibility of every faculty member who deals with graduate students on a day-to-day basis. Dealing with the consequences of their decisions is also the responsibility of the department when it convenes to make decisions on hiring, tenure, and promotion. (Am I suggesting that responsible action is not always in play in departmental decisions? Yes, I am.) If these many areas are attended to, and if the very notion of responsibility for advancing the common good of the academic community ever trickles up to the administrative level, there is a fair chance that the current, less than happy situation might improve.

Donald Hall: How did the perspectives that you've been offering bear on your work as editor of *PMLA*?

Martha Banta: I shall return in a moment to that idea of "voice," but first I want to mention that we have thirty thousand members in the Modern Language Association who get a free copy of the journal, whether they read it or not, but certainly thirty thousand *potential* readers, who have many interests and different areas of expertise. Every day we at the journal had to confront the issue of how to edit the journal so that it was not too generalist (you can't only publish essays that thirty thousand people will be interested in), yet was not so specialized that when you read it you would say, gee, this piece should be in *Speculum,* what is it doing here? In a sense it is much easier for scholars to write and editors to select a very general piece or a very specialized article, but it is very difficult when the journal is attempting, in a sense, to have it both ways.

What I tried to do is convince MLA members at large of how wide a sweep *PMLA* is willing to make. The perception had come into place that a certain methodological approach or list of preferred theorists or a certain set of preferred topics or a certain prose style was required before *PMLA* would give an article the time of day. Whether that was a correct perception or not, it was a powerful belief, and I tried to say "no" to it. *PMLA* really does invite all kinds of approaches, methodologies, theories, all kinds of subject matter, and all kinds of writing styles. All the journal asks is that it be good. (I've always like T. S. Eliot's little quip, "There is no method except to be very intelligent." Perhaps this is part of the man's infamous elitism; then it's one kind of elitism that I don't object to.)

I did all that I could to alter the perception that *PMLA* imposes one bland set of requirements that privilege a particular writing style or "voice." Eric Wirth is the associate editor who handles the copyediting, and he is superb (I wish I had had him, way back in grammar school, to teach me everything there is to know about syntax and punctuation). Certainly he cannot be faulted for seeing that ideas are correctly expressed. Still there has been the notion that all *PMLA* articles "sound" alike; I got this in letters to *PMLA*'s Forum, I had people saying it to me in person, and so on. Although I disagree that everything in *PMLA* has had the same blah style, there is some truth that there has been too much of a sameness. Through the comments I made in my editorials, and in other little ways, I kept reiterating the need for all of us to find a voice of one's own, to free one's self from overdependency on the discourse that seems to be in favor at a particular moment, to even be daring, witty, and brave in how one expresses the ideas which are so passionately (aren't they?) engaging your intellect.

Donald Hall: Any thoughts on how one finds that personal voice? What was your process in that regard?

Martha Banta: If, that is, I've found that distinctive voice. If I have, it has taken a great deal of time to acquire. In the graduate seminars I've taught over these many years, I would say that only once or twice have the students written papers that sound only like them. In saying that I am not denigrating their intelligence. A seminar paper can have everything, can deserve its A or A+, but still be immature, still be new in the game. It may be grammatically sound and have a nice flow to the sentences, but still not be distinguishable from the next one on the pile of papers in front of me.

Perhaps in my case I brought something peculiar to this matter. Before going to graduate school I had been working on and off Madison Avenue for ten years writing advertising copy. During that "first career" of mine, I learned certain tricks of the trade, but they clearly didn't make what I wrote for my living sound like a scholarly article. When I left Madison Avenue and suddenly found myself in a graduate seminar, I was very conscious of the fact that I had to convert from one kind of writing to another. At the same time, I had had ten years of constant practice where I had been very self-conscious of the act of writing. After all my job depended on me thinking about the power of certain verbs, holding back on adjectives, not using the passive voice: all the ploys that go into good critical writing whether it's to sell shoes or Gertrude Stein. (By the way, Stein's sentences and shoe-copy are marvelously akin.) I had certain mannerisms that I had to put aside, but I was also aware that I had acquired a voice, a voice that worked on Madison Avenue, which I could, with care, transform into scholarly discourse. As a result, I may have arrived at sounding like myself more quickly than my graduate school friends who had been in school since kindergarten and had never had the chance to discover a voice that was theirs.

Donald Hall: To return to some of your earlier comments, you spoke about respect and collegial responsibility, which should translate into making decisions and fulfilling duties appropriately and fairly. I'm not sure if you know this, but you are regarded as a particularly generous and supportive colleague. What are your thoughts on what makes a person a good colleague in a department, university, or other professional setting?

Martha Banta: I have something short to say and it sounds a great deal like a sermonette, if not a jeremiad: Don't carry envy, malice, and spite in your heart. Don't cloak personal attacks upon your colleagues with fine sounding rhetoric that calls for "a need for academic excellence" to block a person's promotion or hiring, because you simply hate their guts. I have been in too many meetings, in every conceivable academic setting, where the rhetoric is that "we won't support this person because he/she doesn't meet our standards of intellectual excellence," but if you dredge layers of past history and personal relationships, you realize that the speaker simply can't stand this type of person or that kind of ideological position, though of course they can't come out and say it in that way. Often they are half deceiving themselves; they really *do* believe the sound of their own rhetoric, even if they are engaging in ad hominem attacks. I'm of the mind that few people who engage in mean, spiteful, or malicious things do it all that consciously. Rather it is simply a matter of thoughtlessness and indifference; they come together to pass judgments but they haven't read the material, they haven't bothered to come to the job talks, they have closed down their minds. By failing to think about the seriousness of the fact that they are hiring someone, advancing them to tenure, promoting them, accepting a grant proposal or essay or conference paper, they have dodged their responsibilities. (That word again! As one of my undergraduates once said to me, when I took him to task for plagiarism—one more form of irresponsibility—"Oh, so you're on a moral-kick!")

Donald Hall: Is this getting worse? Have you noticed any changes over the course of the past decades in terms of a general level of collegiality and responsibility? Have we always been a profession at war with itself or have things grown nastier?

Martha Banta: I tend to think that human nature is fairly consistent. I hate to sound platitudinous in the midst of the gritty facts of academic life, but I encounter just as many good people now as I did then, just as many indifferent people now as then. But as I tried to say earlier, circumstances, pressures, the business ethos, et cetera, can simply turn the screws tighter on what you might call basic propensities of character. Character is very important, but so is circumstance, and just as circumstances are important, character has certain ways of responding to them. As we all know—and as Niko, Gordon, and I have tried to point out—particular circumstances are making things tougher recently, have raised the stakes tremendously. Many more people are being weeded out, decisions that throw them out of the profession are more sharp edged today because of impinging conditions: economic, social, political. There is a rhythm, you might say, between circumstances and what we do with the situation that we find.

Donald Hall: Finally, is there a role that can we play in our mentoring of graduate students that can help foster this collegiality and sense of responsibility rather than indifference or divisiveness?

Martha Banta: One of the reasons that I have immensely enjoyed working in the graduate program at UCLA is that the majority of the graduate students there are exceptionally collegial; they actually seem to like one another. Now of course there are some exceptions; there are a few who come in bristling and competitive and antagonistic, and envy any success that's not theirs to win. But the majority are the nicest people possible. And my own graduate school experience was wonderful. I was so naive that when I left graduate school I assumed that all graduate school experiences were as good. Now I don't mean it wasn't terribly hard to get seminar papers in on time and not to have much money to live on, and to have to struggle with the pressures of professional apprenticeship and so on. But in terms of the relationships I experienced between the students and the faculty, and the students amongst themselves, I was schooled to believe that I had entered a profession based on principles of generosity and goodwill. Having coming directly from Madison Avenue, where the opposite ethos was in place, I thought, "What a relief the academic profession is. These are really decent people." Then I moved out of graduate school and began to discover (lo!) that many of the Madison Avenue types exist in the midst of the academic world.

I have many colleagues who couldn't be more warm and personable. Naturally, students generally gravitate toward them rather than the faculty who are cold and seem totally self-absorbed. I might add that I find that those who are decent to their students are usually also decent to their colleagues. They don't make a division, saying "I'm going to be nice to them because faculty are *up here* and not nice to student because they are *down there*." But collegiality across the board is not the sole responsibility of faculty; students have to make the effort as well. Now, I don't think people, whether faculty or students, can be dropped into one another's presence and be redeemed overnight. And the last thing I would want is to have self-esteem sessions in which everyone hold hands in a circle, and learns to be nice to one another, and then ends with a big hug. No. You have to form your character in more mature ways, under more acerbic conditions. But graduate students and faculty alike should think carefully about these things, should think that it is not simply what you are publishing, what job you get, how much salary you get, how fast you are going up the ladder, you should also be thinking, am I a good person?

8

The End of Theory, the Rise of the Profession:
A Rant in Search of Responses

Geoffrey Galt Harpham

*Editor's Note: It may seem odd that I would choose to include a "rant" in a col-
lection of dialogues. Is not a "rant" the polar opposite of the supple give and take
that I extol in my introduction as essential to the health and well-being our profession? Not exactly. Calling any two things "polar opposites" is always reductive,
of course, but in this case such a designation would wholly overlook the possibility of extratextual responses, as well as subtle internal clues to shaded ironies and
fine self-complications. Without a doubt, Professor Harpham's "rant" will be
uncomfortable for many readers. Frankly, I wanted to walk away from it several
times (especially after point 21 or so); many of the trends and even concrete occurrences that he points to with dismay (if not actual disgust) I find laudable and
energizing. Indeed, I could not help feeling an affinity with some of the targets of
his "rant," and even experienced a few surprisingly direct hits: I am, after all, a
self-aware "professional," a queer theory enthusiast, an administrator who would
rebuke the deployment of old style authority in the classroom, and finally (and
he had no way of knowing this when he wrote his piece) an interviewer of LA
adolescents (for my work on the southern California rave scene), whose micro-
deployments of power I find as fascinating as any canonical work of literature I've
ever read. Some of his "givens" are quite foreign to me: I've never even read an
issue of* Sports Illustrated *(I've glanced at a few pictures while waiting in the
dentist's office) and barely remember the Beatles. I subscribe to* Lingua Franca
*(no surprise there) and would point to Trent Reznor and Marilyn Manson as
"geniuses" of the sort that Professor Harpham seems to find so sorely lacking today. At the same time, I find myself nodding in agreement with his reading of the
genesis of the "star system" and his basic timeline of changes in the profession, only
to find in some of those changes the very reason I am working in this profession*

today, rather than, perhaps, a reason to leave it. No piece in this collection allows a clearer perspective on some of the standpoint epistemological differences underlying our profession's disagreements; at the same time it offers a response to the current climate that is incisive and certainly provocative. And in its provocativeness lies this "rant"'s potential for important dialogic work. Indeed, Professor Harpham openly invites energetic response, which his appended "discussion questions" will no doubt help spark, for in my opinion they are as interesting textually (and perhaps tactically) as anything he says in the body of his "rant."

1. If you work in a university, you may sometimes wonder what your administrators are reading at night. I can tell you. Eyes popping, covers drawn up, they are eagerly devouring by flashlight lurid accounts of the bad effects of "the star system," by which a few conspicuously useless queen bees absorb vast resources that might go to building the institution. "The professoriat is being proletarianized," as the late Bill Readings summarizes this argument in his book *The University in Ruins*, "and the number of short-term or part-time contracts at major institutions increased (with the concomitant precipitation of a handful of highly paid stars)" (1). Such comments are echoed everywhere, especially in publications such as the *Chronicle of Higher Education* and MLA's *Profession*. My own institution, Tulane University, recently produced an "Environmental Scan" that noted a "continuing trend toward the development of a winner-take-all market in which institutions vie for the services of 'star' faculty through generous salary and benefit packages. Star faculty," this document continues, "are recruited for their prestige; competition for their presence allows them to craft unique employment contracts which often limit their teaching loads to allow for greater time for research pursuits." A mighty prestige-machine, the university is being gutted by its own product, becoming hostage to "research."

2. Jetting from Berkeley to Bellagio—touching down everywhere, it seems, but at the institution that pays them—stars confer a reflected glory on their universities by virtue of their conspicuous uselessness: what sort of glorious entity must it be, the world wonders, that places such a high value on thought that it could devote such immense resources to supporting someone whose only human function is to think, or at least to talk? What sort of entity, indeed, the "proletarianized" assistant and associate professors ask themselves bitterly, as they rise at dawn to grade scores of papers, having tossed in their beds for hours, pursued in their dreams by vengeful promotion and tenure committees that are skeptical and even contemptuous of their efforts. Stars wreck institutional efficiency, cripple institutional flexibility, and give a wildly distorted

view of the academic life. If only universities could get rid of those wretched stars, this increasingly popular argument goes, the wealth could be spread more evenly, incentives and rewards could be offered to those who need and deserve them, the university could rationalize its operations, and everything would be great.

3. Alas, they're tenured; and the university has not found an alternative currency comparable to prestige. So we're stuck. The whole miserable situation is like Brueghel's *Parable of the Blind Men,* with the entire line of sightless men, led by sightless administrators, tumbling one by one into the ditch. Brueghel does not, in this work, depict the stars themselves, but perhaps the massive composition called *The Peasant Wedding,* with its memorable images of gustatory and amatory repletion, the merry guests served platters of food carried on long boards by straw-haired graduate students, suggests the ethos of life at the top.

4. How did this happen? How did the university, the spiritual home of unremunerated idealism, come to germinate a whole class of overcompensated sybarites? The answer, I believe, is counterintuitive but inescapable: theory. At least in the humanities, *theory gave birth to the star system.*

5. In the beginning—the late sixties—theory promised a new beginning for the humanities, a transdisciplinary enterprise with great implications for future growth. The university was delighted to welcome theory into the fold, in part because theory represented a challenge to the increasingly encrusted autonomy of departments, a principle of communication between disciplines, and, as feature stories in national publications on such figures as Derrida, Foucault, Barthes, de Man, Fish, and the "Yale School" began to testify, a way of making headlines beyond the campus and thus of commanding the kind of respect reserved for celebrity. During the seventies and eighties, theory became a synonym for the exciting, the new, the postmodern. The theoretical "project" was the very site of individual and institutional ambition, the point at which the activities of the academy began to impinge on those of the world, and where the values of the world were most visibly operative in the academy.

6. In its immediate institutional effects, theory represented, then, a point of coalescence between the university and the "real world." Exactly why this might have been so is a bit obscure to me, but one interesting possibility is that, in contrast to other university pursuits centered on "research," the arduous refinding of the various lost objects that presumably represented the essence of the university's mission, theory was in essence a forward-looking and synthetic activity. Theory acted as a solvent on those repositories of lost objects, history and nature, whose hierarchies could be demonstrated to be "in theory" con-

tingent. The theoretical perspective leveled things that, when encountered in the world, had seemed frozen into positions of higher or lower, weaker or stronger, noble or ignoble. In this way, theory was devoted to the business of equalizing the unequal, and so promoted the kind of skepticism about distinctions that characterized its institutional and extra-institutional effects.

7. Moreover, theory was intrinsically skeptical about identity, about the right or capacity of anything to determine what it was or how it could be understood. Theory posed the question of identity by treating all actual things not as themselves but as instances of some emergent general principle. Thus a meditation on a given text might become theoretical by giving way to a meditation on textuality itself, or a discussion of rhetorical figures in Proust might theorize itself by widening the focus to include figurality as such. Theory requires examples, and the theoretical approach treats all particular things as though they harbor theories, general laws yearning to see the light of day.

8. Often, theoretical skepticism takes the form of inverting some claim that had been thought to be crucial to the identity of a given thing or practice. This tendency is especially pronounced when it comes to the issue of whether something is concrete and material or conceptual and ideal. The rule of theory is that whatever a thing has been thought to be, it is in fact the opposite. Nothing is so utterly immured in specific, material, historical materiality that it cannot be seen otherwise, as a mere image, a concept, a tissue or film floating in zero G. "In theory," material things become liberated from the contexts in which they emerged, emancipated from their own most salient attributes, and free to enter into all manner of new configurations and relations. Thus, for example, prisons, when treated by Foucault, are transformed from monuments to the loss and lack of privilege, primitive stone dungeons of banishment from the mainstream, into privileged figures, radiant images of a radically conceptual "modernity." Derrida's account of Marx falls into this category. Derrida emphasizes not the endless statistics of *Capital,* nor the insistence on economic and historical determinism, nor the calls to political transformation, but rather a persistent "spectrality" that runs through Marx's texts, as in the famous first line to "The Communist Manifesto": "A spectre is haunting Europe."

9. But theory can also materialize objects out of thin air. Derrida's early career as a theorist, we may recall, had been based on the insistence that texts, long held to be transparent records of mental events, testaments to spirit and genius, were in fact relentlessly and obdurately material entities, resistant to idealization and antithetical in their essence to anything like "consciousness." Early or late, spectralist or materialist, Derrida is always a theorist.

10. On one subject, theory is unequivocal. From the theoretical point of view,

history can be suspended and the issues approached as if for the first time, with no baggage, no sense of an overriding natural or inevitable rightness in play. In one sense, history is the prey of theory, which relentlessly exposes its operations to be contingent, determined by power or force that has no "theoretical" justification. All historically settled interpretations of literary texts, for example, were vulnerable to exposure by theorists not as the farthest point of refinement yet reached by human intelligence but as non-necessary and provisional formulations achieved by various institutional and social agencies. Whatever research had turned up concerning the whiteness of the whale, Hamlet's indecision, or Satan's dark allure could be shown by some theorist to be a mere reflex. Society or some uncognized force had tapped your knee, theory told interpreters, and you began to reproduce accounts for which no theoretical justification could be claimed.

11. This premise of reconfigurability extended beyond literary interpretation, of course, to all sorts of other matters. Sexual identity, for example, was commonly understood to reflect one's inner disposition, one's "identity"; but, of course, there was no solid theoretical reason why this should be: theoretically, women were fully equal in endowment and rights to men, no matter what their actual condition today; theoretically, men could desire men as well as women. The terms "feminist theory" and "queer theory" condense into suggestive phrases the particularly strong alliance between the theoretical and the minoritarian. And while history and theory are, as I noted, natural predators, it could be said that each requires the other for support at crucial moments. In the case of same-sex desire, theory corrodes the credentials of the historical process that, in our society, has produced heterosexuality as a norm; but history supports the theoretical claim by disclosing other cultures, or other moments of our "own" culture, in which, for example, what we call "homosexuality" was felt to be not inconsistent with "normal" masculinity, even procreative matrimony. Theory is nothing if not systematic, and the consistent argument of theory is that history is either more systematic than it appears to be, or less systematic than it claims to be. In both cases, theory promotes the view, which history—other histories, of other times and places—confirms, that things could be otherwise than they are. The climate of theory is one of free agency, in which all sorts of normative configurations are understood to be historically constructed, pliable, and therefore susceptible to a previously unsuspected individual or collective agency.

12. Perhaps the exemplary instance of theory in the sense I'm talking about is Saussure's linguistics. Saussure posited a new account of language; or rather, he sought to delineate a new thing, which he called "language alone," as op-

posed to the language studied by comparative philologists and philosophers. Comparative philologists had examined the internal evolution and geographical dissemination of various languages; philosophers, the origin or purpose of language—historical in the first case, and radically historical in the second. Together, these two approaches combined to foster a kind of Hegelian view of language as a historical product that yet could be traced to a single origin, perhaps even a divine endowment, an ultimate purpose, a definitively human nature. Saussure, by contrast, concerned himself with language as a present-tense system of signs. According to Saussure, the sign system is fundamentally "arbitrary"; the system could have been constructed otherwise, and could, if the linguistic community so determined, be changed, albeit slowly. From this premise, only parts of which were retained in the discipline of linguistics as it subsequently evolved, other thinkers in various disciplines concluded that pretty much everything that has seemed fixed, given, natural, was in fact arbitrary and could be constructed differently—the essential premise, I am contending, of theory as such.

13. Perhaps the most exciting aspect of theory was that it operated by a kind of lever principle. "Discoveries" in one field could be shoehorned into another. In this way, the linguistics of Saussure could be made the basis for "advances" in the fields of psychoanalysis, political theory, philosophy, and literary criticism. Thus Saussurean premises had a "theorizing" impact on the hitherto empirical-philosophical discourse of linguistics; and this enabled linguistics to have a theorizing impact on other disciplines, as major "theorists" in such disciplines as history and philosophy happily conceded. Literature, the most empirical of fields in some respects, the closest to the untheorized world, was, perhaps for this very reason, the most hungry for theory and the most responsive to Saussure. As Paul de Man commented, literary theory "comes into its own as the application of Saussurean linguistics to literary texts" (*Resistance to Theory* 8).

14. In institutional terms, theory was power. In everyday parlance, theory and power might be antonyms, but within the university they rapidly became synonyms. And, through its sponsorship of theory, literary study went, almost overnight, from being the feminized outcast of the institution to the power center of the humanities, which were rechristened "the human sciences" in order to group them with social science and bring them more into equivalence with the prestige and concreteness of the "hard" sciences. The prestige of theory was remarkably concrete. Theorists, especially foreigners, whose knowledge seemed different in kind as well as greater in quantity than that of natives, possessed the power of decree. Certain texts were literally required read-

ing; smeary photocopies of articles recently published or freshly translated were passed around as samizdat productions. If you knew French or knew someone who did, you could acquire the cachet that accrues to the "subject supposed to know." I remember getting a mimeo on blue paper of a partial translation of Derrida's "Structure, Sign, and Play in the Human Sciences," and the feeling of power that rumpled bundle of paper gave me, even—in fact, especially—before reading it. Barthes's *Mythologies,* de Man's "The Rhetoric of Temporality," Lacan's *Ecrits,* Kristeva's *Desire in Language,* Althusser's *Lenin and Philosophy,* Foucault's *Madness and Civilization*—if you hadn't read these, you just weren't in the game. Thus a dark luminosity spread from literature departments—or at least a favored few in possession of the right "texts" in those departments—outward.

15. Now the point is that this atmosphere of danger and charisma gave rise to the star system in the humanities: yesterday's renegade theorists are today's institutional stars. The most luminously representative American figure in this scene is surely Stanley Fish, whose career reached a point of rare transparency with a series of articles and interventions in the mid-to-late eighties on the subject of professionalism. The most interesting of these, called simply "Anti-Professionalism," argued that since academics were properly and necessarily involved in professional structures, it made no sense to pretend otherwise. Those who for whatever reason deplored the professional context of knowledge-production were simply incoherent and self-confounding on the face of it. Other messages from Fish to the universe, encouraging humanist academics to picture themselves behind the wheels of Porsches rather than pug-ugly Volvos, to think of themselves as players in the go-go atmosphere of corporate turbulence, swelling fortunes, and blockbuster mergers, further encouraged humanists, previously the most unworldly denizens of the ivory tower, to adopt a more aggressive posture, a more sharply delineated profile.

16. In one respect, Fish made a career of being against theory; as he said in the introduction to *Doing What Comes Naturally,* he was, time and time again, making "an argument in which the troubles and benefits of interpretive theory are made to disappear in the solvent of an enriched notion of practice" (ix). But this hardly does away with theory. The most aggressive and capacious claim one can make on behalf of theory is that it is not a separate activity at all, but just ordinary practice, for this claim makes theory unconscious, inescapable, and impervious to critique. No practice would be immune to such a claim, as Fish demonstrated by making identical arguments not just about literature and its interpretation but also about linguistics, psychoanalysis, political philosophy, and legal theory. A thoroughgoing pragmatist, Fish actually instantiates

many of the basic principles driving the theory revolution, including its tendency to level or erase distinctions and its ability to generate a transdisciplinary institutional power.

17. The forward thrust of the theoretical era effectively ended with the deaths of Barthes, Althusser, Lacan, de Man, and Foucault, but by then—1984, with all our Big Brothers gone!—all the elements of today's star system were in place. One of the many signs of the dominance of theory was the emergence of an academic discipline called, simply, "theory," and of various programs designed to propagate that theory. I was hired by Tulane University in 1986 as a "theorist," which was fine by me, and a year later, was given the job of inventing and then running the Program in Literary Theory, which I did from 1987 until 1993. The history of this program suggests the point I'm trying to make, and the next one as well. We got sizable and impressively engaged audiences at our hitherto sleepy university by inviting scholars who were thought to have something to say that was not just empirical but theoretical, not confined to the texts they were discussing but carrying a general import such that if you missed it, you might be history before you knew it, working in an outmoded paradigm. During those years, I invited people I considered to be established and rising stars: J. Hillis Miller, W. J. T. Mitchell, Robert Weimann, Naomi Schor, Jane Gallop, Hayden White, Judith Butler, Mary Poovey, Eve Kosofsky Sedgwick, Christopher Norris, Myra Jehlen, Martin Jay, Stanley Fish, Fredric Jameson, Walter Benn Michaels, Rodolphe Gasché, Slavoj Žižek, Homi Bhabha, and others. We missed a few and placed a few bad bets, but we hit, I think, a fair percentage of the acknowledged heavyweights. And they *were* acknowledged; their stature transcended their fields because that's the way theory worked.

18. What strikes me most forcibly about this list is that if I were running such a program today, I would probably invite the same people. Admittedly, not so many years have passed, but I can think of very few emergent stars who will, in ten years' time, replace these. There is certainly no new *generation* of stars; what we now call the "profession" is not generating stars, so that yesterday's stars remain today's, but older and fatter and generally less stellar than they used to be. (Less stellar, perhaps, but a lot more expensive. We paid $750 and coach fare for a lecture, class visit, and a faculty seminar; today, a certain few on the A team can command $5,000 plus business class for the same gig.) As in the universe, so in the university: *There are no new stars.*

19. Similar things are going on all over. In his last decade, Sir Isaiah Berlin was fond of saying that there were no more geniuses around. And indeed, if one were to go back, say, to 1968, that amazing year, one could point to Martin Luther King, James Baldwin, the Beatles, Richard Feynman, Chomsky,

Nureyev, Nabokov, Sartre, Borges. Another thirty years or so back, and you had Thomas Mann, Hemingway, Beckett, Duke Ellington, Schoenberg, Bogart, Picasso, Dietriech, Franklin Roosevelt, T. S. Eliot, James Joyce, Frank Lloyd Wright, Virginia Woolf. Peel off another thirty and you are looking at the birth of modern art, modern music, modern dance, modern poetry, modern science: Cézanne. Matisse, Degas, Picasso once again, Stravinsky, Dubois, Twain, the Wright brothers, Marie Curie, Niels Bohr, Einstein, Bertrand Russell, Freud, Thomas Edison, Nijinsky, Rockefeller—giants were walking the earth. The world today has both expanded and shrunk; people have "access" to more information, but there is, it seems, less that is truly worth thinking about, less to become fascinated by or deeply committed to. All fields of cultural or intellectual endeavor, once heroic, now consider themselves "professions." And perhaps this is the true meaning of "postmodernism."

20. The portion of the academy that I'm talking about, is, then, not alone in witnessing a certain flattening, or what Fredric Jameson called (speaking of postmodern culture) a "waning of affect." Indeed, the history of literary criticism can profitably be studied from the point of view of the fortunes of affect. Eliot, of course, scrupulously eschewed affect, thereby creating a powerful "St. Sebastian" effect of pathos and fortitude. The most powerful subsequent critics—including I. A. Richards, Erich Auerbach, Edmund Wilson, Newton Arvin, F. O. Matthiesson, Leslie Fiedler, Raymond Williams—were also those whose rich affective life could be read as the photographic negative of their immersion in the facts of textuality and history. The demiurges of the theory revolution virtually drown in affect, sometimes expressed bluntly as in Derrida or Barthes, sometimes perceptible through its repression as in Foucault or de Man. Theory actually represented the liberation of affect; but the rise of professionalism made literary study available not just to aesthetically responsive scholars but to ambitious people who understood the structure and ethos of a posttheoretical professionalism that represents the form of postmodernism prevalent in the academy today. That spirit is corporate rather than controversialist, bureaucratic rather than charismatic, consolidating rather than exploratory.

21. It would, however, be a mistake to blame the spirit of professionalism for the death of theory, for theory was in trouble from the very beginning. The most effective theoretical pedagogue, de Man, himself wrote in a late essay that theory was in fact nothing other than "the universal theory of the impossibility of theory"; "nothing can overcome the resistance to theory," he wrote, "since theory *is* itself this resistance" (*The Resistance to Theory* 19). Of course, de Man had a highly idiosyncratic view of theory as the universal solvent of

all identities, all totalizations, all "premature" thematizations, but it is interesting that, even at the acme of its institutional prestige, theory was attacking itself, issuing challenges to its own integrity. These challenges were taken up and amplified in a far less friendly and ironic spirit by those who, like Fish, Walter Benn Michaels, Stephen Knapp, Gerald Graff, and Frank Lentricchia, had no particular investment in theory's survival and in fact saw theory in a pre-Columbian spirit as an alien virus, an old-world microbe threatening the health of the indigenous peoples, their pristine pragmatism, their naive but sturdy moralism. Thus, during the past fifteen years or so, the antitheoretical reaction has flourished and ramified, and theory has been supplanted by other critical discourses that make no grand systemic claims but do often claim moral rectitude and political efficacy. The nineties have ben dominated by sex, especially homosex; by race, especially minorities; by culture, especially material culture; by performance, especially the performance of identity. The emphasis today is on the local, the particular, the concrete, the minority. Size does matter: the smaller, the better.

22. The discursive mark of the professionalized academy is the disappearance of controversy over fundamental principles and a general concentration on the cultivation of small plots of ground, little fields of specialization. There are no must-reads for a general audience. Instead, we have little in-groups cultivating their social and institutional identities and reward systems. Everybody is preaching, but only to the choir, to smaller and precommitted audiences, because nothing applies generally. I was told by an editor at one of the major presses that the largest-selling book at the MLA convention of 1997 was a book on science and Victorian culture, a fact that confirmed, he said, his suspicion that literary scholars don't buy books in literary studies, but rather books in other fields. The reason for this, I think, is that literary scholars today don't feel the need to read anything else in literary studies—they just need to write. The book on science may help them do that; the others are just competition, clogging the track.

23. The immersion in the specific and material forecloses any effort at speculative system-building and fosters an intense effort at *description*, on the presumption that criticism properly consists of an accurate rendering, an account that "gives voice," "reconstitutes," "celebrates," or "exposes." Cultural studies today is militantly empirical, with a settled preference for the material, the embodied, the visible, the localizable. The strong cultural critic today is typically, if not always, indifferent even hostile to theory. In a 1993 article entitled "Queer Performativity: Henry James's *The Art of the Novel,*" Eve Kosofsky Sedgwick asserted that "the thing I *least* want to be heard offering here is a

'theory of homosexuality.' I have none and I want none" (*GLQ: A Journal of Lesbian and Gay Studies* 1.1 [1993] 1–16; quote on 11). An even more telling sign of the antitheoretical turn in this particular field is the conclusion to Judith Butler's influential book *Gender Trouble,* a book that became influential not through its dense and rigorous readings of Freud, Foucault, Lacan, and others but largely through its *envoi,* which made a sudden pivot toward "performance" as the key to gender identity and the dubious (as many feel) resolution of the "trouble" that had constituted the book's subject up to that point. With this gesture, "queer theory" abruptly morphs into cultural studies.

24. By comparison with such classic theoretical terms as *text, form, determination, ideology, desire, value,* or *interpretation,* the very term *culture* is almost defiantly undertheorized. As Geoffrey Hartman notes in his recent book *The Fateful Question of Culture,* the term resonates with both *cult* and *agriculture,* and suggests, even in contemporary academic usages, a fascination with barbarism or archaism, a keen interest in the retrograde, as if authenticity were only to be found below radar or reconnaissance, down among the phenomena. Recently, as chair of my department, I received a job application that referred to a dissertation entitled "Cannibalizing the Victorians: Racial and Cultural Hybridity in the Brontës and Their Caribbean Rewritings." A full and eager participant in the current academic scene, I could not suppress an involuntary moan of satisfaction, and regretted all the more that the position had not, after all, been funded.

25. Sometimes, I can suppress the moan, as when, for example, theory is retained in ghostly forms as a way of legitimating studies that cannot legitimate themselves. I recently participated in a panel on the impact of cultural studies on literary study, and heard a speaker who, after making numerous judicious prefatory remarks about the importance and complexity of the interlocking questions of race, gender, class, et cetera, finally got down to the nub of the issue, her particular field of research. "White identity," she asserted, is an under-studied component of racial self-articulation; and what is particularly under-studied by the academy is the fact that whiteness is "performed" differentially. Within this general category of racial performance can be situated the further fact that some people seem not just white but super- or hyper-white. And so, the professor settled in to speak of her work, which consisted of trolling the hallways of Los Angeles high schools in search of "nerds" to observe and interview. "The issue of nerd identity," she claimed, "involves many crucial theoretical questions." A trained and credentialed sociolinguist, this professor was in a position to claim that "different identity claims are being made by saying, 'Tyotally cyool' as opposed to 'Totally cool.'" On hearing this,

my first thought, of course, was to call *Sports Illustrated* to offer the incident as a candidate for their feature, "This Week's Sign That the Apocalypse Is upon Us"; but then I reflected that the numerous theoretical issues buzzing around nerd identity, no matter how fascinating and urgent to me, would probably not interest most readers of *SI*.

26. I am not opposed to description. When criticism abandons description it stands in danger of becoming like political philosophy, which neither analyzes nor describes anything concrete at all and is thus the most corrupt of all scholarly discourses. But it is important to create, to mark, and to maintain the distinctions between description and inference, description and analysis, description and norm, description and speculation. Good criticism—that is, criticism that is judged to be good—will make the connections appear to be so tight that there seems to be almost no space between description and its others. But there must be, in the mind of the approving reader, some sense that an object is nested in the judgments or inferences that swarm around it, and that sense is produced only by description that seems to stand clear of those judgments and inferences. This is true even if the "object" in question is description, representation, or language itself, as it is in the case of a literary or philosophical text. Judgments, generalizations, theories have integrity only as generalizations from accurately described details.

27. But, I would insist, those details themselves acquire dignity and stature only in the firm embrace of some reasonable judgment, some tightly articulated general system, some powerful and suggestive theory. When the relations between description and its others are managed properly, the effect can be one of great power. When it is done poorly, when the distance between object and assessment, or description and inference, is collapsed, then the object of description has no autonomy from the mind of the critic; the reader of criticism is coerced, and the effect is one of absolute power, which, as is well known, corrupts absolutely.

28. Parenthetically, I would like to add that a collapse of distance in criticism is being accompanied and reaffirmed by a comparable collapse in the domain of teaching. If, today, one cannot theorize with the freedom of years past, neither can one deploy, in the classroom, old-style authority. It goes without saying today that one cannot claim superior wisdom or insight; one cannot intimidate; one cannot fail to befriend—in, of course, a strictly platonic sense. The only qualities valued are informality, accessibility, approachability, charm. Teaching must be easy listening. How different from my own experience! Most of my teachers, I confess, I merely tolerated, but a few earned my respect, even my fear and reverence. By these I was humbled and inspired and,

eventually, guided. All these men—I had no women teachers after ninth grade!—retired long ago, but if they were teaching today, they would be considered woefully defective; after years of low or at best erratic evaluations with a high standard deviation, they would be advised by their chairs or deans to shape up, to get with the program, to conform themselves to their students' expectations. And whatever those students expected, it would not be a scholar. Students today do not, in general, seek out and read works their professors have written; they have little sense of reputation or lack thereof. Professors are just there for them; they are not intellectuals, but graders. One inevitable consequence of the disappearance of distance in teaching is the disappearance of distance in relation between teaching and research, which, as we are constantly hearing, are virtually identical activities, with the classroom being configured as the proper audience for scholarship.

29. We need, I believe, to restore the missing space. We need, that is, to create, to mark, and to maintain the kinds of contestable and non-absolute distance—between object and description, description and inference, and even between teacher and student—that define criticism and pedagogy at their most powerful and indeed at their most dangerous. Without these distances, it is impossible to make the earth, or the student, tremble, difficult to create the conditions for critical power or inspiration.

30. Critical movements cannot arrange for their own succession, but they are capable of provoking reactions. And so we may hope that current practices might give way to a renewed attention to literature, especially to canonical literature. The big works earn their status not by their serene classicism but by their endless malleability, their generous sponsorship of an infinite number of arguments. The deepest mystery of the aesthetic text is the way in which it combines a profound indifference to its own criticism and to any utilities that are claimed for it with the keenest responsiveness to that criticism, those utilities. Stuck in the past, literature remains open to the future; it is progressive, even radical, because it includes among its energies a deep neutrality. It can provide a critique, a negative knowledge, because it has a certain monumentality, a profoundly material presence. We need to know more about all this.

31. The kind of inquiry I'm encouraging would be, first, an *inquiry*, undertaken in a spirit of passionate curiosity, a powerful desire to know and create knowledge. Theory, or the theoretical impulse, would be essential to the latter, more active desire. I am not simply urging a return to the heyday of theory. To mark the difference, we could recall one of the more widely publicized arguments of those years concerning the "literary" component of philosophy and

theory. Many construed this argument as meaning that literature had a kind of natural authority over these other discourses, but what it really means, or at least ought to mean according to me, is that no discourse is absolutely distinct from any other, and consequently that none has any predetermined priority or privilege over the others. Can we now begin to imagine a kind of dotted line between theory and literature; can we try to regard a theoretical formulation as an "example" of a literary one, or to see a conceptual statement as a clarifying instance of a statement whose native discursive home was literature?

32. I would like to cite the words of a particular hero of mine, my old teacher Robert Martin Adams, who is among the very greatest of American literary intellectuals. At the conclusion of his spacious and imposing work, *The Land and Literature of England*, Adams comments on the reluctance of modern historians to generalize, and the consequent preference for studying family groupings or short-term behavior of actual people. "Putting a single faction, or single Parliament . . . under the microscope," he says, "we can almost persuade ourselves that there are no large-scale patterns in history, and that long-term developments, if they exist, don't count for anything." But, he argues, they do and count for plenty.

> The chief trouble with atomizing history so completely is that it becomes, under these circumstances, an incomprehensible jumble of particulars of which the mind cannot form or retain a model. Schematizing it completely, on the other hand, flattens out all those living and complex particulars which really mark the behavior of men and raise the study of history above the interest of a diagram or a formula. Two simple rules of thumb (unfortunately antithetical if not contradictory) are that one must learn as much as possible of history's gritty details and incorporate them as largely as possible in a coherent vision of the past. Reconciling these two imperatives—one of which looks toward the past chiefly for its own sake, the other chiefly for the sake of our modern understanding—is the art of creative or compositional reading. Without this resilient, constructive activity, the perusal of reading lists, however long and elaborate, is mere accumulation of inert materials, a toilsome vanity. (*The Land and Literature of England: A Historical Account* [New York: Norton, 1983], 523.)

Adams stresses history, and I have emphasized theory, but the general project is the same: to attempt to think in two directions at once, to reach down and in toward a clear grasp of "gritty details" and to extend out and beyond to an understanding of the larger structures. To set the particular and the general, figures and concepts, narrative and notionality, on a flat surface, not in order to degrade or decompose them, but in order to explore what sorts of relations they might enter into absent any presumption of a natural discursive hierarchy—this would be not just to come up with new interpretations but to subject the very ideas of literature, history, and theory to new pressures and to expose each to new opportunities. Such a project would, I submit, constitute a viable and interesting agenda for the next generation, a project whose successful prosecution would make a star of anyone.

☞

If there are, among those who read this, any respondents in search of a rant, or counter-ranters in search of an occasion, they might wish to pursue several lines of attack.

1. You seem opposed to professionalism. But isn't it true that professionalism is nothing other than a necessary attempt to claim respect for academic work in a cultural climate that is indifferent if not hostile to it?

2. Why are you so attached to theory? Theory was a corruption of literary study, not, as you say, a natural or inevitable form of it. How can you advocate both theory and the aesthetic? Your employment as a "theorist," whatever that may be, suggests an ulterior motive.

3. The lines between discourses secure the integrity of all discourses. To attempt, as you suggest, to imagine a "dotted line" between discourses or to attempt to think "in two directions at once" is simply to stop thinking productively at all. Are you contending that one can think omnidirectionally, without frameworks?

4. Postmodern culture is rapidly erasing the high modernism for which you seem so curiously nostalgic, and replacing it with more democratized forms of knowing to which you seem peculiarly hostile. Where do you get off?

5. Your insistent talk of heroes and geniuses and giants suggests a politically questionable and historically retrograde vision of higher education—a vision, in fact, of education as the virtual institutionalization of *height,* with a corresponding place reserved for the lowly. Doesn't this just confirm inequality as such, and work against the true goal of education, which is to eliminate such invidious differences?

6. Your obvious distaste for new areas of scholarly inquiry implies a mind embedded, like that of most boomers, in its own glorious past. You had your day, now why don't you just give it up and clear out?

7. Your touching defense of the aesthetic echoes some of the most mystified criticism of the past century, and coordinates nicely with the "aesthetic ideology" which is now known to have caused such confusion and damage. How

can you distinguish your position from the right-wing ideologies that have allied themselves with the aesthetic?

8. Isn't your argument about the dependence of theory on "gritty particulars" actually motivated by a desire to provide a brake on the kind of utopian theorizing that constitutes the proudest tradition of left intellectualism?

9. The way in which you insistently raise challenges from the left suggests that you feel particularly fortified on this front. In fact, however, aren't you more vulnerable to attacks from the right? Isn't, for example, your corrosive irony about the "overcompensated sybarites" of the star system just a screen for a well-disguised if ill-advised populism that would, if installed in the university, destroy the very idea of merit and achievement and the respect that rightly goes with them?

10. The tone of this essay is difficult to assess, wavering as it does between massive self-assurance and a humble spirit of deference to one's betters. And you seem undecided about your attitude toward the star system. Do you really know what you're saying, or why you're saying it?

9

That Was Then, This Is Now, But What Will Be? A Dialogue between Two Generations of Professors

Donald E. Hall and Susan S. Lanser

Donald Hall: Unlike most of the dialogues collected in this volume, the following discussion reflects a shared personal history of transitions and reflects upon the experience of larger professional transitions that we, of course, share with many of our readers. The history that Sue and I have in common began in 1989 when she moved to the University of Maryland from Georgetown University just as I was beginning work on my dissertation under the direction of Deirdre David. Sue served on my dissertation committee and as placement advisor for my job searches in 1989–90 and 1990–91, and became a personal friend with whom I have remained in close contact.

There are some interesting "divides" that our discussion may reflect, examples of what might be termed "standpoint epistemology"—these include "male/female" (recognizing as well that those terms have been ascribed changing meanings over the course of time), "student/professor" (in terms of our perspectives on graduate training at Maryland), "1991/1979" (the dates of our terminal degrees, separated by a dozen years of very significant changes in literary studies and the profession, and hence my reference to them as a "generation"), "West Coast/East Coast" (my career to date has been in Los Angeles, Sue's in Washington, D.C.), and "M.A.-granting institution/Ph.D.-granting institution" (CSUN has traditionally trained faculty for the local community colleges, though a growing number of students plan to continue on to doctoral programs).

Yet as with all of the dialogues included in this collection, our "divides" are ones whose ambiguous, partial natures warrant the quotations marks around the word. Along with our co-contributors, Sue and I are encountering many of the same national trends in higher education, have had to expand our professional vocabulary to include terms such as "development," "assessment," and "strategic planning." Yet these are minor adjustments given some of the more brutal changes occurring around us, for as full-time, tenured academics, Sue and I hold positions of rare privilege in a profession increasingly dependent upon part-time, exploited labor. However it is important to add that we have not simply been "subject to" such shifts in policy; we have also held positions through which we have been able to effect changes in policy, sharing a background in university administration: Sue was chair of comparative literature at Maryland from 1990 to 1996 and I have been associate chair of English and coordinator of the Humanities Interdisciplinary Program at CSUN since 1995. We have struggled similarly to reconcile the theories (feminist/lesbigay/queer) underlying our scholarly work with our daily professional practices. Like our co-contributors, we take our work and our potential impact upon students very seriously. These and many other parallels are hardly surprising, for Sue played a key and very positive role in forming, and norming, me as a productive scholar, self-reflecting teacher, and hard-working university citizen.

And it is this process of professional formation, in response to and as a reflection of changing "norms," that will largely concern us here. A productive way, I hope, of starting our dialogue is with a few personal thoughts on the profound changes that have occurred in my life in the past ten years or so; in part these reflect larger trends in the profession, but they also reflect the inevitable ways a person's life changes in the dramatic move from studenthood to professorhood. The "divide" that separates one's graduate experience from one's new professorial life can be a dramatic one; certainly mine was, as I made a difficult move across country to a university that I had never even see (the offer came without an on-campus interview). But the geographical divide was nothing compared to that of culture: between that of a Ph.D.-granting institution whose expectations for research and teaching had become central to my professional worldview and that of my new academic home with its modest expectations (and even, among a few colleagues, fear) of the former and very high expectations of the latter (a standard 4/4 load). As a graduate student I had certainly thought carefully about my post-Ph.D. life, but had envisioned only two possibilities: a life wholly outside of the academy (the likeliest outcome, I fully understood, given the realities of the job market) or a life in the fast lane of publication, with the express goal of national prominence (and the inevitable secret hopes of academic "stardom"). What I had neither thought about nor developed strategies for was life in the very congested lanes of nonresearch university education.

In stating the above, I certainly do not wish to denigrate the good work (and very hard work) done at CSUN by my colleagues, nor do I wish to point an accusatory finger at my alma mater, for I was a very willing (and ambitious) participant in the Maryland graduate program. Indeed, Maryland's "problems" (if you can even call them that—"problematic parameters" is probably more accurate) are those of Ph.D.-granting institutions in general. Yet those parameters are still too little explored (most books about the "profession" were and are written by faculty at research institutions, of course). As much as we can talk productively in this book about our "profession," we should also recognize that there are in fact many "professions" within the larger frame, including independent scholars, employed outside of the academy, as well as individuals working at community colleges, state universities, and Ivy League institutions. How can we more effectively prepare students for careers (or just simply talk to them more honestly and knowledgeably about careers) that could take them to institutions and offices across the nation (indeed, the world) and across an enormous professional landscape?

Susan Lanser: I'm not surprised that Donald felt unprepared for the particular career that he partly chose and that partly chose him, even though by the late 1980s our discipline was acutely conscious of the "problem" of preparing graduate students for academic life. For this very consciousness was not only an effort to solve what now seems to be a chronic crisis in academic hiring but a sign of dramatic change in the very meaning of professing literature. The "professionalization" about which we now so routinely speak—whether explicitly in publications, meetings, and our ever more sophisticated departmental placement offices, or implicitly each time we discuss the "job market," identify a student's success as a "resume item," encourage her to "network" at conferences, or weigh the hiring advantages, say, of rhetoric over Renaissance—marks a dramatic shift from my own graduate education in the 1970s. Thus I fully agree that those seemingly brief dozen years separating my degree from Donald's constitute a generational shift.

Job opportunities had already begun to wane by the time I entered graduate school in 1972, and the confidence that students would get "good" academic positions had certainly begun to erode. Yet my graduate student colleagues at the University of Wisconsin—in my own field of comparative literature, in English, in the modern languages—talked about this problem only occasionally and fleetingly; mostly we discussed ideas, books, and of course our professors. Other people did sometimes ask us why we were persisting in our studies when jobs were drying up, but by and large, we simply pursued work that

we loved and for which we expected eventually to get paid. I know of no placement offices on my campus (or on other campuses) in the 1970s. For most of
us finishing graduate school, *placement* as a project and *professionalism* as a
concept did not exist.

This does not mean that everyone got hired; mine was perhaps the first generation of academics who did not automatically find positions or who found
them through more circuitous paths than usual. Nor did we fail to attend to
the same basic requisites that people emphasize today: publish, teach, win fellowships and awards, earn strong letters of recommendations, give a few papers at a few conferences. I did realize that my own job possibilities might well
be compromised by my association with the new and oppositional field of
feminist criticism, euphemized then as the more innocuous simply "women
and literature." And when I got my first tenure-track appointment, I knew that
I was very fortunate. In the spring of 1980, a few months after I'd accepted that
first job, I happened to give a paper at the National Women's Studies Association's second annual meeting, held at Indiana University. In introducing me,
the panel chair mentioned that I would soon be teaching at Georgetown University. To my acute embarrassment, from some corner of the audience was
heard an audible though not nameable sound, followed by the words, "So *she*
got the Georgetown job!"

That comment resonated with more intensity then than it would carry now.
Feminist criticism was just beginning to achieve academic legitimacy in 1979–
80,[1] and only four or five tenure-track positions on the MLA job list, as I recall, mentioned women writers as a desirable specialty. The "Georgetown job"
had been one of only two in the country (the other being San Diego State
University) to insist on women and literature as a primary field. The word
"feminist" appeared nowhere in the job list that year, and it astonishes me that
my graduate students today, who see feminist scholarship as an excellent "resume item," are shocked when I tell them that in the 1970s feminist critics were
more likely to be fired than hired.

This major shift in the critical paradigm is surely one crucial difference between Donald's graduate school world and mine. I served as placement officer
when Donald was "on the market," and one of my central tasks was to help
students create the very best "credentials" and the very best presentation of
those credentials that they could provide. This too was nothing I or my co-
horts were trained to do. My own professors had assured us that if we did good
work, jobs would come to us. Yet two or three of them did take the trouble to
discourage me from writing a dissertation on women because such a choice
would "narrow" me. (That one could proclaim oneself a specialist in gay or

lesbian studies was unthinkable, and although there were several lesbian "items" on my curriculum vitae when I applied for jobs in 1979, I was nervous about them and hoped that they would be offset by my straighter publications and papers. That my three children had been mentioned by one of my referees—a professor emerita unfamiliar with new guidelines for keeping personal life out of recommendations—did, I know in retrospect, get me off the lesbian hook at at least one university that sought to hire me—though not at another one where, since I had already received another job offer, I decided to risk coming out.)

That I ended up writing both on women writers and on narrative theory was never a conscious "professional" choice but a function of my interest. (Believing as I do in the materiality of interest, I would, however, not dream of claiming that no unconscious professional motives were at work.) And I certainly owe my success at getting MLA job interviews and subsequent campus visits to the fact that Princeton had already accepted the first—and more theoretical—half of my dissertation as what became *The Narrative Act.* So although my friends and I were not "professionalized" or "placed," we did for the most part learn to do the right academic thing. But we learned it mostly without great anxiety.

As I contemplate the field of literary studies then and now with particular reference to graduate education, it is this absence of anxiety that makes the seventies seem so privileged a time. Although—and also *because*—feminist studies were then marginal, oppositional, and activist, my graduate years were a time of relative independence, discovery, and outspokenness. Today—and this seems to me a change even from Donald's generation, when he and his peers at Maryland quite regularly challenged professors, argued with departmental policies, and *claimed* an education in Adrienne Rich's sense of the word—I much more frequently encounter graduate students and graduate student cultures marked by worry, caution, second-guessing, strategic moves— in short, a *muted* culture carefully weighing the choice of fields and advisors, more hesitant both individually and collectively to advocate on their own behalf lest they lose a competitive TA-ship or a mentor's support. And this even in a department that enfranchises graduate students in a number of visible ways and that might seem to faculty to be rather egalitarian—but for that crucial rock-bottom difference of power which limits and undermines all structures and gestures of equality, vital as these remain. As a senior professor, I must then also accept that I too am One for whom the graduate student (or untenured professor) Other might well be watching out.

No one prepared me at all for this either, or for the subtle changes in both consciousness and circumstance attendant on reaching a position of undeniable and, on the current job scene, literally extra-ordinary privilege. This place of privilege has two consequences—respectively about power and about responsibility, of which it would be churlish to complain, but which are as difficult as they are critical for me to absorb. The first means remembering that my casual words may have a much more lasting impact than I intend, that my voice may be larger than I recognize or feel, that however close I become to my students or junior colleagues, we are separated for now by the crevice of institutional power. To forget or deny this difference of privilege is, I strongly believe, to risk abusing it.

The second consequence for which no one prepared me is that of seniority as a state of stress. Full-professorhood is often imagined as the achievement that ends professional stress forever, and to a certain extent this is quite true: I now can make certain decisions without being fired or risking rank. At the same time, reaching the state of Professor has meant both an exponential increase in the nature and complexity of the service work the academy asks of me, and a greater sense of obligation to take it on. For a real responsibility to lead and mentor does, I believe, fall precisely upon those of us who are freed from certain hurdles and who are expert in the workings of the academy. Such an increase in professional demands for which no one has prepared me comes, in my case and that of many of my friends, at a time when what we most long to do, as our lives move well past that halfway mark which makes every commitment of time, every choice of focus, a precious one, is what most of us still call, with good material reason, *our own work*. What I long for is the contemplative scholarly practice that graduate school in the 1970s allowed me: wandering the library stacks to see what I might discover (there were of course no on-line catalogues), letting work take *its* time—as necessarily it did in the absence of computers on which to write and so easily rewrite my drafts. I would of course not trade my computer for the IBM Selectric that was a technological marvel in the 1970s, and Web databases not only save time but enable miraculous discoveries. And I know that in the good old days there were lots of people in less than ideal jobs (though far fewer in part-time and non-tenure-track ones). But I think we need to recognize that the corporate model of academic professionalization, generated partly but not exclusively by the downsizing of tenured faculties, has had very major costs.

How, then, might we think about graduate education across these generational differences? How can we accommodate the structures of power that will continue to dominate the academy and inevitably complicate the mentoring of graduate students, especially when, as Donald said, many of our students will not be able to move into the same kinds of jobs that we in Ph.D.-granting departments hold and hold up as ideals, while also providing an environment that prepares students for a multiplicity of rewarding careers? How can we recognize the need for "professionalization" while fostering the bedrock love of the work itself that brought most of us into the profession, the love that is surely the necessary wellspring of our best teaching and writing and with which in my generation "professionalization" did not dramatically interfere? What kind of education, what kinds of individual and departmental relationships between graduate students and faculty, can usher both students and the profession into the new century? And how do our critical and theoretical positions intersect with our generational and institutional differences to foster or inhibit intellectual and professional growth?

Donald Hall: Sue makes some very important points that I would like to acknowledge as I turn now to reflecting on the present and future course of graduate education. Sue's recounting of her own experiences is illuminating, even as some of the experiences themselves seem so very, very foreign to me. It's not that our trajectories (from relative contentment to feeling overwhelmed, and then the reverse, let us say) have been in truly opposite directions, but certainly they have been quite different. Simply put, I never knew that early sense of optimism and freedom from anxiety. As a grad student, I fretted and strategized constantly: about whom to put on my dissertation committee, about how to deal with department politics and factions that were clearly affecting grad students' chances of finishing their degrees in a timely manner, about how to get published, about how to hit the right tone in an interview so that I seemed confident but not arrogant. In some ways, grad school was the worst (or at least most stressful) time of my life.

But in recounting the above I don't mean to imply that I was either wholly powerless or successfully self-empowering. In her opening sentence Sue says that the career that I have today is one that I "partly chose and that partly chose" me. Of course she is right. But tellingly, my initial, "gut-level" response to her statement was a defensive one. My first thought was, "*I* didn't choose this career path; after all, I only had one job offer in 1991 and was warned explicitly by a mentor (not Sue), 'Don't turn it down, Donald!'" But, of course, I did make choices all along, even beyond the ones mentioned above. I could have said "no" to the job, choosing a nonacademic career or taking my chances the following year (though thank god I didn't because the number of jobs declined precipitously), or I could have made any number of choices earlier or later that would have led to a professional life different from the stressful and strategy-filled one that I continue to lead today (though in most ways I love the life I lead today—both on my CSUN job and in my broader professional work—and am very glad I made the choices that I did). In any case, I have clearly chosen to complicate my career at a teaching-intensive institution with a personally motivated, research-institution publishing agenda.

And it is this real, though highly compromised and complicated, fact of "agency" that often gets lost in recent discussions of graduate students, graduate education, and new professional careers. Not for a moment would I deny the grotesque power differentials at work in graduate school—the ones that Sue points out are even more apparent today than just a few years ago—and in the exploitation of adjuncts and freeway flyers that is prevalent and increasing. But unless we are going to suspend the theoretical faculties that most of us have worked very hard to cultivate in our applied criticism and return to a pre-Foucauldian, top-down model of power that recognizes *only* abject victimhood among those who are (in very real senses, of course) "oppressed," then we must recognize that graduate students and young academics exercise power all of the time and are not simply victims of senior professors and administrators. Sue mentioned the anxious strategizing of students today concerning TA-ships and letters of recommendation (which did occur ten years ago too—we talked all the time about what would happen to us if we pissed off Professor X by challenging his ideas in class); certainly this and the other forms of strategizing I mention above represent small but real examples of power deployment. But there are many other ways that students can deploy power and certainly can make responsible and personally fulfilling decisions about their lives and careers. And we, the professoriate, can do much more than we do today to make this possible; we do not have to be perceived or act invariably as the "One" against which the "Other" must strategize.

What might it mean or require practically to create an environment in which such agency can be more fully exercised? In the current job market and era of complex professional transitions, it demands first and foremost a rigorous honesty about and awareness of current professional conditions. We must be able to state to our classes and advisees clearly, often, and without hesitation that *no student should start a Ph.D. program expecting a tenure-track job*. That is a hard statement to make and to accept, but make it and accept it we must. It is unconscionable that professors today still mislead students into thinking that they can expect or should hold out high hopes for a tenure-track position, but some continue to do so. I see and hear it (and hear about it) in my own department, at professional conferences, and in other interactions with colleagues and students. Some professors mislead students out of ignorance and some out of vanity ("of course, *my* students will find jobs"). I'm sure very few, if any, do so out of malice, but even having the best of intentions doesn't get one off of the hook of responsibility.

I'll never forget an incident that occurred during the spring that I did get my job. I was chatting in the hall of the English building with a Maryland professor and administrator who first congratulated me on the position I had accepted, but who then said, with great seriousness, "Well, frankly, it's about time you found a job; I was beginning to wonder what was *wrong* with you." I still cannot think of that comment without my stomach churning. What a thoughtless statement to make, one that cut me to the core and that demonstrated his ignorance of a market in which fewer than half of all applicants found jobs. And that level of ignorance is still prevalent; I see it in colleagues today who urge students to go on to Ph.D. programs because they "have what it takes" to be professors and can, with some certainty, look forward to an exciting and rewarding career in the academy, and I hear of it from graduate student friends who tell of mentors nervously avoiding a discussion of the job market except to say hastily "oh, of course, of course, it should all work out." Well, of course, it *should* work out, but it probably *won't* work out. To my mind, such commentary provides evidence of incompetence and dereliction of duty that requires active redressing through faculty training seminars, through rigorous peer review processes, and even, potentially, through administrative action. This is a harsh response, I know, but I believe that we who hold tenured academic positions bear tremendous responsibilities that come with the privilege, one of which is being as aware as possible of the current professional climate and its norms, and not stating as "fact" something that became illusion years ago. Relaying erroneous information is never acceptable for an educator, and if we consider the relaying of professional information a real and even requisite part of the content of our courses and advising sessions, as I believe we must, then wild inaccuracy and incompetence in that role clearly should be subject to the harshest evaluation.

But being a student also carries with it serious responsibilities, one of the most important of which is *listening carefully.* If professorial egos have an occasional (or more than occasional) impact upon a discussion of the expectations a student should bring to a graduate education, then certainly student egos also have an impact. "I will be the exception" is not an uncommon personal response to hearing about hard professional facts, because so many graduate students have been exceptions before in their lives; they have been the smartest, the hardest-working, the most successful, and the most rewarded in their families and peer groups. But as many of us know well, the smartest and hardest-working among new Ph.D.s do not all get jobs. *Indeed, two-thirds or more will never get a tenure-track academic job.* And it is that hard, ugly fact that not only must we communicate to students but that they must also hear and believe.

But does this mean, practically, that our Ph.D. programs should be forcibly downsized and some eliminated? I'm of the camp that believes "no," and speak again from personal experience. Even when I faced unemployment in the academy (it was a long winter and early spring before the CSUN job offer came through in late March), I was still happy that I was about to receive a Ph.D. I had always wanted the degree and a graduate education even if I had to find a non-academic job afterwards. And this is what I try to make crystal clear (and not once but many, many times) to students contemplating doctoral work: *do it only if you want to do it for its own sake and for the intangible rewards you will receive while doing it (and, indeed, afterwards) in spite of the fact that you will find yourself working, most likely, outside of the academy.* And in writing this I want to point out that a particularly serious responsibility falls on those of us teaching at M.A.- and B.A.-granting institutions, for students here, contemplating doctoral work, often have only our advice and information upon which to base a decision; they do not have easy access to student colleagues already enrolled in Ph.D. programs. We must give such students as much information as possible *before* they start doctoral work. If I send a student to Sue for doctoral study, that student should already understand what the likely employment outcome of her or his course of study will be, as well as the expenses involved in pursuing a Ph.D. For students finishing an M.A. and looking for an appropriate Ph.D. program, part of the decision-making process must involve a consideration of finances; even if one acknowledges the realities of the academic job market, should one really saddle oneself with tens of thousands of dollars of debt (or much more) in the process of getting a degree that is not directly marketable? I urge students to weigh the long-term financial implications of attending a very expensive private university versus those of attending a lower-cost state university, and to think carefully about the cost of living in certain cities or towns and how they can "make do" (or not) on their stipend or TA salary. Most (I hope) hear and think carefully about all of this and make a decision accordingly; some, I know, do not.

Of course, none of the above erases all of the real and continuing anxieties of being a graduate student or of encountering the power differentials within a doctoral program. Always, a few students will find tenure-track jobs (and not always the best and brightest students), which will work to inflate some of their peers' hopes. Furthermore, there are necessary steps that students must take to increase their chances of finding such a job, if they plan to compete for one. That process of "professionalization," in spite of fairly dim hopes of actually securing employment, further complicates any sense of a placid "let come what may" attitude that a student may start with; it can feed a partially or covertly held belief that "if I just do x, y, and z, surely a job will come," even though a tenure-track job probably will not come. But it is also important to recognize that so many of the concretes of such "professionalization"—presenting conference papers, publishing articles, working toward a book contract, teaching a variety of courses—can be, indeed should be, enjoyed for their own reward and performative payoff rather than only for the job that they may lead to. While it is extraordinarily difficult to maintain such an attitude and awareness, I return to one of my comments above: the graduate students in question *are* some of the brightest and most socially aware individuals around. If, as I suggest, professors must be held accountable for their level of professional awareness, then students should be expected to turn their intelligence and awareness to the text of their own lives and futures.

And the "honesty" that I call for above extends beyond being forthright concerning the chances of landing a tenure-track job; it also (to pick up on a concern that I expressed earlier) includes a more open and inclusive discussion of the wide variety of academic jobs and institutions awaiting those students who do secure some form of employment in the profession. All doctoral programs should sponsor in-house panel discussions by "freeway flyers" and adjuncts as part of rigorous professional studies courses or workshops. No one's interests are served (in a morally responsible way) by simply covering up the reality of most academic lives. Departments should also bring back to campus employed graduates of their own programs who have secured jobs at a variety of institutions, including community colleges and teaching-centered universities, as well as research institutions. As I said above, I did not know and had little way of knowing what life would be like at a university with a standard four-course-per-semester teaching load. Former graduate students from the University of Maryland had secured and were dealing with such jobs, but they had never been invited back to campus to speak with the next generation of doctoral students. Employed graduates of programs are a very rich resource that universities rarely utilize. Any student reading this book who does not know what it means in terms of quality of daily life and research to prepare four different courses simultaneously and grade as many as a thousand papers and exams in a semester is being shortchanged by her or his own graduate program and advisor. And few of those advisors, employed at Ph.D.-granting institutions with much lower teaching loads, are well qualified to speak about the lives of those of us employed at nonresearch institutions. Again, these are blunt words, but if we are going to speak bluntly to students then we should also be able to speak bluntly among ourselves. Only by dealing so forthrightly with employment issues can we even begin to cultivate and treat with proper respect the decision-making power of our graduate and undergraduate students.

On a personal note (and with the risk of sounding *very* West Coast), these issues are ones that I continue to struggle with constantly, as I create and re-create my professional and personal life through daily actions. All of us do, whether we are tenured professors, adjunct instructors, or graduate students. My recognition of such lived and potentially disruptable "performance" grows (as you might guess) out of my reading and use of theory; Judith Butler has taught me something about how I can live my life, not just how I can approach a text on a page. Yet as Butler's critics are quick to point out, it is extraordinarily difficult to break old patterns, and certainly we face great challenges in working to "normalize" expanded responsibilities for professional awareness and forthright truth-telling about future job prospects. And it is perhaps most difficult of all not to become defensive, as I admitted at the beginning of this installment. But our responsibility to our students must take priority here, even as we recognize our responsibility for our own choices and lives. Otherwise we as professors and students are simply locked in rigid positions of self-willed blindness, ego, and antagonism.

Susan Lanser: I'm sobered by Donald's response, and on two counts. First, I see that my own position as professor has led me to erase or minimize the agency of students that Donald rightly emphasizes. That means that I've in fact enacted the very power move that I said graduate students had to beware of. So even though Donald is right to remind me that not all professors are alike, it is, as so many of us acknowledge in our scholarship, remarkably easier to inhabit one's position than to think outside or beyond it, and perhaps most difficult to inhabit the position of the Other with whom one is positionally engaged in a deeply ordinary, daily—and hence potentially unconsidered—way.

Second, and considerably more important than my breast-beating recognition of myopia, I'm especially sobered by Donald's passionate plea for truth in educating—for giving graduate students a realistic picture of their career possibilities. I ask myself to what extent I have indeed been as brutally honest with my students as Donald seems to want, whether this honesty is really all that Donald cracks it up to be, and what effects it would have on my students' work. My own practice has been to take what feels like a realistic and optimistic approach. (I know some would consider realism and optimism mutually exclusive, but I'm willing to understand optimism within a Sisyphean framework, recognizing the difficulty of the task and even the likelihood of failure, while still daring to hope, and considering the effort worthwhile). This means that I acknowledge to students that it's hard to get an academic job, that there aren't enough of them to go around to those worthy of receiving them, and that the academy is not a meritocracy (merit being usually necessary but not sufficient, and much of the job search being no more within the student's control than a roll of dice). And so I counsel students to do work they love, in whatever field of interest, since work that is not informed by passion usually falls short; to do that work as superbly, with as much originality, careful scholarship, attentiveness, and lucidity as possible; to understand what a new Ph.D.'s dossier should look like in order be "competitive"; and to prepare themselves for several years on "the market," which means understanding the job search not as a one-time experience but as a phase in a career, one that can be a productive transition between student and professional life. Although at some point I usually do talk with individual students about "alternative" careers—a perhaps troubling term whose potential I will explore below—on the whole my advising has been oriented toward a range of jobs *within* the academy—and, I now see, a fairly narrow range at that.

Indeed, in my mind and thus surely also in my rhetoric, I'm actually preparing students for a very narrow band of jobs, from the equivalent of my own at a large research university to posts in four-year liberal arts colleges or branches of state universities, preferably not in departments with four-course-per-semester teaching loads unless the student clearly doesn't want to do writing or research. And even as I counsel students to be realistic, I thus implicitly define their success (and indeed my own success as their mentor) equally narrowly.

Not only do I not prepare my Ph.D. students for positions shaped quite differently from these, but until quite recently I did not usually introduce the subject of nonfaculty careers. But I would argue, in response to Donald's call for a different kind of mentoring, that within the hierarchical system already at work in the culture of literature Ph.D. education, my reluctance to *initiate* individual discussions about other careers is logical and possibly salutary. First of all, those who evaluate Ph.D.-granting departments, from prospective students to outside reviewers to deans, usually define a department's success by only two factors—the national reputation of its faculty and its record of placement in "good" tenure-track jobs. As long as we (individually and collectively) think the best thing (or worse, the only really good thing) that can happen to our students is to get this one kind of job, then to encourage an *individual* student to aspire differently is to suggest that she or he is not likely to make the grade. In the current climate, in other words, a student to whom I introduce the idea of a different job path may feel I don't think she's "good enough" to "compete"—and I fear that her sense of herself, and indeed her work, will suffer accordingly. After all, writing a dissertation is a terrible challenge, a process that tests in a new way one's knowledge, training, authority, stamina, social life, and mental health. This is true not only because one learns how to write a book by writing one, but because the writer has usually not yet received any kind of academic imprimatur and indeed has lost the short-term boost of A's in seminars in pursuit of deferred rewards. Especially in the face of professional uncertainty, the dissertation is surely the most stressful and lonely, if sometimes also the most exhilarating, project of one's early career. Would one stay with such a daunting task if one were not imagining oneself holding the only job in the humanities for which a dissertation (not a degree, but a *dissertation*) is both requisite and immediately usable? Surely part of what sustains the process is the image of that dissertation between hard covers, or the image of the colleagues who will shower the book with praise and invite one to partake in the high life of the academy.

Is the answer, then, a graduate curriculum in which the dissertation is not the focal point? A few years ago, a *New York Times Magazine* essay argued for a three-year, dissertation-free Ph.D. I remember thinking there was some merit to that proposal but ultimately resisting it as too thin to train people with the depth of knowledge and height of competence for which I still think the Ph.D. ought to stand. And a two-track system in the present climate would inevitably construct a hierarchy of degree programs; how would one make the nondissertation Ph.D. the equivalent in time and rigor to the standard (there I go already) one? The question, then, is whether it makes sense to keep the same structure of graduate training when for the foreseeable future fewer than half our students will find the kind of jobs for which we are currently training them.

Although I may be speaking from conservatism, I'd like to think we can reshape the degree without changing it entirely. But reconfiguring both graduate expectations and graduate education requires first and foremost a change not simply of curriculum or of rhetoric but of professional and departmental consciousness. (Our values about careers cannot be feigned; we who dwell in language know the undertruth will out.) This is perhaps where the word "alternative" in that now euphemistic phrase "alternative careers" might be put to new, if temporary, use. The *OED* helps us: its seventh definition of the term, with usages dating only from 1970, is "purporting to represent a prefer-able or equally acceptable alternative to that in general use or sanctioned by the establishment, as *alternative* (i.e. non-nuclear) *energy, medicine, radio,* etc." From my perspective as a lesbian and a feminist, a Jew, and a critic of "the es-tablishment," alternative careers so defined are the *best* careers.

How might we learn to think about alternative choices in this sense for per-sons holding the Ph.D. in literature? I would begin by taking a humbling, large-world perspective on the work we ourselves do. Most of the nonacademics I know—and the academics outside literary studies—would have no interest in reading most of my work even if they could understand it, and though I pride myself on fairly nonspecialized and lucid prose, I concede that many of them could not. I spend much of my time in a small town in Maine, where I have many friends and neighbors whom I would call intellectuals, some of whom have high school educations and others of whom have graduate degrees. They have been delighted when I have offered, say, a presentation on Jane Austen at the local library, or led a book group for adolescents, or even shared informally my research on sapphism in the eighteenth century. But in the context of our shared concerns and our community's pressing problems, most of what I do "for a living" is of very limited relevance. Were I to leave my academic posi-tion and work, for example, toward improving the state of Maine's abysmal record of sending students to college (almost at the bottom in the nation de-spite very high test scores), I know that I would be doing far more direct good than I am doing in my present job. I am then forced to recognize that I choose my present profession because I so deeply love the work—the particular *kind* of reading, writing, and teaching—that it enables me to do.

The perspective of these friends offers a corrective lens through which I can see my own work and my respectable heft of publications as narrow, fairly esoteric, and relatively insignificant. And indeed the academy does reward the esoteric: our tenure systems, for example, penalize people for producing "trade" rather than "scholarly" books, and the scholarship so many of us con-sider "political" is often seriously attenuated both by the discourse we speak and by the venues in which we speak it. (I recall here both Terry Eagleton's admonition in *Literary Theory: An Introduction* that one is "allowed" to write almost anything in academic discourse because the discourse itself so limits what can be said, and bell hooks's words in "Education as the Practice of Free-dom" about how little that is genuinely challenging goes on in a college class-room, no matter how "radical" the teacher thinks s/he is. We might, then, re-call a humbling definition of "academic" in the *OED* and in such phrases as

"This discussion is academic, anyway": the academic as inconsequential, impractical, of little use.)

I make these comments not to disparage our profession but to encourage the necessary distance, and hence dialectical thinking, by which we might reach a genuinely egalitarian attitude toward academic and public (as in "of or for the people") work. And this, I think, requires remembering that there is another—alternative—view of the academy that may make it a lesser (or certainly not better) choice if one is deeply committed to repairing the world. Nor is the academy the only place where one can use one's Ph.D. training. Graduate education enables people to work intelligently and knowledgeably in a range of careers for which both a knowledge of cultures present and past, of literature and of critical theory, and the *skills* of inquiry, research, writing, teaching, and informed critical thinking are necessary and appropriate.

And as the word "alternative" reminds us, there are more than individual careers at stake. Last summer in the *New Yorker,* David Remnick paid posthumous tribute to Alfred Kazin as one of the exemplary readers as well as writers of our time. In a world where, as Remnick notes, reading is becoming a threatened activity, Kazin believed that the greatest wisdom, the best of human understanding, could be found in books. Surely most of us in literary studies would agree. But Remnick also remarks that Kazin's own books would probably not earn him a Ph.D. these days, because they are not "scholarly" enough within present disciplinary paradigms. At a time of desperate need for public intellectuals—people who can articulate a thoughtful, historically and culturally informed vision in popular forums from the Internet and television to books, newspapers, and magazines, Ph.D. training not only could but should encourage students and faculty to engage in such important work.

One way to begin would be to allow students to write dissertations that, like Kazin's books, follow alternative models, and to understand that this does not mean producing shoddy work. One of the finest dissertations for which I have had the privilege to serve as a reader was written by a brilliant high school teacher, Mary Alice Delia, who was pursuing a Ph.D. with the intention of enhancing rather than abandoning her position in secondary education. She took quickly to postmodern thought, attended the Dartmouth School of Criticism and Theory in 1989, and under the superb mentorship of Susan Handelman completed in 1991 a rhetorically and conceptually innovative dissertation, "Killer English: Postmodern Theory and the High School Classroom," in which she explores mutually constitutive practices of literary theory and pedagogy in a spectrum of sites from the graduate seminar to the high school English classroom to the academic conference, theorizing education deeply and broadly, from its largest implications to its most practical details. Sadly, Mary Alice Delia died of leukemia before she finished turning her dissertation into a published book. But "Killer English"—the name students gave to her senior courses—models the kind of dissertation that both meets the highest of academic standards and makes a genuine difference outside as well as within the academy; certainly it has taught me more about teaching both theory and literature than anything else I have read, and I have always encouraged the teaching assistants I supervise to read it. The dissertation succeeds so stunningly in part because it blends conventional prose with letters, reports of classroom incidents, and conversational dialogues. Fortunately Delia's mentor encouraged her to take rhetorical as well as ideological risks with this dissertation, and I recall that Handelman thought this was safe precisely because Delia was not seeking an academic post in which she might be penalized for her "alternative" methodology. I hope the day will come when such a caveat will not be warranted.

I have learned also that for some students—sometimes the best students—an academic position is simply not politically or psychically suitable, that another career is "alternative" in the best of ways. Marian Urquilla, one of the most brilliant students with whom I have ever worked and the recipient of an extremely competitive national graduate fellowship, chose to leave the academy without completing her Ph.D. A committed social activist with extraordinary credentials in the public sphere, who even during graduate school held positions of national leadership and consultancies almost never given to persons at her age and stage while also editing a volume of conference papers and teaching brilliantly, Urquilla came to realize that as much as she loved and excelled at her studies, the parameters of academic practice worked against her commitments to deep social change. She is now director of the innovative Columbia Heights–Shaw Family Support Cooperative, which is engaged in major systemic reform and in galvanizing community leadership in Washington, D.C., neighborhoods. She has told me how much her training in critical theory and postcolonial studies has enabled her present work, allowing her to take—and to teach—a complex view of the dynamics of class, gender, race, and power in which the delivery of social services operates, giving her ways both of addressing practical difficulties and of analyzing, with an eye toward altering, the systems and ideologies from which those difficulties arise and the practices that maintain them. In other words, her graduate education was in no sense superfluous to her work; rather, it enables her to do that work differently, with a greater capability both to change the organization and to teach others new ways of perceiving what they experienced.

Clearly the work I am doing in the world is not more valuable than the work in which Marian Urquilla is engaged. This is not to denigrate what I do but to put it in its place as one among many options for people educated in literary and cultural studies. Another exceptional student whom I mentored is working in electronic publishing, while another, who authored a prize-winning published essay, opted for family reasons to remain in the Washington area and teach in a private high school. Dissertating students often hold temporary positions that might well equip them for similar permanent posts: internships in organizations of higher education, curriculum consulting in high schools, teaching in business environments. A myriad of public and indeed academic institutions, from museums and libraries to governmental and nonprofit organizations to university centers and offices, explicitly seek persons holding the Ph.D. These organizations recognize that academic training is training in both content and skills, and that these skills are transferable beyond the candidate's specific field. After all, many of us even within the academy are called upon to teach "out of" our fields, and a good number of us change those fields over the course of a long career.

In thinking about graduate training, I have thus found it useful to consider the ways in which the field of folklore studies is already addressing some of these concerns. Folklore had once been an academic field at the Ph.D. level, while training M.A. students for "public folklore" jobs in such venues as museums and state agencies. For a number of years, however, the field has recognized the wider applicability of folklore training for a multitude of careers in settings as unexpected as hospitals and businesses. This recognition, together with the realities of academic placement in this as in other fields, has pointed to the Ph.D. as the desired degree for many kinds of folklore positions in the public sector as well as in the academy. Both the American Folklore Society and graduate departments of folklore have been shaping their training, their career advising, and their professional organizations and journals around multiple careers, recognizing the important interrelationships among those careers and the equality of these options in relation to the field's larger goals of producing knowledge and furthering understanding, shaping the future and preserving the past. The integration of different career objectives into both graduate training and professional organizations has not been without tension, and certainly vestiges of academic superiority linger on, but public-sector folklorists are now galvanizing the field and helping to reimagine its academic vision and practices. And the expanded conception of careers in folk-lore has generated not only new options for folklorists but new recognitions of their expertise; it may not be coincidental that recent heads of both the National Endowment for the Humanities (William Ferris) and the National Endowment for the Arts (Bill Ivey) hold folklore degrees.[2]

I would suggest that we in literary studies look to fields like folklore that have been grappling with these issues much longer than we have and that have already taken practical steps to address them. First, we might consider in our graduate education the equivalent of an internship or fieldwork component that would give students experience in some venue outside college teaching: work in undergraduate advising, administrative assistance in a research center, internship at a national organization such as the NEH or the AACU, teaching in a high school, working on the staff of a journal, museum, library, or publishing company, undertaking field research in another country, producing a video, developing Web sites. Those students who might opt for, or end up in, tenure-track positions will surely gain valuable expertise and understanding from such experiences. Second, we can open up the dissertation to a wider notion of intellectual production, giving graduate students opportunities to enter a range of influential public positions from editorships to directorships—or even, to the envy of many of us within the academy, to make writing a full-time career. Third, we can make sure our students are not only taught a wide range of skills—bibliographic, critical-analytical, compositional, pedagogical, textual, et cetera—but taught to recognize these skills as transferable and "marketable" attributes that can be adapted across fields and disciplines.

Any practical changes we implement, however, will succeed only to the extent that they accompany—that is, either instigate or culminate in—a change in our own consciousness. Several years ago, Jamaica Kincaid published a scathing critique of colonialism and tourism called A Small Place. Perhaps because I live part-time in Maine, which is itself a kind of colonized environment in which I am implicated, the book affected me profoundly. I teach it in my "Problems in Comparative Studies" seminars as well as in some undergraduate courses, and it generated the framework for an essay on comparative literature that I wrote a few years ago.[3] Kincaid's book is also about what it means to live in a small, isolated, and insulated community. People living in a small place, she says, have a distorted vision, a confused sense of time, of history, of causality. Those of us who see the same people each year at professional meetings, or meet new colleagues who often turn out to be friends of friends, know what a small place the academy really is. Let us acknowledge that it is also a small place in perhaps less cheering ways, and let us recognize that Kincaid could only see her small place clearly by leaving it. Let us, then, listen to those who are outside the academy as we consider its future, and the future of our students, in the next century.

Donald Hall: To Sue's eloquent words, I wish to add just a few more thoughts specific to and growing out of my own life and career. Sue writes near the end of her first contribution to this dialogue that "many of our students will not be able to move into the same kinds of jobs that we in Ph.D.-granting departments hold and hold up as ideals." As she goes on to explore, some will end up in the publishing industry, others in governmental or public agency work, and many others at schools like mine: where one teaches, advises, or administers relentlessly and does the best one can with one's research and one's larger professional life. And as Sue notes, the common practice is for graduate and placement advisors to avoid even mentioning teaching-intensive positions "unless the student clearly doesn't want to do writing or research." The result of this silence is the shock I felt when I entered my new career. But if a general silence reigns on the realities of life "under" a 4/4 teaching load, at least some of the responsibility for breaking it rests with those of us who have the experiential background to speak with authority on the topic. And this sense of responsibility prods me to return to this topic in the few paragraphs I have remaining to me here. While certainly I cannot do full justice to the complexities of teaching-intensive positions in a page or two, I nevertheless would like to speak briefly and honestly to graduate students contemplating the possibility of a career at a nonresearch institution, and also to new faculty members at such institutions, about what they need to bring with them to their new jobs if they "*want to do writing or research,*" as I and many of my colleagues do.

For those graduate students who work several academic jobs while in school, perhaps holding a TA-ship and one or more part-time positions simultaneously or, as was the case with me, who teach a couple of classes and hold a library job in order to pay the bills, it will be relatively easy to imagine what a position at a school with a 4/4 load entails. It means relying upon some of the most important skills acquired during graduate school, ones that were often practiced in the writing of a daily schedule as much as in the writing of a dissertation: carefully compartmentalizing and prioritizing the various demands upon one's time and attention, making precise judgments about how many hours or minutes to devote to a specific task (and then calling it "done"), and setting realistic daily and weekly goals. A research and professional life *is* possible while grading hundreds of papers and preparing three or four different classes, but it must exist in the interstices of the day and the academic calendar: in an hour or two in the morning before leaving for classes, on a Saturday reserved and utilized especially for it (with grading put off until the evening or until Sunday, twelve hours of which will then be filled with paper marking and course prep), on holidays and during summers, when every moment must be used efficiently. And in domestic situations where caring for dependent children or seniors is also a factor, these negotiations and scheduling challenges can be even more difficult than I have encountered in my own experience. But in talking with colleagues whose domestic situations are even more complex than mine, we all agree that our ongoing struggle to construct rich professional, as well as personal, lives can be exhausting, but it can also be exhilarating, if you thrive on such challenges, as some of us do. But if you don't (and only you know best what your past experiences in such situations have been), it can be paralyzing and embittering, unless you adjust your goals accordingly.

And this is where honesty is, again, crucial. New and would-be faculty members should be told and should know their institution's precise expectations for tenure and promotion—whether it is a book, half a dozen articles, or some combination of professional activity and publication—and know as well that the path of minimal but adequate scholarly achievement is always a viable one (and is probably the most reasonable one given the many other institutional demands on their time). Faculty at teaching-intensive institutions must set *achievable* goals for themselves—an article a year or an edited collection such as this one in two or three years. If they set unreasonable goals and then fail to reach them, they may not risk institutional approbation (if their goals exceed all institutional expectations anyway), but they will perhaps encounter something far, far worse: a personal feeling of failure that is difficult to recover from. We must be honest with ourselves about our own capacities, the demands on our time (caring for families, children, and dependents), and our own work habits before articulating a private research and professional agenda. We can have an active writing and research life with a 4/4 teaching load, but it cannot be precisely the same as those of our graduate school mentors or others with half our teaching responsibilities (and for a more detailed discussion of these matters, see my essay "Professional Life and Death under a 4/4 Teaching Load" published in MLA's *Profession 1999*).

In many respects, my years in graduate school did prepare me very well for my career at CSUN. My hectic daily schedule now is practically the same as my hectic daily schedule then. My worries over article placements and book contracts then were the same that I encounter now. The negotiations with committee members and administrators that I had to engage in then trained me to deal with committees and administrators in my life today. But now, the big difference is that I get paid adequately for what I do, and I have a secure position at an institution that values my work. The local successes—teaching awards, congratulations of colleagues, and positive evaluations by peers and administrators—augment my modest professional achievements. Indeed, most careers are always largely local even if they do have national aspects. And at a nonresearch institution, the local support and rewards for even very modest achievements can be extraordinarily positive.

Thus as we think about and envision differently graduate education and the careers it prepares students for, let us not forget that there is no one path to success and happiness, as Sue reminds us beautifully above, that the values and worldviews of one's Ph.D. program are neither "real" in any metaphysical sense nor even "real" across the landscape of our multifaceted profession. Indeed, to understand, move beyond, and in some fundamental way forgive the inevitable limitations of my own graduate training, while at the same time appreciating fully all that it did do for me, has been essential to my growth as a professional and my sense of contentment with what my career currently entails and what it may hold in the future. And thus to Sue and others—Deirdre David, Martha Smith, and Neil Fraistat, as well as Dottie Bozman and Rhoda Hyde, who employed me at McKeldin Library—I owe an immense and ever deepening debt, one that can only be offset through my own mentoring of students and young colleagues.

NOTES

1. It is after the publication and hoopla around Sandra Gilbert and Susan Gubar's *The Madwoman in the Attic* (New Haven: Yale University Press, 1979), I [SL] believe, that feminist criticism became academically legitimate. See my essay "Feminist Literary Criticism: How Feminist? How Literary? How Critical?" *NWSA Journal* 3:1 (1991), 3–19.

2. I [SL] thank my partner Jo Radner, current president of the American Folklore Society, for my knowledge and understanding of this field.

3. See Lanser, "Compared to What? Global Feminism, Comparatism, and the Master's Tools," in *Borderwork: Feminist Engagements with Comparative Literature*, ed. Margaret Higonnet (Ithaca: Cornell University Press, 1994), 280–300.

10

A Changing Profession:
Interviews with J. Hillis Miller, Herbert
Lindenberger, Sandra Gilbert, Bonnie
Zimmerman, Nellie McKay, and Elaine Marks

Donald E. Hall

VITAL DIVERSITY: AN INTERVIEW WITH J. HILLIS MILLER

Donald Hall: As you know from our correspondence leading up to this interview, the general impulse behind the *Professions* project is to explore possibilities for dialogue in an academic environment that is often strife-torn and seems constructed around a model of polemics and reaction, rather than productive communication. I hope this interview will illuminate some of your perspectives on our collective work in literary and cultural studies, as it has changed over the course of your career, as well as what you may hope and fear concerning the future of this work. So I would like to begin by asking you to reflect on that truly remarkable career; what would you point to as perhaps the most positive, and alternately, most troubling of the changes that you have seen?

J. Hillis Miller: I read this question and thought to myself that you probably are not interviewing anyone else who started college before the New Criticism. I went to Oberlin College at a time when the New Criticism was just beginning to be institutionalized. My wife-to-be had a course at Oberlin a year or two later in which Brooks and Warren was used, but when I began, the required freshman course at Oberlin was still one on Victorian prose. It was considered vital that all Oberlin students read Newman's *Idea of a University* and Matthew Arnold on the function of criticism, so as to acquire a common idea about a "humanistic" inheritance that was specifically English; we didn't read any United States writers. That was a standard university course in American colleges and universities before the New Criticism, and it clearly functioned as a form of indoctrination. The textbook we used—I remember it well—was edited by a man named Frank Aydelotte, a professor at Princeton who had been a Rhodes scholar. His book presented the ideal of British culture—worldwide British culture—for which the Rhodes scholarship stood.

Of course, that was replaced by the New Criticism, which was a brilliant heuristic move. At the time it was institutionalized you had all these students coming back from World War II, who got into college through the GI Bill. They were a new kind of student, middle-class and working-class, who for the first time had the money to go to college and were far less aware of cultural history than the people who used to go. Now my first instinct would have been wrong, which would have been to give them a crash course in the Western tradition. That is not what Brooks and Warren did. Just the reverse. They said, "Don't worry that you don't know anything. Let's just look at the poem itself." Of course today everybody knows that the politics of these New Critics was southern agrarian conservative and that most of them were church-going Christians. On the other hand, it seems to me the effect of the New Criticism was really quite different from that politics. Inadvertently those New Critics invented a methodology of reading that was language oriented, that could be applied to anything, and that detached literature from biography and history. So you can blame the New Critics for separating literature from its context and for creating an instrument that could be used to interpret movies, newspapers, and other texts. And it even had as its background something like a scientific methodology. Instead of the impressionistic criticism of the older sort—where you could say that this poem makes me feel good or bad without evidence— the New Critics said that you had to cite evidence. That tool had long-lasting effects in making later developments like structuralism, which is even more overtly a pseudoscientific approach, more acceptable. It also corresponded, in spite of the authors of the New Criticism, to what was happening in the United States at the time, which was a breakdown of the presumption of universal consensus. Of course, I don't think that New Criticism or later developments like deconstruction caused this breakdown (as deconstruction's detractors often say). Instead they were a response to the breakdown and were attempts to account for it. The appeal of deconstruction and structuralism is that they help people to understand something that has already happened.

You ask about what I would point to as the most positive and alternately the most troubling of these changes. I think the most positive thing about the changes I just mentioned is that they have corresponded to a genuine commitment on the part of most people who have participated in them, a commitment that is the real vitality of our profession. These are all people who have loved literature, have wanted to explain it and teach it, to transfer it to the people, and to understand its role in society. A tremendous amount not only of intellectual but also ethical and political vitality lies behind much of this work. This for me explains and justifies the shift now to what is called "cultural studies." We are in the presence today of professors in departments of English who are the first generation of scholars who were brought up with television and cinema and pop music. It is not that they don't love literature, it is that they have also been decisively influenced by these other forms. It is natural that they should want to study them, to study film and popular music and culture in general.

The one thing I find troubling about some of these changes might be considered a reflection of my own biases and sense of vocation. I went into the study of literature in the middle of my sophomore year at Oberlin. I was a physics major but realized that what I really wanted to do was to study poems and novels, that they were what I cared about. Incidentally, this was a choice I thought meant a commitment to poverty, but one that I wanted to do so much that I would give up a money-making career as a scientist. I remember I had many conversations with my wife-to-be, and she would always say "Oh, I'll go live with you in a little cottage somewhere." [laughs] It was all very idealistic.

Why did I make that shift to the study of literature? I was fascinated by the strangeness of the works of literature, that is to say, their unaccountability, their peculiarity. As I read a work of Tennyson, I would say to myself, how could anyone use words in this very peculiar way? That need to explain was to some degree a scientific transfer. You might say it came out of a motivation similar to that of an astrophysicist who gets data from a quasar and says, "This is very peculiar, there is more energy coming out of this body than a million suns—how could this be?" And the astrophysicist goes on to hypothesize that it must be a black hole even though he can't see one. The discoveries of science go by way of discovering peculiarities. The same thing has always seemed to me to be the case for literature. What interests me is the strangeness of the work, the way it doesn't fit historical generalizations about a period, nor does it fit what other critics, no matter how learned they are, say about it.

That peculiarity lies in details that are not accounted for by generalizations you make—about Victorian novels, for instance. You could say generally Victorian novels use omniscient or first person narrators, et cetera, and that they tend to be multiplotted. These are true generalizations, and the formal features are fundamental to the ways those novels make meaning. On the other hand, what is really interesting about these novels is exposed when you set Trollope against George Eliot, both of whom use the same conventions, but whose other assumptions are extremely different, for example about the way one mind can know another mind. It is those differences that interest me. Therefore what is most troubling for me in the changes that are taking place now is that in the urgency that lies behind cultural studies and its intent to account for literature and other cultural forms in terms of large-scale historical conditionings of a period, those peculiarities are sometimes lost and that the habit of needing to do what I would call close reading, paying attention to the details, no longer seems to be so necessary. In particular, I am thinking of essays in cultural studies which either make no citations at all or simply summarize the plot and describe the characters. That's what people did before the New Criticism. It is this loss of concern for detail and attention to peculiarity that I find troubling.

Another anxiety I have about cultural studies, in spite of my admiration for the intellectual energy and commitment such studies have generated, is the way a disquieting circularity sometimes characterizes it. The categories of gender, class, race, and ethnic or national identity are posited as constructed features of a given culture and then, behold! they are discovered in the works that are claimed to be determined by that cultural context. Those works, however, are presupposed as important evidence about the gender, class, race, and ethnic or nationalist assumptions of that culture. An example is the way the novels of Anthony Trollope are praised for representing so accurately Victorian class and gender relations, while the historical studies that establish what those relations were draw in part from Trollope's novels as primary evidence. This is having it both ways with a vengeance. This means that some assertions in cultural studies are not open to disproof, though they tend to claim a quasi-scientific validity. Another way to put this is to say that such assertions are performative, not constative. Whether or not they are felicitous or infelicitous performatives, whether or not they "work" and are a way of doing things with words, is another question. A proponent of cultural studies might reply that formalist, rhetorical, or "intrinsic" readings are subject to a similar circularity, since meanings are projected into the words on the page that are then claimed to be objectively there, in the words. I reply that formalist readings are at least more open to being tested, for example by appeal to rhetorical terms that are traditional and relatively neutral ideologically. (Note that I say "relatively"!) Intrinsic readings are much closer to the scientific ideal that demands that false hypotheses can be tested and shown to be false. You cannot make words mean absolutely anything you like, whereas categories like gender, class, and race are constructed and ideological, by the cultural studies scholars' own account of them. A full investigation of this contrast would require many pages of careful discrimination. It would involve putting in question the more or less direct causal link that is presumed in one way or another in most cultural studies to bind a work to its cultural "context."

Nevertheless, in spite of my reservations and anxieties about cultural studies I greatly respect the energy that goes into them. I would only urge that they be made methodologically more sophisticated. I favor institutionalizing cultural studies in a more serious way than we have done so far. This would mean establishing standards of provability and asking what sort of training one needs to do such work. This might, for instance, include training in anthropology. We may need new protocols and requirements, such as the linguistic ones that are taken for granted in anthropology. In that discipline if you want to do fieldwork in a given country you have to learn the language. Our youngest daughter has a Ph.D. in South Asian anthropology. Before conducting her re-search in Nepal she studied with a Nepalese family to learn the language. In cultural studies within the humanities, however, it hasn't become taken for granted that if you want to work, for example, with African Anglophone lit-erature, it would be good idea to learn the original African languages of some of the writers. There are also rules in anthropology about the use of human subjects, about getting signed permissions from them, et cetera. We don't usu-ally do that in the humanities even though more and more of what we do in-volves human subjects. Some people to whom I talk become quite anxious when I suggest that cultural studies should be institutionalized in this way. They don't like the social science model, suggesting that it is complicit with unjust power relationships, imperialism, and so on. This may sometimes be true, but it is also something that anthropologists have been self-conscious about for years now and have elaborate procedures to resist.

Let me say a word now about what you began with, about the polemical side of our present situation. I certainly agree that it is contentious. This may come from the urgency I mentioned earlier. On the other hand, here at the Univer-sity of California at Irvine, at least, people with very different opinions are able to dwell amicably together and respect each other's opinions. This situation may be a model for the larger professional dialogue that you want. I agree it is a model that is very difficult to embody and institutionalize, not only because of people's sense of commitment and urgency, but also because the tradition that I and most of us in the profession were brought up on says that if you talk long enough, eventually you will come to consensus—it is the Habermasian model. Consensus rarely occurs, however, without doing violence to some of the positions that people started out with. I don't see why consensus should necessarily be the goal. What I favor instead is a Lyotardian model, rather than a Habermasian one, a community that is one of dissensus. This model recognizes that groups must have cooperation with each other within an institutional setting, but that they may have critical methods and goals that are fundamentally incompatible with each other. After all, in much of our scholarly and professional work, we don't finally come to agree. Nevertheless, a situation of dissensus goes against the ethos that we have been brought up with, the assumption that we ought to continue talking until we all agree or the assumption that at some point the majority will finally make a decision. I would argue that a minority group that is good at what it is doing ought to be allowed to have its place in a department or in a profession in which there is great diversity, and in which professors and students have goals with particular and very different positions, vocations, and commitments or ways of doing things, ones that they, I would hope, do with their whole heart. All these individuals could reside amicably within the same department, if each is courteous and respectful of those people who hold positions with which he or she disagrees. That does not mean that forceful argument should not occur, but that this disagreement need not have consensus as its horizon.

Donald Hall: But how does that "dissensus" dovetail with the necessity of finding something like a common voice to represent departmental or university interests to administrators, stakeholders, donors, or governmental entities?

J. Hillis Miller: That is often a problem. I believe, nevertheless, that we can go to legislators or administrators and say our department is "vitally diverse," that we don't try to do everything, but that we have groups within the department which do many important different things, and that we provide students, both undergraduate and graduate, with a critical mass of teachers within each group who support one another. In a similar way a department of biology might say, "We don't do everything in the field of biology but we have great strength in four or five different subfields of biology, and they fit together." It is never going to be absolutely neat—you will always have some people who are working alone, but at least as a model the notion of diverse research and teaching groups makes sense.

I also believe you need to defend what it is you do in relationship to your geographical location and the makeup of your student population. So, for instance, a research university on the edge of the Pacific Rim, with an undergraduate body that is over half Asian American, like the University of California at Irvine, has the possibility of being distinctive in doing something in that specific context. Of course, this doesn't mean that we should stop teaching Shakespeare or Chaucer or doing European comparative literature. Nevertheless, we have a great opportunity to become distinctive in doing Pacific Rim Anglophone literature, or even world Anglophone literature—Australia, New Zealand, Anglophone literatures of East Asia. This would also go along with the orientation of my university in science and social science areas as they look toward the Pacific Rim. I think such an orientation would make sense to the people to whom we are accountable.

Donald Hall: To talk a bit more about this notion of the "vital diversity" of our profession, I would like to turn to one of the arenas in which that vitality is explored and expressed. As a past president of the Modern Language Association, what are your thoughts on the successes and challenges of that organization as a representative body and as an arena for productive dialogue?

J. Hillis Miller: The MLA has gone through enormous transformations since I first had anything to do with it. These mirror the changes I was discussing earlier. When I was first a member of the executive council of the MLA in the 1960s it consisted exclusively of men. They were, moreover, men of a particular sort: "heads" (as they were called) of midwestern or western state universities. By the time I got off the executive council a few years later, the membership had diversified to include, among others, a nontenured woman. This change happened almost overnight. Though in principle there always could be nominations from the floor of the MLA's annual members' meetings, it just didn't happen. It was an "old boys" network. The "old boys" were the only ones nominated and were always elected without dissent at the meeting. Certain politically active people in the late sixties recognized that you could take over the executive council of the MLA very easily, just by having enough people at the election meeting who would nominate somebody else and raise their hands to vote. That "take-over" was a good thing. Today it is hard to believe that the MLA was the way it was, that the officers were almost all male, all of a certain kind, all representing a certain kind of institutional structure. The old boys network was also the way in which people got jobs. In those days a professor at Wisconsin would call his old teacher or friend at Harvard, Yale, or Princeton, and ask "whom do you recommend that we hire?" The person he called would name one or two people, his own students, of course. These would be interviewed at the MLA, and one would get the job. That was the way I got my job at Johns Hopkins. I remember I was interviewed under a potted palm in a Boston hotel. Incidentally, I almost lost the job because I was reading

Faulkner at the time. The job was in Victorian literature, and I made the mistake of telling the interviewer that I was also greatly interested in Faulkner. I discovered that my interviewer was one of those men who didn't believe that there was such a thing as American Literature. He would say about Emily Dickinson's works, "those little things aren't poems!" But I did get the job. That was simply the way it was done in those days and it was wrong. There was essentially little competition. Now all that is different, partly at least through the efforts of the MLA.

Of course that is not the only way that the MLA has changed. Every year there is an article in the newspaper that makes fun of the apparent craziness of some of the presentations, but I think that representing somewhat wild diversity is just the point of the annual MLA meetings. Again, members have done the right thing. If there are enough people interested, they request a panel on a given topic. The MLA has decided that its job is to reflect the diverse interests of MLA membership rather than to try to determine them.

Part of the MLA's work now is in assembling accurate statistics about enrollments in English department courses and foreign language courses, about employment prospects for graduate students, and about shifts to part-time and adjunct labor. Those statistics are unsettling, to say the least. The enrollment in French courses between 1991 and 1997 went down 25 percent. German went down 28 percent. The rise in the use of adjunct and part-time instructors is tremendous. Less than half of new Ph.D.s in English literature and literatures in other modern languages get tenure-track jobs. The MLA has at least tried to tell the truth about that forcefully. I'm an instructor of graduate students myself. I look at these wonderfully dedicated, bright, and talented young people. When I realize that only about one in three will get a tenure-track job, I find that highly distressing. This is not theoretical distress; it comes from having students who are doing wonderful work, whom I know and admire, who have a strong commitment to our profession, but who are not getting jobs. Or getting badly paid part-time or non-tenure-track work, without proper benefits, without any voice in their departments.

One thing that stands out for me is that it is not necessarily the best people, at least in my judgment, who get jobs. There are so many candidates now for every job, that any one candidate who is really original and who might become distinguished—who has a particular and unique way of doing things—may be perceived as a threat by somebody on the hiring committee or in the department where the job is sought. If you've got a situation where there is almost always the possibility of finding somebody that nobody objects to, then the people who are original or a little rough around the edges, and who might therefore offend somebody, tend not to get jobs at all. These are among the best students and often the ones with real senses of vocation.

Donald Hall: Do you warn students away from graduate school?

J. Hillis Miller: What I say now is you had better look at the facts and go to graduate school only if it is what you really want to do and with the understanding that it may have to be an end in itself. That was the case for me. If I had been told that I would get a Ph.D. in English and still not get a job, I would have done it anyway. Then I would have done something else. Today, especially, getting a Ph.D. in English is simply not a wise thing to do if you are doing it just for a job.

My advice to graduate students is simple: Don't do something just because it is fashionable or because you think you might get a job if you do it. Do something that you really want to do. Your dissertation requires several years out of your life. If you are doing something that you can't do with your whole heart and with a sense of commitment to it, it is going to be painfully difficult, and you won't even do it well. On the other hand, you can take advantage of the fact that you are marginally supported for a few years (with at least enough income to live and eat on) and do research that you really want to do.

Nevertheless, we must talk more to our students about other things that you can do with the Ph.D. in English or other languages. Most of us are bad at that right now. One of the faults of graduate instruction in English departments is that professors give their students the idea that there is only one honorable thing to do with a Ph.D. and that is teach at a university. All three of my children have Ph.D.s or doctorates. One has a doctorate in education from Columbia Teachers College. She is the only one doing anything directly related to her degree. Our son has a Ph.D. in medieval English from UCLA and is teaching reading to grade school children. Sally, the anthropologist, while she was finishing her dissertation, started saying that she didn't want to go into "academics"—and I could tell by the way her lip curled when she said "academics" that the jig was up with that. She is now a wholesaler of organic foods in Toronto. Now you could say that it isn't at all clear why a wholesaler of organic food needs a Ph.D. in South Asian anthropology, but in many ways that training prepared her very well for dealing with and understanding people. I think the people who hired her are proud to say that they have a Ph.D. from Cornell working for them. Alternate careers is something that the MLA has started paying some attention to, but we are not very good at it yet, partly because we don't know what the alternatives are. For a Ph.D. in English, however, there are all sorts of alternatives—here in the LA area, in communications and media, for instance. These professions have links to many of the things we do in graduate programs.

Of course much of the current employment problem stems from funding and resource problems that we have in universities. What we do in literary and cultural studies programs is not well understood by the scientists who, for the most part, run research universities today. Some of them secretly, or not so secretly, think that what goes on in the humanities simply doesn't matter. That is one of the things we have benefited from in the past. Because the humanities don't matter anyway, they assume any changes that we make in the curriculum don't really matter either. The shift to cultural studies and the changes in the kinds of appointments we are making, which strike me as radical changes in the curriculum, have not caused much fuss among administrators, perhaps because they don't care. I may be exaggerating this a little bit, because certainly those scientists aren't stupid, even in humanistic areas. Many them read literature and have a broad sense of culture, but they tend to rely upon publications like the *New York Review of Books* for their information. In other words they only have a journalistic understanding of what goes on in the humanities, or what ought to go on in the humanities. It is very hard to talk them out of that. This can be illustrated by an anecdote about an experience I had when a Nobel Prize–winning economist came to lecture at UCI. There was a reception for the economist and a group of scientists including the distinguished guest approached me and said, "Oh, we're glad to see you; we were just talking about you and deconstruction; we know all about it." I said, "That's interesting, how did you find out about deconstruction?" They said they had read about it in the *New York Review of Books*. When I told them that really was not the best place to learn about deconstruction because it is notorious for its bias and misunderstanding on the topic, they reacted with genuine surprise, asking "Oh, what should we read then?" I suggested the works of Jacques Derrida, de Man, even my own books, which are not all that difficult to read. They looked amazed by the suggestion that in order to make up their minds about something like deconstruction it might be necessary to do some primary reading, and that the *New York Review of Books* is not exactly an authority in the field. It is as though I said to them, "I know all about genetics; I read the *Scientific American*." They would quite rightly say "You're an idiot if you think that gives you authoritative knowledge." The difference is that *Scientific American* is not ignorantly hostile to genetics. We have to face this misinformation about what we do. As I said earlier, we need to communicate better to others what our department's strengths are and just what we do in teaching and research.

Donald Hall: There was a wonderful phrase that you used in an article in *Profession* a couple of years ago in which you say what we in literary and cultural studies do best is to create and explore the "ungoverned" and "ungovernable." To find a way to explain that to "governments" as well as to administrators is an enormous challenge. Any final thoughts on how to meet that challenge?

J. Hillis Miller: There is a parallel with what goes on in the sciences. I read *Wired* magazine and Nicholas Negroponte, a professor at MIT, said in a column in *Wired* a couple of years ago that corporations should exploit the potentials of universities. Certain kinds of research in the sciences are by definition wasteful—especially really cutting edge research—which corporations and R&D corporate laboratories can't do, because they have to ensure a payoff for clients and stockholders. Universities have another type of client—students— that justify their existence. They give students degrees and prepare them for jobs in the real world. Therefore you can have wild and imaginative research conducted in a university that includes collections of people who cut across departments and fields, and who have really bright imaginative ideas, maybe only one out of a hundred of which will pay off. Negroponte says the university is the place for that kind of innovative thinking and research. Such "wasteful" research is necessary to society and has an absolute economic value, as well as a spiritual and cultural value. We know one of the payoffs of the huge cold war research funding of universities was the things that were invented under that kind of pressure—space capsules, forms of miniaturization, et cetera— which turned out to have enormous social uses. The same can be said in a somewhat different way for teaching and research in the humanities. What we produce and what we should be paid to produce are original ideas, original readings of works that no one has done before. That for me, I might say in passing, was the value of the seminars of Paul de Man that I went to at Yale, and the value now of Derrida's seminars I attend here at Irvine. The important use to me of those seminars is not the theoretical/conceptual side, as you might think, but the fact that they always had or have surprising things to say about the texts they read, things that I wouldn't know or anticipate ahead of time, even if I know the works well. An example would be some brilliant segments of Derrida's recent seminars on Melville's "Bartleby, the Scrivener" and Proust's *Recherche.* I recognize Derrida is an exceptional case. Nevertheless that is what we should try our best to do and the sort of thing we must try to defend to the powers that be. This is the best response to the people who think that tenure ought to be abolished. Some of the most creative and innovative people would be fired. You would have fewer new ideas.

You might say we need institutional setups—in our profession and in our universities—in which every potential Derrida that comes along can flourish.

PROBLEM SOLVING: AN INTERVIEW WITH HERBERT LINDENBERGER

Donald Hall: Let me ask first for a few general impressions concerning how the profession has changed over the course of your career.

Herbert Lindenberger: I started TA-ing in 1951, so I'm just hitting the half-century mark in my career. And obviously there have been many changes, but I think the first thing one has to do is accept the fact that in any kind of career there are going to be incredible changes over the course of time. In some the technological changes are so powerful that your career ends early, and certainly that hasn't been the case yet in our field. And I never even think of changes as being for the "better" or "worse," which is something I often see afflicting others. You have a lot of people in my age bracket, and even younger than I, who are unhappy because they feel the profession has been "betrayed" by younger people. But that has always been the case. When a new critical mode comes in, it displaces the old one, and people often deal with their discontent simply by demonizing the young or the old. That was certainly the case when I was young. I was in one of the first departments doing comparative litera-ture. It was actually housed within an English department, one of the first that had become New Critical. Robert Heilman came in the late forties to head the English department at the University of Washington, and I started in 1950. As an undergraduate I had read a lot of New Critical essays, so I was prepared for this approach. But there was a whole faction of unhappy older professors; they didn't like it, they felt themselves marginalized, and most of them were not allowed to teach graduate courses, because they belonged to the older histori-cal school (what we then called the philological method). So early on I wit-nessed the sort of situation one has today. The big difference between then and now is that then there were only two critical modes in the United States that were clashing with one another: the philological mode (which had variants of course) and the New Critical mode (which too had its variants). Now there are multiple modes which clash with one another. Critical modes have prolif-erated incredibly in the last twenty-five years.

Donald Hall: And many of those are based on identity positions, which can certainly heighten the sense of loyalty to and, at the same time, defensiveness concerning those modes.

Herbert Lindenberger: You are right: when they have to do with identity, there is a special edge to it, but on the other hand, you were always expected to be loyal to the group to which you belonged, the one that was going to further your career. People have always worked in groups in this profession, though I've felt uneasy with that because I hate to be manipulated by other people. So I've resisted and remained a loner. The pressure to conform is powerful and unfortunate; you are often made to feel that you are betraying somebody if you move in your own direction.

Donald Hall: It certainly stifles innovation.

Herbert Lindenberger: It does, and some of those critical modes based on identity are already old hat, and the people practicing them may not even realize it; it is just too difficult for them to extricate themselves. I once was interviewed (this was in the 1960s and was the only job that I interviewed for and wasn't offered) at a big midwestern university and as I was introduced to the various people there, someone said "oh so and so belongs to the New Humanism," and "so and so made his name" doing this or that, and some of these modes had died out years before, but here you saw all of these people still identified with them and they weren't publishing anymore. It was pathetic; you saw the ghosts of old ideas, and people were tied to them for life.

Donald Hall: And no doubt training graduate students in that same old mode.

Herbert Lindenberger: Oh, yes.

Donald Hall: But even if certain professional dynamics have remained fairly consistent over the years, do you see any significant differences between young academics at the beginning of their careers today and their senior colleagues at the beginning of their own careers, in terms of their senses of professional "selves"?

Herbert Lindenberger: Let me take an economic point of view here, because with a half century in this profession, I really think one can make correlations between the job market and the way people see themselves. When I went on the job market in 1953, you didn't go to the MLA. It was the "old boys" network, and I was placed by my department chair at the University of Washington. It was a big state school and most people were not getting good jobs, in fact most were not getting jobs at all. I had decided that I would probably end up in law school after finishing my degree. But then a good job fell into my lap, at the University of California, Riverside, the first year it opened. They wanted someone in comparative literature because they thought that I would be what my new employer called a "utility infielder," somebody who could teach German, freshman English, and all kinds of literature courses. The job market was so bad, I felt lucky to have anything. And I remember that a fellow graduate student asked me "is this a regular (tenure-track) job?" And I said, "I'm afraid to ask." I had no idea if I would be back the next year. It took me about two months to get the nerve to ask my boss, the head of the Division of Humanities, "Do I get to come back next year?" And he said "oh, of course," and I actually stayed there for twelve years. The economic situation was such that I felt myself lucky to have anything, and it seemed so precarious that I feared the job would blow away if I said something. Then the situation gradually changed in the late fifties, and people developed quite different professional selves along about 1958/59. Even beginners started talking confidently. People knew that even if they didn't make tenure, there were lots of other jobs out there. Their sense of a professional self was tied to that, I think. And then beginning around 1970, it went in the other direction, and I watched this awful thing happen, as people who had entered the profession with total self-confidence suddenly found themselves having a hard time getting tenure. You saw people in the seventies with Ph.D.s and six years of teaching literature applying to law schools. Some who were starting graduate work in that climate actually went into it the way I did, thinking, well, I might as well enjoy my education while I'm doing it because I may or may not end up in the profession. But a lot of people, vast numbers of graduate students, dropped out because of this feeling of hopelessness during the seventies.

Donald Hall: So what you are saying is that the level of anxiety that seems pervasive today among graduate students and young assistant professors is more a reversion to type.

Herbert Lindenberger: It is what I remember from the early 1950s and from the seventies; it was really bad for about fifteen years, from the early seventies through the mid-eighties, and then a new confidence came, though the market never got back to what it was in the sixties. Still, it got a lot better than it had been, and the reason people gained confidence was that demographics were very much in their favor, and they knew there would be a lot of retirements and that would result in many new jobs. So even if things were not terrific by the late eighties, they were going to get increasingly better and that would make tenure easier and so on. And then something totally unexpected happened: yes there were lots of retirements, and yes there were lots of new students, but colleges had become corporatized, they were using business school manuals to make decisions about how they treated personnel, and they realized that having people as part-timers or adjuncts was economically more viable than using long-term employees (and it certainly *is* economically more viable, and educationally also disastrous).

I try to talk to students today about all of this. I tell them to enter this with a sense of adventurousness, for you don't know where you are going to end up. You may not have an academic job or you may have one that you don't really want; you may end up doing the kind of teaching that you did not foresee yourself doing. You might also end up becoming an expert in rhetoric and composition and not doing much literature teaching. Or you might choose to go to law school. And it won't necessarily be the brightest person who gets the job that you most want, it is a matter of many factors coming together. So one can't predict these things; you just have to see your life as an adventure, a narrative, whose high points, climax, and denouement you have no way of predicting. It might even be a postmodern narrative without any high points or resolution at all.

Donald Hall: This leads to a topic that I wanted to ask you about, namely, the size of graduate programs given the current job market. In your opinion, should those who run doctoral programs deny students access to programs "for their own good," even if they are fully informed and still wish to pursue a Ph.D., or do we provide them with as much information as possible and then maintain relatively large doctoral programs, if the demand is there, even though few graduates may secure jobs in the academy?

Herbert Lindenberger: Well, you know you are talking to someone who has strong feelings about this. This was a big debate in the MLA's Committee on Professional Employment, and the head of the committee, Sandra Gilbert, who is a close friend, disagrees with me and gives very good reasons for her position. She has had wonderful experiences at UC Davis with older students who do not really expect to get academic jobs and for whom graduate school is an enriching experience. I tend to disagree with that as a model. The two departments I deal with, English and comparative literature, as long as I have been at Stanford, have taken in very few people, no more than we think are likely to get jobs. In English we have had between three hundred and six hundred applicants a year, and we average ten or twelve new people per year. In comp.

lit. we will take three or four people out of (the most we've ever had) one hundred or so applicants. The chances of any one person getting in are minute. That doesn't mean that all those who enter pan out. It also doesn't mean that those whom we have refused might not be very successful. Some of these had poor undergraduate records, and some didn't know how to write an application. But ours is the same model as that of many professional schools: MBA programs at the top schools and medical programs. My feeling is that the resources of a university are limited. Staging a graduate program, especially a Ph.D. program, is an extremely expensive undertaking if you do it right. If you think of the library holdings and all of the support facilities, the personal attention that you are supposed to give, it is a huge investment. The Ph.D. is such a big commitment financially in every way for a faculty that it should only be undertaken by relatively few places.

But I also know that the university system (not just in literature but in all fields) operates on cheap labor, especially in the big state schools. They do it in the sciences to get lab help, and they recruit large numbers of graduate students for that reason. The same things happen in literature and language because of the need to staff classes in freshman composition and beginning languages. This is a system that is economically, not intellectually, motivated. And that is unfortunate, for it takes advantage of the romantic desire of young people to emulate their mentors. If students are at all intellectually inclined, with a deep commitment to ideas, at the undergraduate level those students will probably entertain the idea of an academic career, because they have had little exposure to other careers except perhaps for their parents' careers (and often they are in rebellion against those very careers). Their idea of a role model is their favorite undergraduate teacher. That was true of me; that's what pushed me into academia. You would like to be doing precisely that thing your teachers are doing, without realizing that there are many more possibilities out there and that you might be better, or at least just as good, at some of these other things. There's no way of knowing because you're not shaped fully at that point. And yet this economically motivated system opens the doors to all of those people to enter Ph.D. programs whether or not there is a job for them later on. If I could legislate these things, I would say that we should go back to the same number of programs that we had thirty or forty years ago before they started proliferating.

And let me add here that a lot of the motivation for keeping graduate programs big comes from within departments because professors want to teach graduate students (though I only give one graduate course every two years—I happen to enjoy teaching undergraduate students). So part of the responsibility for the present situation lies with the professors, as well as the administration. The latter wants cheap labor, and professors don't want to teach beginning courses. This has created an evil system: not that the people doing it are themselves evil, but the system itself is evil in the effects it has on human beings. And there is yet another factor worth mentioning here and that is the desire for prestige. This often happens in the universities that are not the main state universities, Western such and such, Eastern such and such, Northern such and such . . . I remember in the California system when they made the distinction between the three levels, the community colleges, the CSU, and the UC; there was an attempt in the early sixties to allow the CSU to offer the Ph.D., and the decision was made not to, and it was a wise decision, because who needs more Ph.D. programs? I can name a different type of example, though, a Western such-and-such university, where a former student of mine is teaching. He said that they were forced to create a new Ph.D. program by the administration, which wanted it for two reasons: cheap labor and, just as importantly, prestige. "We want to put Western such-and-such on the map," they told his department.

Donald Hall: As a bad Ph.D. program?

Lindenberger: Actually the department made the best of a bad situation and decided to keep its program unique: it proposed to specialize in rhetoric and composition and train students to teach in small colleges; there are a lot of small religious schools in that area, which they thought they would have a market for. And I also know of Ph.D. programs at quite nonprestigious universities which, by targeting a market (and I'm deliberately using the language of business), actually have better placement records than some of the elite places do. So there is something to be said if you target this way, and we certainly advocate this in the CPE report—that you try to occupy a niche and seek to supply Ph.D.s of a particular kind for a particular market. But I'm still dismayed (even if they manage to place most of the people) by that motivation, of putting "Western such and such" on the map. They want the Ph.D. for their own economic reasons and for reasons of prestige. So they play with the lives of students who come into this quite naively, and that's wrong.

Donald Hall: This discussion of graduate education leads to another topic that I wished to ask you about and that is your opinion on the health and well-being of the field of comparative literature today.

Herbert Lindenberger: I'm probably one of the earliest Ph.D.s in comp. lit. in this country. Early in the twentieth century Columbia had started a program, as well as Wisconsin, plus a few others. But as a commonly awarded degree it is really relatively recent. When I did my graduate work in the early fifties, people still wondered what it meant—comparative literature, what are you comparing? But for me it just meant having the freedom to do what I wanted to do. There were no rules about it. In fact, I created the basic rules that we live by here at Stanford when I started our program in 1969. I left the chairmanship after thirteen years in 1982 and although the personnel have changed, the structure of the Ph.D. has basically remained. It is a structure that you can fill in your own way. And the structure seems to work for people, because they can be imaginative and original within it, but there still is some structure to it. And we can guarantee to other universities who are thinking of hiring someone from our program, that they know several languages and that they also have an in-depth knowledge of one national literature from the medieval to the modern. You must be able to compete with people working in a single national literature. And I think that's been one of the secrets to our success on the job market. Now some of our people have gotten interdisciplinary jobs too, even a few real comp. lit. jobs, but there are few of those. The majority of our students have taken jobs in departments in the traditional national literatures. They learn to identify themselves and teach in that national literature. So when people ask "What can I do with a comp. lit. degree? I can't get a job," I respond, "you *can* if you do it right." Our comp. lit. students have as good a job record as you can expect in a bad employment situation.

Donald Hall: Why would a German department at a small school hire someone out of a comp. lit. program with an emphasis in German rather than out of a German program; what would they see as an advantage?

Herbert Lindenberger: Well, first of all, students have to look as if they would fit into a German department, so all of our students who go into foreign literature departments have had time abroad; they know the language well. We even had one student who kept both German and Russian going at the same time, spent a year in Germany and a year in Russia, and went on the market in both; one school interviewed her in German and she took a job in Russian. She is now tenured in Russian at Columbia. And she has important things to offer in their contemporary civilization program, just as other students have important things to offer to a small college that wants someone to do German, but who is also going to teach all kinds of general education courses, which a comp. lit. degree, if it is well done, really trains them to do successfully. Because I was starting to create the program here just as the job market was turning bad, I was particularly conscious of this, and we have continued to insist that our students understand the realities of academic employment. Some of them have objected to following the structure so rigidly, but then they give in because they really want a job. And we can demonstrate that the structure works.

Donald Hall: This touches on my next question, which concerns the tension between standardization and innovation, which many of your published pieces seem to address. Do you have a perspective to offer on where the boundary between necessary common practices and new ideas lies, in our writing and our professional lives overall?

Herbert Lindenberger: You need both. It is like rules and procedures within department meetings. One may want to change the whole orientation of the department, and maybe you can do it, but you have to do it by means of rules and procedures and the ability to persuade others. And the same thing with scholarship. If you want to change the whole way that one looks at a period, you do it by means of rational argument, documentation, and the like. Which doesn't mean that you don't write in unconventional ways. I've done several quite serious pieces in dialogue form, and I've recently mounted a hypertext narrative that can be read in three different sequences. One of my books, *Saul's Fall,* can be viewed either as a piece of fiction or as a piece of critical theory, though my other books tend to be heavily annotated and use fairly standard modes of argumentation. But I had one chapter in my last book that I had the hardest time organizing until I realized that I had a whole lot of little topics, seventeen of them, so I just put them in alphabetical order with titles; actually there is an argument that goes through the whole chapter despite the unconventional form. I like to play with form, but if you are going to get someone to listen to you, you also have to do a certain amount of documentation.

Structure is very important on all levels. I like contentiousness and debate, but the best way that debate can take place is when you have institutionalized rules and procedures for debate, as you have in a parliamentary situation. I've spent more than half my years here at Stanford in the academic senate, which works in a parliamentary way. I've argued very hard on lots of issues and I was deeply involved in the Western culture debate, when we got all of that national attention, but it all took place within a context of rules and procedures. Some departments know how to operate in that way, but I think that is the exception. I was once a part of a department—at UC Riverside in 1964—when more than half of the department left in the course of a year and a half. Tenured as well as nontenured. Rules and procedures simply weren't working. It started when two paranoid people who had known each other years before found each other there again and manipulated some vulnerable assistant professors to revolt against the rest of the department. The fights we had, though they pretended to be about intellectual matters, had nothing to do with these at all. The two paranoids created an incredible situation that none of us who were present will ever forget. It is what can happen, professionally, when structure breaks down completely.

Donald Hall: This discussion of publication and professional responsibilities brings me to my last question and that concerns any advice you may have to offer to new assistant professors or others near the beginning of their careers, about priorities, about mistakes to be avoided or productive ways of juggling their responsibilities . . .

Herbert Lindenberger: I would hope that the mentoring and acculturation process in a department would be structured in such a way that it would bring the best out of each person. At Stanford we are all assigned as mentors to new assistant professors; it is formalized, we have to report to the chair, there are luncheon meetings between mentors and mentees, and so on. But even years before that I was mentoring informally, and then as now, the first thing I tell young assistant professors is that they should be doing very little, if any, administrative work. They should be advisors to students, but they should not be running time-consuming committees. We made a terrible mistake at Stanford years ago with somebody who did not get tenure (but who got a good job elsewhere), who had been made head of undergraduate studies. That was absolutely wrong. It isn't just that you need time to publish, you also need time to mature intellectually, to create your courses, to develop a scholarly point of view, to acculturate yourself, and you should only gradually move out of that into other duties. I also tell people that they should be careful about spreading themselves too thin in other ways, when they should be developing one larger project. There are some people who spend all of their time writing ten-page conference papers on the most diverse topics depending on the conference, and they never focus on any one thing. A conference paper should be a product of what you've been doing in a serious way rather than something you do to get to that particular conference. Go only to those conferences where you can build on what you have been doing anyway. I always tell people to become focused and to avoid the temptation of trying out too many different things at once.

On the other hand, I'm a person who has never been focused on any one thing for long; I get tired of an area I've been in and I move on. But what happens is that I become temporarily focused for five to ten years on something, and I immerse myself in that and don't let anything get in the way. And actually when I look back at it I see there is a certain continuity to my work, because I always ask similar types of questions and am obsessed by certain types of problems that I revisit from project to project. But you see those connections only with hindsight, of which I've accumulated a good bit at this point in my career.

NEW USES FOR OLD BOYS: AN INTERVIEW WITH SANDRA GILBERT

Donald Hall: I've asked several of my interviewees the same opening question, namely for their impressions of how our profession has changed over the course of their careers; what past challenges do you feel have been met successfully and what present ones demand immediate attention?

Sandra Gilbert: I think that's a wonderful question. This profession has changed so radically over the course of my career! I can't imagine what future I thought I had when I went to graduate school in the sixties. I had never in my life even had a professor who was a woman! As far as I knew, when you became a professor, they issued you a tweed jacket, a pipe, and a pair of extremely heavy, expensive, leather masculine shoes . . . and maybe after a while you got to have a gray beard too. (That was a sign you'd got tenure.) I'd never seen a woman academic—and not only that, at Columbia, where I was a graduate student, and where I was in many ways treated well, nobody thought I should be in graduate school! I'd married at the age of twenty, right after I had graduated from Cornell, and I had three children rather quickly. As soon as the faculty found out about my husband and children, I was a nonperson, a nonstarter. To be sure, I got to go to Columbia free because at the time my husband, Elliot Gilbert, was teaching in the college and faculty members' families didn't have to pay tuition. But I remember all too well the first party that we went to as a couple. One of my professors came over to me and asked what I was doing there. I answered that Elliot was one of his junior colleagues—at which he looked surprised and asked incredulously, "What are you doing in graduate school then?" That was what the profession was like in those days! Of course the academy itself was much smaller, much less professionalized, and considerably less diverse. So obviously I think that many of the changes that we have seen—in particular the diversification of students and faculty, the expansion of fields, the multiplication of opportunities—all of these things have been very good and extraordinarily dramatic.

The problematic part, I think, is the super- or *hyper*-professionalization we've experienced, so that, as John Guillory has noted, graduate students feel that *they* are nonpersons, nonstarters, if they come out of graduate school without having been to ten conferences and published a couple of articles. I'm sure that the good things—the multiplication of opportunities, the diversification, the expansion of the academic population—are in fact related to this whole issue of hyper-professionalization. When I started out, the profession liked to think of itself as the home of gentlemen scholars, and basically what we've seen over the last forty years has been the disappearance of the gentleman scholar and the rise of the technocratic professional. After all, there is a kind of technocracy that is associated with hyper-professionalization, specifically with the increasing centrality of theory. In contemporary academic institutions, where humanists have to be competitive with the sciences, expertise in "theory" seems to me to be a way for people to certify themselves by showing that they have access to a highly technical specialized language that is every bit as arcane as the language of the sciences.

And I suppose one has to come to terms with the fact that there probably never will be any possibility of really eliminating that kind of hyper-professionalization. What would be the alternative? A regression to the rule of the gentleman scholar and the domination of the old boys' network?

Donald Hall: What was the process by which you got your first job? Was it a dramatic break with that old boy's network?

Sandra Gilbert: Oh absolutely. There was not one old boy who lifted one old finger to help me! In the middle sixties I followed my husband to California. He was going to be a faculty member at the University of California at Davis, and I was so naive! I thought, "Well, Elliot's going to be teaching at Davis, I should apply to Berkeley. But of course I'll have to explain to these people at Berkeley why an excellent Columbia graduate student like me is living in California and not writing to them from New York." So I wrote this crazy letter saying that I was married and living in Davis with my husband and children but I'd be very happy to come and teach at Berkeley. I might as well have written to a stone wall! Indeed, it was just as if I'd written to a bunch of ivy-covered buildings that couldn't possibly pick up a pen to respond!

But I did finally get a job by sending out a million letters to every school in the area, most with that kind of naively pleading tone that I guess my letter to Berkeley had: "I am a Columbia graduate living in California with my husband and children, et cetera et cetera." First I was offered a job at Sacramento State, where I had been teaching part-time; they offered me a position as a temporary but full-time lecturer, the kind that people are getting now. And then Cal State Hayward actually offered me a tenure-track position. So I went and told the chair at Sac State that I couldn't accept his job offer because I was going to go to Cal State Hayward. He asked, "But what about your husband and children?" I told him that we were going to move to Berkeley so we would be halfway between the two institutions. And he responded, "My goodness, isn't that nice of your husband!"

Donald Hall: How well do you think the MLA has responded to the problems that have existed over the years?

Sandra Gilbert: I am very impressed with how responsive the MLA has been for the last few decades. But I do remember going to my first MLA meetings with my husband, just tagging along as a wife, and it seemed as though you were issued a tweed jacket and a pipe in order to get into the convention, too. As a woman—and a quite young, newly married woman at that—I felt very self-conscious and peculiar. But then in the late 1960s and early 1970s, when there were revolutions all over the world, the MLA was transformed, and groups like the Commission on the Status of Women began to be heard. A lot of the old boys experienced "those" people as taking over the MLA, even while "those" people experienced themselves as still marginalized and oppressed. My long-time collaborator, Susan Gubar, and I used to talk about what we called the "MLA syndrome," which was the perception of many men in the MLA that the women were taking over and the perception of many women in the MLA that the men wouldn't let them say a word. Completely at epistemological loggerheads!

But I have seen firsthand how hard everybody today tries to make room for every possible point of view, and not just the staff at MLA headquarters but most of the people on the executive council and on the various committees that I have worked with. I think one reason that some groups who are so angry about the job market continue to be outraged is that they can't seem to understand that an organization with thirty thousand members has to try to be responsive to views that are at least *somewhat* representative of positions held by almost all thirty thousand. Obviously the MLA isn't going to be responsive to morally evil points of view, but the organization can't adopt a monolithic perspective on most issues precisely because its membership is extraordinarily diverse.

Donald Hall: I'm curious, what did you like most and least about your experience as MLA president?

Sandra Gilbert: I think what I've always liked about the MLA is the opportunity to interact with really interesting people outside of the usual institutional settings. When I was on the executive council in the early eighties I used to refer to the group as the "big department in the sky," and in many ways it *is* like an ideal department, because even when there are disagreements, meetings for the most part seem to lack the usual sort of in-fighting as well as the usual kind of bad faith. Even the way in which the MLA has been embattled lately—attacked both from the right in the course of so-called culture wars, and more recently the left in the course of what Cary Nelson has called the job wars—even *that* brings people together in a certain way; you begin to have a fairly clear vision of what you can do and what you can't do, which is ultimately very salutary. And precisely because officers and members of the council don't see each other on a daily basis, there's a collegiality in the group that's much harder to achieve even in the happiest departments, where there are too many territorial issues. So that is what I liked best.

What I liked least was the downside of what I've been describing, which was how we were constantly being attacked and all too often being called upon to do things that weren't in our power as a professional organization. Even with the best will in the world the council and the officers can't change the economy. Here's an example of what I mean. As Herbie Lindenberger may have told you, we had dinner the other night with Phyllis Franklin, the MLA's executive director, who told an illuminating story about somebody from one of the graduate student caucuses who called her to insist that the MLA should "stop" CUNY from doing some exploitative thing. Phyllis asked this person, "Do you vote?" and he replied, "No, why would I, all those politicians are so corrupt!" "You mean you didn't vote for governor? You didn't vote for mayor?" "No, why would I, they're all corrupt!" To which Phyllis responded, "But it's the mayor and the governor who fund CUNY! What do you think the MLA can do? Parachute in?"

Actually, though, that would be a very good use of the old boys, parachute them in, in their tweed jackets and pipes and heavy leather shoes!

Donald Hall: Is there any way that the organization, or those of us who teach graduate students, can better address that level of anxiety that graduate students feel?

Sandra Gilbert: Well certainly the report of the Committee on Professional Employment was a passionate effort to address such anxiety. We really tried to indicate our concern and our care. But we can't unilaterally change the world or the economy, even as we hope that all our students and colleagues—along with parents and voters in general—will join with us in making a *concerted* effort to improve the situation. One way to do that is to be politically active on the larger scene—in the state, in the nation, and in political arenas where decisions about funding really are made. The MLA can't produce the funds out of nowhere, but the MLA can work to advance its members' interest: we can try to expose the situation, and then we can try to urge everyone—tenure-track faculty, adjuncts, graduate students, even undergraduates—to become militant in speaking for the needs of higher education. After all, the current situation—the cutbacks in tenure-track positions, the increasing reliance on part-time and temporary instruction—is a disaster for undergraduates as well as for people in our own profession. This isn't just an issue of self-interest for a few rarefied humanists, it's a problem that touches every American who wants to go to college, who wants to have a decent college education for herself, himself, or his or her kids.

Donald Hall: Regarding that committee report, when I talked to Herbie Lindenberger yesterday, he was clear that you and he disagreed on certain issues, especially access to graduate programs, which he believes should be restricted.

Sandra Gilbert: I think that the question of access to graduate programs is a very vexed one. And interestingly some of the people on our committee most opposed to the idea of downsizing graduate programs were themselves graduate students or lecturers. They felt very strongly that such downsizing would create an elite and would harm efforts toward diversity. So I have to admit that I find this question very disturbing. On the one hand, I can see all of the reasons why we should "control the graduate student population" (although that sounds pretty Orwellian, doesn't it?), but on the other hand I also worry that such a move might promote elitism. After all, the first thoughts people tend to have about graduate program cutbacks is that the places to "downsize" should be the less elite schools, while the most elite institutions should go on churning out the usual number of Ph.D.s. But in fact, I know from my own experience teaching in the Ivy League and from the experiences of friends that "top-tier" institutions don't necessarily place as many students as some of the less elite schools in the heart of the country because some of these places with weaker reputations actually have fairly strong local—"regional"—markets.

Of course, I can understand exactly why Herbie feels as he does, and why a lot of other people feel the same way. But I really do think the question is more complicated than it may at first seem. In fact, I can trace the complexities of the issue back to the problem of the "old boys" that we were discussing earlier, and I feel as though I myself might have been one of the people affected by the kinds of restrictions currently being proposed. Suppose when I had applied to graduate school in 1963, the admissions committee had learned that I had a husband and children and said "Well she's got a husband to support her and kids to take care of, therefore she already has something to do with her life, so why should we let her into our program at Columbia?" That kind of constraint would probably have a powerful effect on reentry students, who are more likely to be women or minorities, and who are some of our most interesting minds.

Even while I make these points, however, I have to concede that yes, we undoubtedly will have to consider cutbacks of some kind, but in the context that the committee report recommends—meaning this: if a department does a self-study and discovers that its students aren't getting placed anywhere, that they're jobless and miserable, that their degrees are useless or worse than useless, burdensome, then clearly that department ought to be thinking very rigorously about its commitment to graduate study.

Donald Hall: What are we doing well in terms of graduate education today? And what are we doing not so well?

Sandra Gilbert: I think what we're doing well can be summed up in that one, often overused word "diversity." I really believe that the old boys' system has vanished almost everywhere, and that we are dealing much, much better with women and minorities than we used to. What we aren't doing so well is really forcing ourselves and our graduate students to confront the economic realities of our institutional situation today. I think we really need a truth in advertising policy in graduate schools! To the extent that students are still told where they are trained that they're all going to replicate the careers of their professors, we're violating truth in advertising laws. I think people on our committee felt that while of course nobody wants to reduce the intellectual quality and rigor of graduate studies, programs ought to try to dramatize economic realities through a range of strategies: symposia on the job market, internships at community colleges, and visits to campus by alums who could talk about the many kinds of teaching (and *non*-teaching) positions they've held. We really do need to equip students to confront market realities—and more specifically to understand that many of them are not going to be teaching at Ph.D.-granting institutions if they do get academic jobs, and many will even have to think about so-called alternative, nonacademic jobs. The vast majority of our graduate students, after all, will be teaching at schools where they have to approach literary studies in ways that are often very different from what many of them have learned in most of today's graduate programs.

Donald Hall: This brings up a question about the trajectory of your own career and how well equipped you were to negotiate with the demands at a place like Cal State Hayward.

Sandra Gilbert: Well in a certain sense I had a great advantage in teaching at a place like Cal State Hayward, precisely in having been educated in the old boys', tweed jacket, pipe-smoking way, before the rise of the technocracy. The kind of teaching I'd experienced at Columbia and earlier at Cornell, and that I knew my husband was doing, was very old fashioned, commendably old fashioned in certain ways—and it was very easy to translate what I'd learned in college and graduate school into the kind of work that I did at Cal State Hayward. And at that point, too, I had very few professional prejudices: I didn't have any snobbish preconceptions that would have made me differentiate what I now know are "Research 1" institutions (like Cornell and Columbia) and four-year state schools like Hayward. And anyway, I found that the CSUH students were eager to read everything I assigned. I loved teaching them, and from doing it I learned that you could make all kinds of demands on students who would seem to be hierarchically "lower down" in the great game plan of higher education. My next job was at Indiana, which I soon learned was a step up on the academic ladder, but I was so comfortable with students from the CSU system and indeed from the community colleges, that when I first came back to California I taught the material of what would become *The Madwoman in the Attic* in a little community college course that I was doing part-time in the spring of 1975. My students were mostly reentry women and I could talk to them easily about, say, the then fairly new ideas of "the anxiety of influence" and other, similarly theoretical issues.

Paradoxically, then, I think I was probably rather lucky in having had an old-fashioned education from all those old boys because I never learned any high theoretical jargon. Right now, I'm afraid, a lot of our students come out of graduate school with so much hyper-professional, theoretical baggage that they don't know how to formulate ideas in a way that is accessible to the average undergraduate. Obviously there *are* ways of communicating fascinating theoretical questions to popular audiences but unfortunately many of our students—often some of the best of them!—don't know how to use language that is lucid and jargon-free though that's the language they really need to use in the classroom as well as in much of their writing.

Donald Hall: So how do we train our graduate students to be engaged with the world, instead of very narrow specialists and sometimes polemicists? Are we doing that well?

Sandra Gilbert: Well, I guess I've been saying that we aren't doing a good enough job of teaching students how to communicate ideas to younger people and to general, nonspecialist audiences. I feel quite strongly that there is entirely too much virtually unintelligible—sometimes even meaningless—jargon around. And I'm not sure what can be done about the situation because part of the problem is not just that our students use it but that our students continue to learn it from *us*! Just read what is published in learned journals and in academic "bestsellers" (if that term isn't an oxymoron) to see why our students use so much needlessly complicated language. And here I have to say that in my opinion such an inability to speak clearly to larger audiences is inextricably related to the failures of self-representation that have put us in lamentably bad positions economically. Until we can speak directly to our fellow citizens in language that they can understand, we're going to be the losers in the culture wars—which means we're going to be the losers in the funding wars. So the issue of language is a very urgent one.

Donald Hall: I believe that related to this whole issue of language is one of collegiality and how we talk to each other. Of course these things are hard to predict, but when you are interviewing job candidates, how do you get a sense of whether a person is going to be a good colleague?

Sandra Gilbert: I think that some of the best questions that people routinely ask at interviews are the ones related to teaching: "what courses do you want to teach," "describe your dream course," and so on. And it often astonishes me to hear the answers some candidates give! We once interviewed someone for a teaching position in the English department at Davis, who said that what he really wanted to teach was a seminar on Nietzsche . . . just Nietzsche. Those of us on the committee sort of rolled our eyes at each other! I mean, this young man could have come to our campus and taught a course on Nietzsche and literature, but just Nietzsche? Who did he think he was going to be teaching? I remember a very funny exchange at an interview when I was on the recruitment committee at Princeton. We asked the candidate what her dream course would be, and she said she would like to teach a course in "theory and—and, um—" (there was a long silence) "theory and *non*theory." Our chair asked, "*non*theory, what's that?" And she said, "well, nontheory—like, *you* know, poems, stories, plays." And he said, "Oh yes, what we used to call literature."

I guess what I'm saying is that there's quite a lot you can learn about people from an evolved answer to the "dream course" question; it can tell you a lot about them as potential teachers and therefore as persons. Because after all the most "*people*-thing" we do is what we do with our students. Everything else really revolves around that. Certainly the way we treat our colleagues is intimately related to the way we treat our students. What we think of our students, how we want to talk to them, and what we want to do for them, has everything to do with what we want to do in our departments and with our associates.

Donald Hall: Speaking of that issue of language and meeting the needs of various audiences, I would like to hear your thoughts on the field of feminist literary criticism, as it has evolved, and where you see it going.

Sandra Gilbert: Well, on the one hand I think that I shouldn't complain: feminist criticism, women's studies, and gender studies more generally have achieved a real centrality in our own fields and in the university as a whole. I think we've achieved a position that we could hardly have imagined when most of us began this work in the seventies. On the other hand, however, I fear that there's been a certain degree of co-optation. I'm afraid that what *was* feminist criticism and what is now more likely to be gender studies (and that's fine with me) have become just another sector of the academic technocracy, that they have lost their political urgency and become "established" in a really clichéd ivory-tower way. Some of the leading gender theorists speak in the most arcane ways and are the least capable of addressing public political issues that continue to be centrally urgent in our culture. I see that as a truly major problem. I want to feel that there's a broad social mission for feminist studies, queer theory, gender studies, and all of the other spin-offs of the intellectual revolutions that shook academia to its foundations a few decades ago. I want to feel that we have a social impact, that we make a difference in the world off campus. And it begins to feel sometimes that the world on campus isn't just a microcosm of the world off campus, it's a different universe—and that upsets me. I teach a course in the female literary tradition in which I use *The Norton Anthology of Literature by Women* and my students often come up at the end of the quarter and ask me to sign a book for a sister or cousin or an aunt—or even an uncle. And *that* makes me happy! When I see that there's an outreach like that, when the kids don't sell their books at the end of the course, when they want to keep them and share them with their families and their friends off campus, *that's* when I feel as though there is some kind of point, some kind of political coherence, to what we're doing.

Donald Hall: Do you see it as a matter of all of us finding a way to speak that public language and wholly avoiding theoretical jargon, or is it a matter of better valuing the range of discourses that we can deploy.

Sandra Gilbert: The ideal is obviously to better value the range of discourses. Of course I realize that some things have to be formulated in rather complicated—perhaps formidable-sounding—language. But I do think that a lot of the formidable phraseology we hear or read is just needlessly complicated. What upsets me, in other words, is when people complicate ideas that could be put quite simply and don't seem to have a clue that there might be a straightforward way of conveying a key point.

Donald Hall: What should that mean as we serve on tenure and promotion committees, in terms of what we value by our junior faculty and reward? Have we set up standards that make this aggressive, off-putting language inevitable?

Sandra Gilbert: Oh, I think very often we have. A friend of mine who's a regular columnist for a major newspaper in California submitted a dossier for promotion that included a group of 30 or 40 wonderful columns that she'd written, but was told that since those didn't appear in refereed journals they didn't "count" toward academic advancement! Here she was, speaking as a highly regarded public intellectual—conveying important information about feminism, about our university, about academia, about crucial political issues to the electorate of the state of California, significantly representing the accomplishments and the ideas of higher education—and she was told that such writing "doesn't count!" We need to rethink a lot of those assumptions about what "counts" and what "doesn't count."

Donald Hall: With that in mind, I want to turn finally to what advice you may give to people at the beginning of their careers, about mistakes to be avoided or ways of approaching their many responsibilities.

Sandra Gilbert: Well, as far as I'm concerned that's the hardest question you've asked so far! But okay, I'll do my best to answer it. I guess that, to begin with, I'd have to urge a certain measure of political caution at a time like this, a time when if somebody doesn't get tenure at a first job it's so very hard to get a second one. I don't think that I could argue to my junior colleagues that they're the ones who have to change things along the lines I mentioned earlier; it is more likely that those of us who are established can do so with some impunity. I actually lost my first real job—the one I told you about at Cal State Hayward—because I tried to change the system and offended a lot of old boys in that department. These were people who felt very status deprived and angry at having an uppity young assistant professor, a woman no less, come in and tell them how they should approach their students and teach their courses. I wouldn't want other people to go through when I went through when I lost that job (at a time in the seventies when the job market was just about as bad as it is right now). So I'd have to counsel a certain amount of caution, advise beginners to get established before making too many waves.

And finally I'd tell people to keep writing! Find time, in the summers, on the weekends, wherever and whenever possible, to keep working on the Great Book! When I look back on my early career I remember working on my first book, on D. H. Lawrence's poetry, all the time I was at Hayward. I was determined to finish it no matter what, not just because the material fascinated me but also because I sensed something bad was going to happen to me in that department. And even though I had three little kids and was teaching a 3/3/3 course load, I struggled to keep my focus and finish that book. My kids might tell you that maybe I wasn't there enough for them, though I certainly hope they don't feel that way, but that work was what I *had* to do at that time. We'd go away on family vacations and I'd sit on the beach and write while they made sand castles. So when I urge my students to keep on working on the Great Book, even in difficult situations, they know I'm not saying something in bad faith. They know that I have done the same thing.

A SENSE OF MISSION: AN INTERVIEW WITH
BONNIE ZIMMERMAN

Donald Hall: Is the career that you have had to date that which you imagined you would have as a graduate student?

Bonnie Zimmerman: If I think about what I am doing now, it conforms very much to my idea of what I would be doing before I entered graduate school, when I was an undergraduate thinking about what I wanted to do with my life. Of course, when I fantasized about the future, I saw myself at an institution that was like the one that I was at as an undergraduate, a Big 10, research university, in a small town, where the campus is beautiful and dominates the city. I've ended up making my career at a commuter university in a major city, so it really is in a very different location, but I am not doing things that are different from what I thought I would be doing.

What is interesting to me is that it does not conform at all to what I thought I would be doing once I got to graduate school. I started graduate school in 1969 and within a year two things happened. First of all the job market crashed. I don't know if people today realize that the job market in the first half of the 1970s was probably worse than it ever would be again. We have lived with a lot of really bad job markets over the past twenty years, but nobody, I mean nobody, at that time was getting a job, partly because of massive hirings in the sixties that dried everything up. That became apparent to all of us in graduate school very quickly, and we finished our degrees under a specter of unemployment. The other thing that happened was that I became politicized and deeply involved in women's studies and radical politics. And increasingly I felt that academic life was unlikely to be my future. So in a sense the stumbling into an academic career later—and I was five years underemployed until I got a job here—really was a big surprise, because I honestly believed that my graduate education was not so much a preparation for a career as it was marking time until I ran out of money. And then I would have to do something else.

Donald Hall: Talk a little bit more about that time period, the five years underemployed after graduate school; what sustained you during that period?

Bonnie Zimmerman: When I finished my Ph.D. in 1973 and no jobs materialized, I was already deeply absorbed in "the revolution." I was doing political activism and cultural work, I had found some part-time teaching, mostly freshman comp in community colleges, and a little secretarial work. It started out exhilarating. I loved what I was doing and actually thought that maybe I would do this for the rest of my life; it seemed a great way to make a revolution and still keep my finger in the academic world. But it soon became exhausting and debilitating, and I realized that I really wanted an academic job. I spent time working on parts of my dissertation and got a couple of things published, but by the end of the five-year period I was deeply depressed and was on the verge of giving up. I think that what kept me going was the fact that this was what I wanted to do more than anything else. So I made one last ditch effort to get a job and it was not until May of that academic year that the job at San Diego State emerged; it was a one-year temporary job with some possibility of it turning into tenure-track, as it indeed did. I guess I had come to a point where I accepted the possibility of having to leave academia, and I don't know, in some kind of cosmic spiritual way, maybe you have to give it up before you can get what you are looking for. I told a colleague once that it took me five years from finishing my Ph.D. to getting this job—five years of underemployment. And she also kept trying and at the end of five years she got a tenure-track job. I doubt that the five years is significant in any way, but I do think that sometimes we simply have to stick with it and at the same time do everything that we need to do to make ourselves desirable candidates when jobs do open up.

Donald Hall: Do you think academics' senses of their professional selves have changed dramatically since you began your career? Is there some larger sense in which what professors "are" has changed?

Bonnie Zimmerman: Well it seems to me that the notion of what it was to be a professor twenty-five or thirty years ago was entirely more rarefied than it is today. There was a sense in which professors were unlike anything else. We were professionals, like lawyers and doctors, but also we were not; we had an intellectual connection that went all the way back to Socrates, Plato, and Aristotle. I'm sure the reason I wanted to be a professor, in addition to the fact that I was smart and I loved to read, was that it was also the most romantic job imaginable. And it is still a great job—I wouldn't want to do anything else—but I also recognize that the notion of the professor as some kind of independent, creative promulgator of unbiased knowledge is thirty or forty years out of date. What we are being asked to do today is prepare the work force for the next generation, and to do so in a way that is cheap and cost effective. And that is a very different sense of one's self than being the heir to Aristotle.

Donald Hall: Do you think it is an unequivocally bad thing to leave behind that notion of ourselves as purveyors of inspired knowledge? The move toward a corporate sense of a university may be pretty grim, but are there other ways in which professors see their responsibilities toward students in positive ways today?

Bonnie Zimmerman: Oh I think that is probably true. But I would say there is considerable diversity among faculty today as far as that goes. I think there are many people around today who continue to hold students in basic contempt. And in fact as student preparation for college degrades I notice a rising sense of frustration among faculty and more of a "what are we going to do about them? They just can't learn" attitude, which often translates itself into a complete dismissal of students. Sure, more faculty may be concerned with the learning process and how to best reach students and make learning meaningful to them, but then I think to myself, yes, but some of my professors back in the sixties wanted to work with me and empower me and certainly respected me—so I don't really know if the professors of my undergraduate days were any more tyrannical or authoritarian than some of my colleagues. I'm not sure that's changed as much as we might like to think.

Donald Hall: This leads to my next question: what past crises across the landscape of the profession do you feel have been met successfully and what emerging ones demand immediate attention?

Bonnie Zimmerman: Well, the first that comes to mind has been the challenge of minority knowledges. And here I'm talking about the various "studies" areas: women's studies, African American studies, Chicano studies, as well as peace studies and labor studies and so forth. I think those challenges from the sixties and seventies have been fairly well responded to, some would say absorbed, by the academy and they are not only ensconced in their own little places but there is more and more of that knowledge that is spread throughout the academy. It is not perfect yet, but nobody can look back from education today to, say, 1968 and not see a profound transformation in what counts as knowledge. So that is something that I think universities have responded to very well.

The big challenges—and I suppose these started in the early nineties—are economic and increasingly demographic challenges. They are challenges of periodic recessions and budget cutbacks; they are challenges of right-wing politicians controlling state legislatures and attacking the universities. They are challenges of increasing numbers of students, many of whom are simply not being prepared by the K–12 educational system for a wide variety of social reasons. And these are challenges that universities have been really very very slow to respond to. We have yet to come up with the political strategies to deal with legislatures and a public who simply perceive us as the training ground for jobs, and to educate students who need incredible amounts of remedial work, and to do all of this with fewer and fewer resources. These are the new challenges, and of course to talk about the luxury of the disengaged academic life in an environment like this is ludicrous.

Donald Hall: Any thoughts on how to meet those challenges? Specifically in finding a way of communicating to the public at large, the taxpayers, and legislators, how we do what we do successfully and how we can do certain aspects of our jobs more successfully with greater resources?

Bonnie Zimmerman: Well, the first thing that we do wrong is when we get up and complain about how terrible our working conditions are and how unfair it is that we don't get our salary increases and that we deserve lifetime tenure and all of those kinds of things that stun the public, many of whom a few years ago were being laid off from jobs after twenty or thirty years or were getting cuts in their salaries. We should never think that by protecting our privilege, we are connecting to the public. We are much better off than the majority of people. The way that does work successfully is showing people what we do, and showing it and explaining it to them in their language and in ways that people can understand. Universities in general haven't seemed to think that they need to publicize what they do. Some big research universities that get vast amounts of money and have Nobel laureates get publicity all of the time, but people don't really understand what the purpose of a state university is other than "well my kid goes there and gets a B.A. so that she can get a job." We need to publicize our successes better and explain our work in ways that people can understand.

Donald Hall: Speaking of that issue of language, how are we doing with each other? Are we able to speak productively to each other or are we hopelessly divided into factions and entrenched positions?

Bonnie Zimmerman: Well, here I would like to speak directly from my women's studies experience because that is where I know that I can answer this question best. Just a few years ago I felt that we in women's studies were in very entrenched positions, particularly between people whose theories and pedagogies were rooted in identity politics and those whose theories and pedagogies were rooted in postmodernism. I was at sessions at the National Women's Studies Association where people were screaming at each other around those theoretical issues. I don't think we are screaming as much today; I think something has changed so that people are recognizing that there are strengths in many different positions and that if we listen to each other and talk to each other we are going to see certain commonalities where we might not have before. There are still entrenched people, mostly from the side of identity politics, but there are many of us, and I consider myself one of them, who have moved beyond that position and who are no longer interested in contentious arguments but rather in productive debate. So I actually think there is a lot more collegiality than what we found just a short time ago.

Another encouraging change along these lines is that there is much more talk today about interdisciplinary and cross-disciplinary work. Even if you look at the narrowly academic divisions like social sciences, humanities, and sciences, there are more attempts to move across boundaries and traditional disciplines. And I think that too is very positive, and interestingly enough in my mind, was probably generated by the budget crisis of the early nineties when positions disappeared. A department recognizes that they may never again have twenty-five people specializing in American literature so they had better think about ways in which they can cooperate and collaborate. I tend to study it as a materialist, because I do believe that material conditions determine consciousness. Scarcity in the economy can generate a state of mind of "give me mine," but it can also generate a recognition that "few resources mean we had better learn how to share." And that means having productive conversations about the meaning of sharing. So I'm very hopeful about that aspect.

Donald Hall: Working in an interdisciplinary field, you have served on many hiring committees in the past twenty years. When you are sitting on that side of the hiring table, and many of the readers of this book will be sitting on the other side, it would be interesting to hear what you look for, what sorts of qualities in applications?

Bonnie Zimmerman: Reviewing vitae in women's studies is particularly interesting, because we don't get vitae that all look the same; we get incredibly different ones and trying to compare this person against other people is an amazing process: looking at the different types of research, the different stages that people are in, their different experience in teaching, and then finally asking about that unquantifiable entity in women's studies—what is their commitment to women's studies? So what do we look for and therefore how should people present themselves? It is very difficult to say. Obviously you've got to make yourself stand out and articulate what it is about you that is unique and wonderful and fits this job. And you need to do it clearly and concisely. I'm more and more convinced that a one-and-a-half-page letter and a vita is better than a three-page letter. I can't finish a three-page letter. Frankly, I get bored by the end of the third paragraph. And then—I hate to tell this to people— but it has a lot to do with what interests the committee members have. Somebody will look and say "oh I have a real interest in that topic" and then push that person. And sometimes it is the smallest thing that somebody might notice, that someone on the committee might know. When I applied for the job here, it was in the days when I still wasn't sure if it was okay to be out as a lesbian, so I wasn't going to say anything explicit in my materials. But I had somewhere in them that I had worked with and written for *Lavender Woman,* and two people in reviewing files here noticed that, and knew that *Lavender Woman* was a lesbian newspaper, and said, let's interview her! And that is just how it happened.

Donald Hall: That leads to our next question, which has to do with challenges facing women's studies right now. You mentioned a moment ago about evaluating job candidates and judging that person's level of commitment to women's studies. How is this field changing and what do you mean when you say a commitment to women's studies? How would a lack of commitment manifest itself?

Bonnie Zimmerman: In the past five to ten years there are increasingly institutional avenues for doing women's studies: M.A.s and Ph.D.s or graduate minors or concentrations where you actually learn what women's studies is. Prior to that, people like me did all of our work within the preexisting disciplines, and were able to do women's studies by selection of a dissertation topic. But then we were also the ones in the process of creating women's studies programs and creating the women's studies curriculum. So nobody in my department until recently even had a degree in women's studies. But now we have two people who have masters' degrees in women's studies and some people who are applying for jobs have Ph.D.s in women's studies. So at this point, thirty years into the history of women's studies, there is a meaningful distinction between people who see their professional identity and their careers as being in women's studies as a field of academic expertise and those who do feminist research in the disciplines. As a women's studies department, I think it is important that we hire people who see women's studies as their academic field. That means looking at vitae for things like did they take a degree in women's studies? Do they belong to women's studies associations, do they teach women's studies courses? Are they interdisciplinary? Because a lot of people are very focused on their discipline—history, English, political science—they do research on women and they do research on gender, but they are not doing interdisciplinary work. But others are doing interdisciplinary work because women's studies is where they want to be, not because it is a fallback position, from a job in an English department. That's what I mean by a commitment to women's studies.

Donald Hall: So what do you think are some of the most exciting challenges facing the field today?

Bonnie Zimmerman: What excites me the most right now is how to move toward true interdisciplinarity. We talk about the "interdisciplinary" field of women's studies, but as most people will acknowledge we really are still multidisciplinary. I really want us to think about moving across the disciplines and toward a sense of not just how do we bring the disciplines together but how do we rethink disciplines entirely and perhaps start our knowledge from a different place. That is extremely difficult to do but is a conversation that I want to be part of. Another thing that is very exciting is the internationalizing of our work. Women's studies is everywhere and some of the best work is being done in Asia by Asian feminists. That is scholarship we Western women need to learn from, and we need to think about how it changes the ways that we understand feminism. I teach theory courses here and my theory courses are rooted in Western theory and Western theoretical concepts; what would it mean to start from other theoretical traditions and other places and reshape what we mean by theory?

Donald Hall: Talk, if you would, about that teaching and your own growth as a teacher. How has your pedagogy changed over the years?

Bonnie Zimmerman: What has changed significantly for me as a teacher is that after many years, I am finally comfortable with my style of teaching, and I don't care whether it is the correct style of teaching. When I was a beginning teacher, I was not confident; I attempted to do things that just were not mine. But now I am comfortable doing what I do best, and what I do best is lecture.

Donald Hall: Oh, that's surprising!

Bonnie Zimmerman: It *is* surprising, because it is counter to what feminist pedagogy is supposed to be. But I'm terrific at lecturing! My students love it, and they really seem to learn. Simply put, I believe in telling students what they ought to think. I tell them, "I'm going to preach to you, because I want you to think about the meaning of books and I believe that literature makes you a better person. That is why we read, that is why we go to school, to be better people!" Okay, so I'm not putting them in collaborative projects and I'm not using the "smart classroom," and they don't have email discussion lists and I don't put them in small groups and such; other people do that and they do it very well. I don't do it very well. And I think what is really important to recognize is that everybody has a teaching style and we should work toward figuring out what our best style is, what works best for us, and stick with it. And it is no better or worse to be a dynamic and wonderful lecturer than it is to be a dynamic and wonderful facilitator. They are different styles and different people can make them work.

Donald Hall: So talk a little bit more about what makes for a good or successful lecture. What do you bring to it?

Bonnie Zimmerman: First of all, I bring a great deal of comfort and confidence in the knowledge. I do what I know you are not supposed to do—I've basically taught the same syllabus now, with tinkering, for seven or eight years. I have the syllabus where I want it. I teach the same course every semester—women in literature—and I think that it works very well, the students seem to think that it works very well, and I know the literature inside and out. I don't use notes, I don't even necessarily need to use the book. I'm talking to them and focusing directly on them, and I think that's important; if you are going to lecture you have to be totally focused on the students. I also convey a great enthusiasm for the material, and it is infectious. I ask a few pointed and direct questions, and have an overall sense and plan for how I want the class to go. And students are very predictable. They ask the same questions all the time. They have practically the same responses all the time. So I know what I am going to get, which means I can also shape the class in ways that I think maximizes the learning. I start the semester doing a lot of modeling about how to read. They really don't know how to read yet, so why should I say, "Tell me what you see in this poem"? They don't see anything in the poem; I show them how to see something in the poem and by the end of the semester I expect that they will be able to do it themselves or at least do it better than before. And that is what works for me.

Donald Hall: Finally I would like to spend our last few minutes talking about your local career, teaching in an institution that is not Ph.D.-granting and where resources are more limited than in some research institutions, and the types of personal priorities that you have had to arrive at, trade-offs, joys, and perhaps disappointments.

Bonnie Zimmerman: San Diego State University has made for itself far more of a research mission than the rest of the California State University system has historically. So on the one hand, I have felt validated as a scholar at this university. On the other hand I am also very much aware that we have nothing like the resources that Research 1 universities have. So I'm more than a little envious of my UC San Diego colleagues, and am dismayed by the class difference between the UC and CSU systems. I think that the hierarchical structure of the American university system overall is simply outrageous. But it is what you have to live with. So how do you do it? You have to set priorities for yourself and compartmentalize. Even if it is part of the postmodern condition and much that is wrong with society, you cannot survive unless you can organize your life very carefully. When I started writing my book—*The Safe Sea of Women*—I was chairing the department and would come to school Monday through Thursday and work on all the department stuff and my teaching, and then Friday and Saturday I would stay home at my computer and work. And you've simply got to do that without fail. In recent years, I've chaired the department, been president of NWSA, been graduate advisor for the department, and finished a major project, and that juggling has almost become second nature after twenty years. Every day I look at what I have to do for the department, what I have to do for NWSA, what I have to do for the book, and do them efficiently; that is a skill you have to develop if you are going to survive in this environment. The other thing I would say is to take every advantage you possibly can of all the goodies that the university provides for you, and take off as much as you possibly can to write. Always use your summers, always use your semester breaks—that is when most of us do our writing.

But as difficult as the juggling has been, frankly I think that one of the reasons that I have retained such joy and a sense of purpose is that I kind of like being a big fish in a small pond. I think I might have been less happy had I gotten a job at a major university where I was a minor person that nobody was interested in. But I'm a fairly major player at San Diego State and it is nice to feel that your colleagues respect you. We may never feel like we get enough respect, but I know that people know who I am and think that I'm a good and productive person. So I think that is another thing to consider when you are looking for a job: yes, it might seem terrific to get hired at Harvard or Stanford or UC, but consider what your competition is going to be there. I've liked doing my work here because everything that I do gets credit rather than being compared to some kind of ideal number of articles and a certain number of books and all of that. And, frankly, I'm not sure I would have wanted to have dealt with that kind of pressure.

So I love what I do and really wouldn't be doing anything else, but, of course, I have had my moments of demoralization. I think all of us in the CSU have. People are tired much of the time. I've worked very hard, but I'm also aware that, as productive as I've been, I've not been as productive as I could have been. I think I would have a couple of more books had I gotten a job at the UC instead of the CSU But in the vast scheme of things I guess that is not terribly important. I mean the books will get written, if not by me then by somebody else. In the meantime, I have a real sense of mission about being at the CSU because I like the students and teaching. Those students are the future; they represent a genuine cross-section of the city of San Diego. They are the first-generation students, they are the new immigrants, they are the working-class students, as well as the middle-class and everything else. These are the students who are like my father, the first one in his family to go to college, at a public university at night, while working full-time and having a family. Those are my students, and I feel a profound sense of mission to them.

So I've had a very fulfilling career. But still sometimes I'm amazed to think about the fact that I'm going to end my career at San Diego State—that I'm going to be one of those people with the little gold pin after thirty-five years—because I always saw my life in very transient terms. But here I have been and I'm happy and I will continue to be here, as a productive person. Even with all of the uncertainty and hard work and challenges I've talked about, I can't think of anything that I would have done differently.

A LOVE FOR THE LIFE: AN INTERVIEW WITH NELLIE MCKAY

Donald Hall: I would like to start by asking about your perspective on how the profession has changed over the course of your career. Has it done so dramatically?

Nellie McKay: I went to graduate school in 1969 and finished in 1977, and the profession I see today is completely different than it was during those years. When I was in school, I studied no women, I studied no African Americans, I studied no other minority writers, and even among the white male writers whom I studied, the majority were British and the few Americans were mostly nineteenth-century. In some schools American literature was hardly considered fully within the realm of legitimate literature. So certainly the curriculum has changed completely since then.

A lot of things were happening while I was actually in graduate school. We reached the peak of the civil rights movement during the early years of my graduate education, the Vietnam War draft was a problem for many of my male colleagues, and there were great disruptions across the country. There were guns and riots on campuses, and in many ways, the institutions themselves were under fire. Those pressures helped force people in higher education—faculty as well as administrators—to begin to rethink education. African American students were at the hub of the strife; they were demanding that curriculums change to meet their needs, which meant they wanted to read and study about what it meant to be an African American in this country. They wanted courses that addressed their history and their literature. So by the time I graduated, there were a number of institutions that were in the process of hiring new faculty like me to teach this literature. It is interesting that most of us never even had courses in African American literature, though most of us ended up with dissertations that focused on African American experience (about which our dissertation advisors were learning along with us); this is the work that in fact helped launch some of the massive curricular changes that were to occur within the next decade.

And, of course, along with changes in curriculum have come recent developments in the way we read texts. We now no longer think only about print texts as texts. We now read photographs, architecture, and even performance as part of our work. As cultural studies becomes more and more embedded in English departments, our profession is taking as its province the whole nature of human experiences rather than cordoning off what appears on the page. And that, along with the various new theoretical methodologies that have also come into play in the last twenty-five to thirty years, means we have a real polyglot of work in the field of literature and the arts that did not exist thirty years ago.

Donald Hall: Given the fact that it didn't at that time, what drew you to this profession? What was there already that made it seem so appropriate and exciting?

Nellie McKay: I was drawn to the profession because I like to read. It was that simple. And I had a great time in college even though I wasn't reading about me; it was a wonderful opportunity to read a lot of books and to develop a sense of the meaning of literature, and I enjoyed that very much.

But I began to change somewhat in the late 1960s. I had originally thought that I would go to graduate school and study Shakespeare, which was where my love was at the time. Near the end of the 1960s, I diverged from that, and started thinking that I wanted literature to have something to do with real life and that I did not know enough about what real life in America was. As an undergraduate, I attended Queen's College, which was one of the branches of CUNY. When I entered Queen's College there was a very small number of African American students and no other minorities to speak of. In my first two years, it was pretty calm on campus, but I entered right ahead of the first sizable class of about 150 African American students and by the time I became a junior, all hell broke loose. And I was distressed about some of what I was seeing and hearing on all sides of the issues; I hadn't given it much thought before. That was when I decided I needed to study American literature—and at that time I was really talking about nineteenth-century American literature—to find out something about my own country and where we were. So off I went to graduate school to study nineteenth-century American literature so I could sort out for myself what it meant to be American and perhaps discover why we had come to the place that we were as a society, which was a kind of chaos of hate and anger. I certainly felt that those who had been denied had every right to be angry, but I wasn't at all sure that I understood why those who had done the denying were angry too. And so for me graduate school was a time of turning to literature to understand what real life was like, not just life in the text.

And what happened after that was very fortunate. The English department at Harvard was recruiting black students into its program, and I found I had a number of African American colleagues in graduate school. Now I'm only talking about a half a dozen fellow students, but considering that I was the only African American English major in my class at Queen's College, to have six colleagues in my graduate class was having a large number of colleagues. And some of them, especially those who had gone to historically black colleges or had come from the South, knew a great deal about African American literature already. In many ways they were my best teachers and they got me very excited about the prospects of working in a literature that was really ours. I had never even considered that that was an option. I remember a day when one of my male colleagues (whose name everyone would recognize if I mentioned it) said to me, "Do you realize that we are going to be the first people to train the Ph.D.s in African American literature?" I can still recall where we were standing when he said that and feeling shivers go down my spine. I had gone to graduate school to study and teach my classes and just be a citizen of a profession that I liked. The notion that I was going to be part of a group of people who would be breaking the kinds of boundaries that he was referring to was both frightening and exhilarating. It seemed at that moment to give a kind of meaning to what I had been seeing still as a rather esoteric profession.

Donald Hall: Do you find that same level of or potential for exhilaration among graduate students with whom you work today, or is that a past moment that can never be recaptured?

Nellie McKay: Certainly the African American graduate students that I work with here in Madison do have some of that exhilaration, because they are breaking new boundaries as well. My students are moving well beyond the kind of work that we did in the late 1970s. The students that I work with, both white and black actually, find it extremely exciting to be working in this area. They are expanding our horizons and are moving well beyond where we were when we started our careers. There are still so many areas to be explored even in terms of the literature that is already known. And some are exploring virgin territory by looking not only at African American but also at Native American as well as Latino and other kinds of literature. They have frontiers that they are exploring well beyond us and most are in fact very excited about what they are doing.

The other reason that I know there is still a sense of excitement is that although students have heard how difficult the job market is, we still get more applications for graduate school than we can handle. And I have to believe that these young people are not simply naive, thinking that this is going to be an easy life. There is still a love for the life, as hard as they also see that life is for their teachers these days. They know we are bogged down day after day, week after week, and month after month, with the various and sundry obligations that go along with being professors. That doesn't seem to be fazing them one bit. They're still going on.

And that too is one of the things that has changed over the years. When I was in graduate school I don't remember knowing anything about the professional lives of any of my professors, all of whom were white men, mostly middle-aged. But now as a middle-aged woman myself, I know that my students know a lot about my professional life, that my colleagues and I talk to them about the up and down sides of what we are doing. Most of us who are working with graduate students are always tired, and our students see that. They know that we serve not just them and the undergraduate population but also the university and the community. We are constantly on the job, and our students know this. And sometimes they get to substitute for us when we simply cannot do what we'd like to do. In this way, they get a bit of experience of their own so they know what it feels like to be a professional. Nobody shared that with me when I was a graduate student.

Donald Hall: Do you find that the pedagogy you bring to your graduate seminars is very different from that which you experienced when you were in graduate school? How so and how did you arrive at your sense of pedagogy today?

Nellie McKay: Well, much of my sense of pedagogy today comes not out of studying African American literature but out of having studied women's literature and having worked with other women. When I came here in 1978, I was very excited about our women's studies program and how people in the program were approaching their teaching. We saw students, especially graduate students, as being in training with us. This was very different from graduate seminars I took at Harvard University. I don't tell my students what they should think or how they should think. I don't expect them to mouth back things that they think I want them to give back. We have debates; we have conversations. We agree on a lot, but sometimes we don't agree at all. And one of the first things that I learned from my women's studies affiliation is that I needed to make my classroom a place that was safe for everyone. What happens in our classroom happens just in our classroom. We can have arguments, we can disagree with each other, we can say what we feel. The classroom is a safe space for learning, it is a place where we will exchange ideas and hash them out and leave with, "well, now I know why I think what I think. And I don't necessarily have to agree with anybody else's opinions." When we read critical materials, I keep telling students that none of it is the Bible, it has been published, it is there, it is your job to agree or disagree. And to the extent that it differs from what you are thinking, do not believe necessarily that you are wrong. And I can't imagine anybody who was a teacher of mine ever telling me that in graduate school. I simply can't imagine it ever happening. So we have come a long way—I don't know we have answers for all the ills—but we've certainly opened up and made spaces easier for people to enter and leave without feeling put down or stupid.

Donald Hall: Do you find that the same qualities of speaking openly, honestly, and productively within the classroom setting are equally true now for how our larger institutions—our departments or universities—operate?

Nellie McKay: No I don't think that it is as true. It seems to me that there are actually a lot more factious differences in departments now. I don't know if it is just because I pay more attention to them now than I once did, but it seems to me that I see a lot more unhealthy disagreements, disagreements where people can be insulting to others, in ways that are completely unnecessary, where a faculty person, especially a woman or a junior person, feels humiliated by a senior person. One thing that I took away from the old system was that there was a kind of civility that was possible, and it may not have been an honest civility, but I don't even know that. But I do think there used to be a great deal more civility among colleagues than I now see. And I don't know how one gets this across to some colleagues, but a house divided is always a weakened house. You see the fallout of these kinds of behaviors that divide: departments always get weaker because they can't stand together. I just don't know how to get that across. Sometimes people are intractable and just "know" that they are right about whatever it is they are thinking.

Donald Hall: Do we who teach in graduate programs do an effective job at training our students to be good colleagues? Do we do enough?

Nellie McKay: I don't know what is enough. I try to tell my students when they're getting ready to go out to find jobs, that the first thing that you do when you move into a new situation is to remember that you don't know anything about the people who are there as your colleagues. If you discover that there are painful disagreements on the faculty, do not join sides, be a good listener. You don't want to begin your career by being partisan in ways that can in fact be very harmful to you in the long run. When I was in graduate school, one of my professors said something to me that I now tell students: never enter a fight that you don't intend to win. Which means, you stay clear of most fights. You can't win most of them anyway and winning may end up costing you more than you are willing to pay for the winning.

How we can train students to be better colleagues? We have a system here that is really good in which dissertators work together. They don't have to be working on the same thing, though they have to have some common interests, so you will find four or five dissertators who are all interested in American literature forming a dissertation group. They meet and read each other's work, give each other feedback, and support each other during the process of finishing the graduate project. We also have groups that form as they prepare for prelim exams in which the students study together. And I think that these are great ways in which they are learning to work with their colleagues and to know how to be colleagues when they move away from those groups.

In fact, some of the greatest influences on my life, in terms of finding a purpose in my life, were my own colleagues in graduate school, largely my African American colleagues. They were extremely helpful at a time when we were all together and were using each other as the sounding boards upon which we were going to establish our careers. In my estimation I think that the greatest impetus to do what I have done started with my peer group in graduate school. Had they not been there, my life might have been very very different. And I tell that to graduate students a lot: these are the friends that they are going to have for the rest of their lives. However divided they are from each other in terms of geographical space, they're going to meet at MLA meetings, they're going to meet at other conferences, they're going to remain connected. And with the advent of electronic communications, they need never be separated from the people they want in their lives no matter how far away they are on the geographical landscape.

Donald Hall: The transition between studenthood and professorhood can be quite dramatic. One aspect of that is the process of developing or discovering one's own scholarly voice; what was your process?

Nellie McKay: It started about a year or two after I got out of graduate school, when I was applying for fellowships to get time off to write. I started to look around for people to ask to write letters of recommendations for me, and I discovered that the professors whom I knew in graduate school and who knew my work best really did not know anything about what it was I was going to be doing. I had left that nest and they could not write for me because they had no clue about the work that I was beginning to embark on. And that was quite an eye-opener for me, because I had to find another path. I was very fortunate because in those days African American studies was so small in terms of people who knew anything about it that I knew I could turn to some of the people who were ahead of me even if I didn't know them. Someone like Houston Baker was very important. I had never even worked with Houston, but he and others were willing to make a commitment to helping a new scholar up the ladder so to speak. That was one step, discovering that I finally had to move away from my graduate career completely. And I think the second part of moving toward my own voice was largely the result, again, of women's studies. Women's studies was very instrumental in helping me begin to understand that there was nothing wrong with the "I" word. Whether you used the "I" word or not was not the point, the point was that you had something to say and that you needed to say it your own way. So I found people like Elaine Marks and Susan Friedman, who were not trained in my field, but who were willing to read my work and encouraged me to write what I felt and how I felt, rather than depend on some other source to write through. I've been here now for almost twenty-three years and I think that coming to this university at the time that I did was probably the smartest thing I could have done, because I landed in a community. I knew when I was coming here that the Afro-American studies department was putting into place a literature program of its own and I was hired to set that up and establish it. And that was challenging and wonderful. But I hadn't figured on the women's studies part of it. I had good colleagues in Afro-American studies, but they were mostly men. And even though it was a cross-racial group of men, they were at the time nowhere close to understanding women or able to understand that women's professional needs might be different from men's. If you came into the club you were going to have to be like a man in the club too. That was not easy for me and in many ways women's studies saved my life. I found myself in a group of women who were supportive, who were eager to have women succeed, and who said, "Just be who you are." And that for me was very important in those early years.

Donald Hall: What do you say to students today who are faced with a choice about where to go and where to start a career? What sorts of factors do you encourage them to consider?

Nellie McKay: Well, frankly, I encourage them to take the best job offer that they can get. In the market that we have, we tell students that you may not get a job in the place that you would like to get a job, but it is more important to have a job. So take the job, do your best at that job, and see if you can write yourself out of it if you don't like it very much. But first and foremost: take a job!

But I also encourage them a lot when they are out in those first years to try to get some time away from the job, so that they can work on their writing, because until they have established themselves as having voices of their own and important things to say, the competition just keeps on increasing as newer and sometimes smarter people come into the market each year. I really do have a lot of sympathy for these students, especially for those who get one-year appointments. And we've seen some get as many as three one-year appointments in a row. And sometimes they give up and sometimes they don't. These are the days when the jobs were supposed to be flourishing and we don't have the jobs at all.

Donald Hall: You talk a little about these issues in your May 1998 *PMLA* essay, about the field of graduate education generally and about the specific challenges facing the field of African American literary studies. Have you seen in recent years any changes in our universities or professional organizations that give you some reason for optimism?

Nellie McKay: I still think that the pipeline issue is a very serious one. And it is so serious because for many years most institutions of higher education, including this one, did not see that a part of what they needed to do was to recruit students of color. I once asked someone who was chair of the English department—this was more than a decade ago now—"what are we doing to recruit African American students?" At that time we had no African American graduate students at all. His answer to me was very flippant: "we don't do anything to recruit any graduate students!" And I was simply taken aback, because of the answer and because of the way the answer was given to me. We didn't recruit graduate students so why should we recruit or do anything special to recruit students of color? It was very discouraging to hear that. That attitude has since changed and we do try to recruit African American graduate students. Over the last four years we have recruited now more than a dozen whom we currently have in our program. That has taken some effort, but it is also getting easier because the students help to recruit each other; students now tell students from elsewhere about our program. The other thing that has changed in our English department is that we have a program now that links African American studies to the English department, so that students can come into African American first, get an M.A. in African American literature, and matriculate into the English department. That does two things for us. One, it has been bringing better students into African American studies to begin with, because the students now know that they can come here and get their basic foundations in African American literature, history, and culture, and stay here for their Ph.D.s. And it also means that the English department is able to use this "Bridge" program as a recruitment tool, to encourage students who are definitely interested in pursuing African American literature to get M.A. in African American and then without leaving here move into English and finish up their work. They can do it all here and have the benefits of both departments. So the bridge program has helped us to make considerable strides in terms of recruiting minority students in this field.

    And part of what I was trying to address in that article is that English departments need to do a better job of recruiting students who have been on the outside of the mainstream for so long. And not just African American students but those from all groups who have been on the outside, because we are not going to get them otherwise. I used a statistic in that article; I pointed out that if every Ph.D.-granting English department over the last twenty years had graduated just one student per year, we wouldn't have a pipeline problem now. We simply wouldn't. And if we didn't have a pipeline problem, nobody would be fighting over the newest minority group hotshot coming out of graduate school, African American, Puerto Rican, Native American, or whatever. Minority faculty would be teaching exactly what they want to teach, not feeling necessarily that they *have to* teach African American or any other ethnic group literature. You know, every year there are one or two extremely sharp African American graduate students who come out of graduate school somewhere and every school seems to fight over these one or two students. Totally ridiculous! Totally ridiculous! We shouldn't be doing that. Nor should African American students need to feel that they have to study African American literature. It is just the flip side to the discrimination. And you know it is late, but I'm hoping that in one way or another some people who read this will take some of it to heart and understand that. Are we going to leave it for another twenty-five years?

Donald Hall: Some of what you also said in that article refers to the pool of white graduate students who are studying African American literature; what does one say to those students?

Nellie McKay: We have several white students here studying minority literatures. We don't discourage it because they need to follow whatever they feel passionate about, but we also encourage them not to focus only on minority literatures. And I also give my black dissertators the same advice. If you are writing a dissertation on modernism, let's say, you balance it and do comparative work using writers from different groups so that when you are on the job market you can demonstrate that you have a broad range of knowledge in what you can teach. If you are an Americanist, for example, you should be able to teach American writers across race, ethnicity, or gender. I encourage my students not to get pigeonholed, to take courses in a number of areas, and to show the breadth and depth of their knowledge in their dissertations. Students interested in minority literature should also know about nonminority writers, and of course balancing genders is also important.

Donald Hall: What are the greatest challenges facing the young African American academic or literary critic in terms of the decisions she or he has to make about career priorities and the many demands placed upon her time—how do you talk to students about that?

Nellie McKay: Well I like to think that most of the time my students are a lot more worldly wise than I was. Among women students, white or black, one of the things that I really see is that they seem less afraid of claiming their own lives than my generation was. For instance, a lot of graduate women are very good about deciding and planning if they want to have babies at this time. They are clear that they don't want to give up their whole lives for the profession, but they also want to be taken seriously. I think they are more sophisticated about it than my generation was anyway. And maybe they are because they now have models. They can say, "Well, I like how you are doing that, but I don't like what you are doing on that side of it, and therefore I am not going to do what you are doing on that side of it." I think it has been very useful for them to have models. They are better able to evaluate their options and decide what they want to make of their own lives.

And I try to be as supportive as I can. I joke with them a lot about it. They will say to me, "Don't worry, I'll be gone in a few years." And I say, "Oh no, I know better than that, you actually never go away. You might not be here in body, but whenever that phone rings it might just be you calling to ask, 'what should I do about this?' 'How would you do that?' 'Can you write a letter for me?' So I know you don't ever go away." I certainly don't want to say that men don't do it, but women are very good at giving students the privilege of staying connected. I and a lot of women I know in this university work hard to keep the lines of communication open with former students so that they feel free to ask advice, to ask for help, to feel that we can be trusted to take their interests seriously.

Donald Hall: That's a tremendous burden for you.

Nellie McKay: It is both a tremendous blessing and a burden. Every year more students join the group, but fortunately they don't all come back at the same time. And, of course, we are interested in them and we are warmed by the trust that they have in us.

Donald Hall: As you contemplate the future of African American studies, what do you see as the emerging challenges that this next generation of scholars will have to address?

Nellie McKay: There is one problem that I see that I certainly don't have an answer for. One of the benefits that African American literature has had over the last twenty-five years is its position as being the most established of the fields of minority literatures; we are the largest group, we have the most scholars in the field, we've done the most work. And in terms of sheer size, we may remain larger for sometime to come. But even if we were always to remain the largest, we don't want to see anybody left out in the cold. What we want for ourselves as African Americanists, we would like to see happen for other groups. I don't know how this is going to work in the twenty-first century, in terms of resources for everybody. As fewer and fewer resources come into higher education from the states and the pot gets smaller and smaller, it has to be divided and redivided. I think it is going to take a lot of courage and good moral and ethical thinking, so that we don't end up in a situation where the competition between African American and the others is a source of closing out anybody. How do we continue to expand our own boundaries in what I see as the multicultural era ahead and maintain the kind of integrity that we have always wanted others to have toward us? I see that as a real issue. We tried some years ago to think about a broad ethnic studies program here and we were encouraged to think about how we could pool together with the Native American, Asian American, and Chicano studies programs. It didn't work. It didn't work because the institution itself could not find a way in which African American studies could see any benefits for itself in that pool. I'm not convinced that there isn't a way of doing it that would benefit all of us, but I think that's going to be something that needs to be given careful thought so that one group doesn't say "I don't want to join with you because you're weaker than I am and the resources that I should be getting are going to be split off with you." As the strongest area of these minority studies, African American is going to have to face up to what this means and to make itself a part of the solution to how we get through it without creating more schisms than exist. I think relations are pretty good now between the various groups, but I think that the other minorities will have to grow and that is where I see the absence of adequate resources as a real issue. I can think of four or five faculty positions that our Afro-American studies department needs and should have right now. Is the dean going to say, "but I can't give you any of your spaces because I have to give Asian American one and Chicano studies one?" I see that as an administrative problem, but also one that African American studies has to be involved in the solving of. My field can't just sit back and say well, let them take care of it up in that big house on top of the hill.

Donald Hall: Even with all of these challenges, do you still love the work you do?

Nellie McKay: I still love it a lot! There is just too much of it, and I often wish the work were less. But I love it. I have more graduate students now than I ever had before and they take up a lot of my time. I am very concerned that I leave at least another couple of generations of African American scholars behind me, scholars who are going to be able to push forward the agenda that my generation set in motion but could not fully accomplish. I hope too that the generations that come after me will dream larger worlds than we are able to imagine.

But, you know, I feel at peace with myself and the work. I have absolutely no regrets about having gone into this profession. I feel fortunate to have entered it when I did. These have been exciting times. At the same time, I don't think our profession is an easy one to be in—and it gets harder and harder as we go along—but I am also convinced that in teaching we are helping to humanize younger generations, whether they end up being professors or not, whether they are going to be computer tycoons or medical doctors or whatever. Maybe especially if they are going to be computer tycoons or medical doctors or world financiers. We have an effect on their early lives and hopefully the effect is for the good. And I find that worthwhile doing! I have much younger friends who went into the business world and they are already very anxious to get out and claim retirement and leisure time. But I suspect that while many of them made a lot more money than those of us in liberal arts education will ever make, their jobs were not as personally rewarding as ours have been. I still look forward to every day on my job. And I'm not just being a Pollyanna, I do look forward to every day and want to continue doing this work for a long time to come! I don't think I personally could have chosen a field or an area of work that I would have liked better than the one I have! My students know that; they take advantage of that. I let them.

SOME FINAL WORDS: AN INTERVIEW WITH ELAINE MARKS

Donald Hall: I want to begin with something that I've been asking many of the others whom I've interviewed, and that is about your perspective on how the profession has changed over the course of your career. Have you found that academics' senses of their professional "selves" have metamorphosed significantly or have they remained relatively stable over the years?

Elaine Marks: Let me start with what I know best, which is French studies. I got my Ph.D. in 1958, so that I have been working in this area for a very, very long time. I think that the biggest change for the field is that those of us in the 1950s who went into the study of French literature, and it was more literature than culture, found ourselves in an area that was perceived as being extremely important. That partly had to do with the effects of people like Sartre, Camus, and de Beauvoir after the war, but certainly it brought with it the sense that to be engaged in French studies was to be engaged in the most important intellectual activity possible. We were interested in the "big questions," the big metaphysical ones that had dropped out of Anglo-American philosophy: life and death and the meaning of love. That's what we discussed and talked to students about and read texts looking for. This has obviously changed dramatically over time. When ideological and cultural concerns came into the field in the late sixties, the "big questions" suddenly became for many people non-questions or at the very least questions that had to be reformulated in very different ways. And some of us in the field changed as the profession and flow of discussion changed, as I did myself, becoming interested both in women's studies and in theoretical fields that later came to touch women's studies. But many people did not. They were not interested in the new theoretical directions and were violently opposed to women's studies. And these were people who really lost their moorings. I am the oldest person in my department and it is interesting to note that in last few years people in French and Italian departments have generally retired much earlier than in previous generations. First of all because there are deals, so that it is financially interesting to retire, but also because many have felt left out or left back or not appreciated for the kinds of work that they were doing or the kinds of questions that they were asking. I don't think that this has happened to the same degree in other fields within the humanities. Certainly directions have changed enormously, and perhaps in general the humanities have gone through a kind of disregard over the past fifteen to twenty years within institutions as far as funding is concerned. But French studies have been particularly affected. I think that the individuals within the field feel that they don't have the same kind of prestige, and for some people that was very important.

Now my reaction to all of this has been somewhat different. I have found that it has been an extremely exciting period intellectually, extremely exciting. But I would be remiss if I didn't say it—it has also been difficult. The excitement of the talking about the "big questions" I mentioned a moment ago was replaced for me personally by the equally intense excitement of the initial years of women's studies. But frankly that has not born the fruits that I thought or hoped it might. In my women's studies courses now, the undergraduate students, in particular, have developed a very narrow line. They seem to me unable to read

texts as texts. They read only to find sexism, racism, anti-Semitism, or whatever, and of course it is just about always there—it's endemic—but they don't
see other things nor do they seem to be interested in looking for other things.
In my opinion (and Biddy Martin has discussed this too) there has been a widespread negative effect of women's studies and cultural studies, and that is an
inability to read for ambiguities. I have a real concern about this move into a
looking for the ideological monster in society/in the text, the evil one or ones,
and always finding them, because then, what do you do with it? There are other
sorts of questions to ask about texts and it concerns me that students seem less
interested in intellectual pursuits than they are in reading to condemn. This is
a real concern of mine professionally—students seem so narrowly indoctrinated
that they are hostile to all other ways of thinking about a text.

Questions of gender, sexuality, ethnicity, religion—I think it is wonderful
that these are discussed, but they can also generate serious problems in the
classroom. Let me offer a personal example here. In the course that I teach on
French and Italian Jewish writers of the twentieth century—a course in translation—many of the Jewish students want the texts and the professor to be
Jewish in a particular way—not to be secular. And I suffer a great deal from
this because I am very secular (I actually prefer the word "atheist" but nobody
says that anymore). This raises a very difficult but important question for our
profession. Do we encourage people to think about questions of identity *as
questions*—when should it come in and when not?—or do we, because of the
labeling of courses that have words such as "Jewish," "women," "lesbian" in
them, encourage students to think only from that position? A discussion of
these questions in socio-political/cultural terms is very important, but too
often in the classroom when one is dealing with complicated texts, as soon as
questions are presented through the texts and not single and simple readings,
the students who are speaking from that identity position are often very uncomfortable, but I would even say more than uncomfortable—hostile and
angry. That may be the greatest challenge for professors who teach such matters, to figure out a way of retaining—"ambiguity" may not be the best word—
retaining what is *disturbing* about reading texts and yet carrying the students
along with you who want to feel validated. Though quite frankly I am not
certain at all that the classroom is the best place for students to feel validated
about being Jewish or lesbian.

Donald Hall: But I have found with some of my own politicized students who
may be speaking out of a certain identity position that I want to retain or tap
into the fervor, because the energy that they may bring with the politicization

can be remarkably dynamic, while some of the students who don't have that political attachment are rather lackadaisical, saying "Oh, everything is fine; oppression doesn't even exist anymore." I suppose the challenge is taking that energy and finding a way of breaking it down and problematizing or making it multiple.

Elaine Marks: But I think it is difficult, because I think the danger is that identity in a kind of flat way becomes as deadening as anything that we have known before. When the class has an identity focus, there has to be a way that students can read these texts and take into account that they are texts and not mirror reflections of the identity problems as the students have already conceived them, because usually that means that they simply can't read the text. They can't even see it because what they feel and what they have in their heads is so projected onto the text. I find that a serious problem. You talk about energy, and I agree with you, but it is very often that "identity" is the only motivating thing for students and if you unhook that they are left with no energy— it is like a believer to whom you tell there is no god. And even though I mentioned the Jewish writers class earlier, frankly, it was a lesbian culture class that was the worst experience of this sort that I have ever had in the classroom, because that is where I found the identity problem the most overwhelming. I could not even get the students to read Foucault because he was a man. And that was only the beginning of the problem, because obviously I was asking them to do serious intellectual work on sexuality. But it's as if all the work had been done and all people wanted to do was sit around and tell coming-out stories or such. It was not a good experience. I have not gone back.

Donald Hall: Mentioning Foucault, I had a follow-up question to something you said a moment ago, about individuals who started out in French studies with a belief in their own intellectual centrality given the prominence of Sartre and Camus. But today and for the past twenty years, we have been influenced heavily by people like Foucault and Derrida in our profession. French theorists are still very central to what we do. Why has that not translated into a continuing belief among your French department colleagues in the importance of what they are doing?

Elaine Marks: Because I would say in the French department here and many other places (but certainly not all), at least half to two-thirds of the people are not interested in that kind of theory. *Really* not interested in that kind of theory. I think the other thing is that although it has translated into importance—the importance of theory in the academy—it has also been "translated." That is to say my colleagues who use these theories—particularly those in the English department—read them in English, which is fine; I read them in English and in French, because the English often acts as a sort of textual commentary on the French. But that doesn't translate into an importance for French studies. And beyond the fact that many of my colleagues don't read Derrida and Foucault—that that is not their idea of what French studies is about—the general public doesn't read them either. After the Second World War, the many people who talked about Sartre and Camus were not only in the academy. French culture had a position within the United States that it no longer has. French culture today tends to be pretty consistently either ignored or denigrated. And frankly, even in France Foucault and Derrida are not read today—within certain intellectual groups, yes—but they have not taken over the country the way Camus's *The Stranger* or Sartre's novels or Gide or Flaubert or Zola did.

Donald Hall: In thinking about such changes and how we react to them, I would like to turn now more directly to the fields of feminist and gender studies. How comfortable are you, for instance, with the rubric of gender studies, and how it could institutionally or programmatically subsume or supplant traditional women's studies programs? Do you even see that as a possibility or cause for concern?

Elaine Marks: Now that is a good question, because fifteen years ago I would have said, "oh, gender studies, out with it, we're going to lose the specificity," but now it troubles me less. It troubles me less first of all because I think it has already happened. We have a women's studies program, but people who work on women writers or questions about women are often referred to as being in the field of gender studies. So I think one reacts less to something that has already been accepted in the language. It is simply in the discourse now. So "gender studies"—I have no problem with that in more traditionally constituted departments. The real question would be if I think that our women's studies program should change its name to a gender studies program and there I think I would still say no. I think that it would lead to more problems than it would solve—cross-listing of courses and funding, among others. So I would still hesitate about that, and I actually surprise myself when I say so, because it is not that I think we are doing cutting edge (and I don't really like that expression) work in women's studies—I think we were but I don't think we are now. That edge has moved into certain groups within ethnic studies where people do women's studies–like work as well as work on race.

Donald Hall: In terms of the broader field—the national/professional field of women's studies—how do you assess the health of that—do you see any crises that have been successfully met and others perhaps that are lingering or imminent?

Elaine Marks: Certainly I think that the bringing into the field in general of African American women, Hispanic women, Asian women has been a very good thing. I think that also there has been a general raising of consciousness among male colleagues who thirty years ago would never have thought of any of these questions, but who now, without having been asked to do so officially, include more women writers in their courses. That has been one of the good effects of the inclusiveness of women as colleagues—in our department here we have about ten people on the French side who are female, and that is about eight more than twenty years ago. So as far as the presence of female bodies in departments, of female writers in the curriculum, that has been a good thing. And I think that is clearly related to the successes of women's studies and the women's movement generally.

But as far as the field is concerned, I don't see signs of anything having moved recently. I'm talking about intellectual work within the field. It seems to me that much more interesting intellectual work has been done by people in queer theory and African American studies. And it may have done by people who were in women' studies but who then moved out to add other strings to the bow. But I don't see it happening purely within women's studies programs nor do I see women's studies programs as the center of the most exciting intellectual work that relates to women's studies.

Donald Hall: Is there any way of revitalizing that?

Elaine Marks: I'm not so sure. I think that the energies of peoples have gone elsewhere. I think the energies have gone into postcolonial studies and queer theory, but carrying along with it a kind of feminist underbelly. Again it's the people who started in women's studies who have very often moved out into these other areas, or if not the same people, then they taught people who moved out into other areas. But I don't see women's studies anymore as vitally strong. I may be sorry I said that but I don't.

Donald Hall: We have been talking about some rather dramatic changes here, and they are ones about which you take a very matter-of-fact attitude. I am wondering who or what had the most profound impact on your own sense of a professional self and, perhaps, greatest influence on the ways that you have processed the changes that you have seen?

Elaine Marks: I think the answer there is Bryn Mawr College, where one got a very particular kind of training in self-reliance and independence, and acquired a fundamental sense that one was very important as a person and thinker, and as a female person and thinker, no matter how a context may change. And this is partly a question of generation. I should start by saying that I am an only child from a Jewish family. I had my parents and three sets of aunts and uncles who had no children, and, I suppose, when you get that much attention a sense of your importance is already there. The danger is that whatever you say everyone is going to respond "oh, isn't she marvelous!" So you have to recover from that. But I think it is much better in life to have an overbearing sense from the beginning of ego and importance than not to have it at all. And then I also went to a progressive school in New York, where we never "did" plays, we wrote our own plays, and where we were encouraged to picket General Motors when there was a strike in the middle of the winter. I suppose that too helped lay a certain foundation. And then . . . Bryn Mawr, which was very traditional, but where we talked a lot about women as scholars and thinkers. And I think all of that gives one a sense of assurance and equality. It is interesting that both Kate Stimpson and Elaine Showalter also went to Bryn Mawr, and it certainly gave me, perhaps all of us, the notion that to be a professional academic person was also a very good thing. At Bryn Mawr one was aware of teachers/professors who were married, who were single and seemed asexual, who were lesbians—it was sort of all there. All of these were possible paths. Mind you we also had male professors at Bryn Mawr, but they made less of an impression on me and on many of us than the female professors. It was a defining place for me.

Donald Hall: You mentioned the sense that you acquired that being a professor was a "good thing"—what have been your joys and disappointments in that regard? Are there things that you expected to find in this career that you didn't find?

Elaine Marks: Oh no, I think I found much much more than I expected to find, especially as I don't think I had any expectations. It was not even my idea to be a professor, it was really my idea to be an actress. Professor was a fallback position. I got an M.A. because that seemed like a good thing to do and then

I went to New York to be an actress. And that did not go very well at all. I worked with a little French company and then with an American company and the first thing that happened was that the guy who was directing it was all over my body. And I thought, "This is *not* going to work out!" So I went to New York University to see if I could get a job as a teaching assistant, and did not know, because I had never thought about it, that you couldn't be a teaching assistant unless you became a graduate student, and I did, and that's how I became a professor of French. I came to it by accident, because I needed to earn money, though certainly it was not an accident that I studied a lot of French, and teaching was, after all, acting and performing. So I have been really rather surprised at how well it all turned out for me. I don't think I have had anything other than surprises that it was all better than I thought.

And let me be very clear about something here: I know well that our graduate students now have anxieties that I never had. When I got my Ph.D. in 1958 I had people writing to me asking me if I wanted a job because there were very few people receiving the degree. It was just before the explosion of the sixties and it was really a whole other world. My graduate students today have such tremendous anxieties and they so desperately want to be professors. They have a sense that this is truly a very good and privileged thing to be and I think that that is true—if there is any sense that I have about the profession, it is that when one gets into it and has a good job, the privilege is extraordinary. Tenure is an incredible privilege—most professions don't have anything like that; if people don't perform they get kicked out. Most people do perform well in our profession, but not all, and even if they don't, after tenure they're here for life. But except for that, or rather, those people, it is really very wonderful. And you have to be careful; I wouldn't want anyone to read this and say, well she doesn't really need a salary she likes it so much, because it is both pleasurable and constantly challenging at the same time. But it has more than met expectations because I didn't really have any in the beginning.

Donald Hall: Thinking back, what do you think of as your most satisfying accomplishments and how did those come about?

Elaine Marks: You know, it is like my expectations, I don't think I think in those terms. I really don't think in terms of personal successes. I think in terms of good moments, pleasurable moments, and in a sense, although outwardly I've had a very good career, I don't think of it as a career. I simply think of it as what I do.

I think that the most pleasurable thing that can happen as an accomplishment is to come out of a class with a very good feeling. It doesn't always happen; there are classes that for whatever complicated reason, I think I blew it, they blew it, we blew it together. But when it does go well, that is really a wonderful feeling, whether it is an undergraduate class or a graduate seminar.

I think that probably in terms of publications, what has given me those moments of pleasure are things like *New French Feminisms* and *Homosexualities and French Literature,* though the latter was not as much a personal accomplishment. I mean George Stambolian did much more moving and fighting than I with publishers on that book because the University of Chicago Press had asked us to do *Homosexualities and French Literature*—and then when we did it, their board said, "This is simply a fad and won't be taken seriously!" But then we got it to Cornell and talked them through it—George really did—and it was all very exciting because it involved French writers, and critics and scholars, and George. That was a lot of fun, and I've very keen on having fun in all of these things, though "pleasure" may sound better. And it was also a good thing to have done, and *New French Feminisms* with Isabelle de Courtivron was too, but where exactly the same thing happened. A commercial press had spoken to me and when we finished it, they said again, "Hélène Cixous? What is all of this?" And we went to several places before the University of Massachusetts took it. So the fact that one had to fight for it was enormous fun, knowing that we had something that was a good thing, and particularly so in the case of the book with Isabelle, because we had used many of the texts in classes. *New French Feminisms,* which is now old, still sells, one still gets royalties, and that's nice. But of course one doesn't think of all of that. At the time it really just gave one a lot of satisfaction to be doing it.

So, you know, I don't think of it as a career, and I suppose at some level, I don't think in terms of profession or institution. It may be that when one is in the academy a long time, it is like home. It can be dysfunctional like a family, it can have good or better moments, and certainly one can be in good or better places. I've read enough of Althusser to know all about the ideology that goes on in this, so I know I also have a level of comfort that younger people couldn't, maybe shouldn't have, but that you do have when you have been in the academy for that long. And it may be again, Donald, that I came in at a moment when you didn't have to fight to get in, you had really rather to choose where you would go and be, and what you would do. I know that one has to fight now and I know what the political goings on are, and I know the different kinds of issues that one has to face today, but my experience has been different, and in a sense, I would be one of the people, and there aren't many, who have had an easy time. Personally an easy time. So that even if you know that other people are not having an easy time, there is some way in which the ease that I have had colors my way of thinking about it. And I'm very conscious of that, that it is not at all a model itinerary, that it is a special one that has to do with a particular moment in time. Others, for instance, have asked me questions about sexuality and the problems that one has in the university when one is lesbian, and certainly I know people have had terrible problems. But I didn't. If people said terrible things about me, I didn't even know it. I always felt that I could say what I wanted to say and did. Some people might respond, well you didn't say enough and you should have said this, that, or the other, and I suppose that's all possible.

Donald Hall: At the same time I think that other people have had good fortune and great careers, they may be in situations that are even easier or perhaps more difficult, but I think there is something to be said for how you have approached this, with an attitude of what pleasure and satisfaction can be garnered from it, even with the dramatic changes occurring that we discussed earlier. Because what has struck me in this project, talking with some people who didn't participate, and overhearing many different conversations, is that it is not a very joyous profession much of the time. I usually have tremendous fun in my teaching and writing, and in my existence as a professional, but a lot of people don't. As we all know from our departments and professional organizations, there are some very tortured souls among us. And at times I simply feel like shaking people and saying find some way of garnering joy, because this is all there is!

Elaine Marks: Well, that may be my secular sense. This is all there is, so why have that sort of spleen? And I'm sure it has had something to do with the fact that my expectations were practically nonexistent. We, of my generation, studied Sartre and Camus, but we didn't think that we were going to be the next Sartre or Camus. We just thought of ourselves as teachers. That is so very different today; people do think of themselves sometimes as perhaps the next Barthes or the next Foucault. It is an entirely different mindset.

Donald Hall: There is good reason why "careerism" is a term of opprobrium. If one is so obsessively concerned with standing, ranking, these little incremental hierarchical moves up or down in one's professional reputation or whatever, it destroys any sense of equilibrium or pleasure in the doing of our teaching, scholarship, and other work.

Elaine Marks: Oh, don't misunderstand me, in a particular situation, I can be as competitive as anyone else, but I don't think of it totally in that way. Mostly I have simply enjoyed it and am still enjoying it.

And you know, I never even think of myself as a scholar, which is very interesting, and I hate the word "research." We read books and we think about what we do and we put things together. Certainly I think of myself as a teacher, but I don't even really think of myself as a writer. I mean I write, but "teacher" is probably the operative word. And I think of myself as an intellectual—I like that word because it is very much used in France. "Intellectual" and "teacher"—and I guess before I retire I still would like to be able to give some people who control monies—the chancellor, the state legislators—a better sense of why those activities are so important. Mind you, not really why the "Humanities" are important, because that is too big for what I mean. I really do mean why what we do in language and literature is so important, because I think that is much more under attack and less appreciated. I know historians feel that nobody understands what they are doing, but "history" just by the word has sort of inherent prestige. You know, this lack of a word for what we do may be why so many people among us feel so unmoored. You can say you are a "historian," but what do you say you are if you do literature—a literary critic? That is not much of a rubric. It is not like being a "historian" or a "philosopher" or a "psychologist"—we don't even have a word—"teacher" is fine and "intellectual" is fine but those doesn't say that we are teaching literature and language. So maybe what I should set out to do before retiring is simply invent a word. Voilà—what about that! A word like "historian" or "philosopher." Then we could have yet another kind of exciting crisis or problem! But it is really very telling. What word is used? A reader? I mean everybody reads; we are all readers. Textual critic? Good heavens no! That is not going to move anybody!

Donald Hall: Nothing comes to mind. To recognize our interactions with texts, you have to go back to that word "critic"—whether it is cultural or literary critic.

Elaine Marks: But that is not a word like "philosopher" or "historian." It really doesn't do it. Well, maybe you can think of something when you read over everything everyone has done. You will come up with the word and you will put the word on the book!

[Editor's note: But, unfortunately, I did not . . .]

Contributors

DENNIS W. ALLEN is professor of English at West Virginia University and the author of *Sexuality in Victorian Fiction*, as well as articles on queer studies and popular culture.

MARTHA BANTA is professor emeritus of English at UCLA, the author of numerous books on American literature, and was the 1997–2000 editor of *PMLA*.

JUDITH JACKSON FOSSETT is assistant professor of English and American studies and ethnicity at the University of Southern California and the co-editor of *Race Consciousness: African-American Studies for the New Century*.

REGENIA GAGNIER is professor of English at the University of Exeter and the author of *The Insatiability of Human Wants: Economics and Aesthetics in Market Society*, as well as works on nineteenth-century Britain, social theory, interdisciplinary studies, and women in the profession.

KEVIN GAINES is associate professor of history and African American studies at the University of Michigan and the author of *Uplifting the Race: Black Leadership, Politics, and Culture in the Twentieth Century*.

SANDRA GILBERT is professor of English at the University of California, Davis, and past president of the Modern Language Association, as well as the author of works of feminist theory and criticism, a memoir, and six collections of poetry, most recently *Kissing the Bread: New and Selected Poems, 1969–1999*.

GERALD GRAFF is associate dean of curriculum and instruction and professor of English and education at the University of Illinois, Chicago, and the author of works including *Beyond the Culture Wars* and the forthcoming *Clueless in Academe: How Schooling Obscures the Life of the Mind.*

DONALD E. HALL is professor and associate chair of English at California State University, Northridge, and the author of *Fixing Patriarchy: Feminism and Mid-Victorian Male Novelists* and *Literary and Cultural Theory: From Basic Principles to Advanced Applications,* among other works.

ROBERT VON HALLBERG is professor of English, German, and comparative literature at the University of Chicago and the author of works including *Poetry, Politics, Intellectuals.*

GEOFFREY GALT HARPHAM is chair of the Department of English at Tulane University and the author of works including *Shadows of Ethics: Criticism and the Just Society.*

GORDON HUTNER is professor of English at the University of Kentucky, the author of numerous studies of American fiction, criticism, and culture, and the editor of *American Literary History.*

JAMES KINCAID is Aerol Arnold Professor of English at the University of Southern California and the author of numerous works on Victorian literature and contemporary culture, including *Annoying the Victorians, Child-Loving,* and *Erotic Innocence.*

SUSAN S. LANSER is professor of comparative literature, English, and women's studies, and former chair of the Comparative Literature Program at the University of Maryland. Her books include *Fictions of Authority: Women Writers and Narrative Voice.*

HERBERT LINDENBERGER is Avalon Foundation Professor of Humanities in Comparative Literature and English at Stanford University, the author of works including *Saul's Fall* and *The History in Literature,* and past president of the Modern Language Association.

ELAINE MARKS is Germaine Bree Professor of French and Women's Studies at the University of Wisconsin–Madison, the co-editor of *New*

French Feminisms, the author of *Marrano as Metaphor,* and past president of the Modern Language Association.

JOHN McGOWAN is professor of English and comparative literature at the University of North Carolina, Chapel Hill, the co-editor of the *Norton Anthology of Theory and Criticism,* and, most recently, the author of *Hannah Arendt: An Introduction.*

NELLIE Y. McKAY is professor of English and African American studies at the University of Wisconsin and the co-editor of the *Norton Anthology of African American Literature.*

J. HILLIS MILLER is UCI Distinguished Professor of English and Comparative Literature at the University of California, Irvine, the author of books including *Ariadne's Thread* and *Speech Acts in Literature* (forthcoming), and past president of the Modern Language Association.

MARJORIE PERLOFF is Sadie D. Patek Professor Emerita at Stanford University and the author of numerous works on poetry including *Wittgenstein's Ladder: Poetic Language and the Strangeness of the Ordinary.*

NIKO PFUND is former director and editor-in-chief of New York University Press and currently academic publisher of Oxford University Press (New York).

JAMES PHELAN is chair of the Department of English at Ohio State University, the editor of *Narrative,* and the author of works on narrative theory, including *Narrative as Rhetoric.*

JUDITH ROOF is professor of English at Michigan State University, the author of *The Lure of Knowledge,* and co-editor of *Who Can Speak?*

JANE TOMPKINS is professor of English at the University of Illinois, Chicago, and the author of works on theory and pedagogy, including *A Life in School: What the Teacher Learned.*

BONNIE ZIMMERMAN is professor of women's studies at San Diego State University, the author of *The Safe Sea of Women: Lesbian Fiction, 1969–1989,* the editor of *Lesbian Histories and Cultures: An Encyclopedia,* and former president of the National Women's Studies Association.

Index

Typeset in 10.5/13 Minion
with Minion display
Designed by Dennis Roberts
Composed by Barbara Evans
at the University of Illinois Press
Manufactured by Maple-Vail Book Manufacturing Group

University of Illinois Press
1325 South Oak Street
Champaign, IL 61820–6903
www.press.uillinois.edu